Pax in Bello
Peace in War

The Reverend Doctor Robert Ernest Osborne,

**B.A., B.D., S.T.M., Ph.D (1920-1986),
Captain Royal Canadian Army Chaplain Corp, C.D.**

Pax in Bello / Peace in War
Copyright © 1982-1983 Robert E. Osborne. All Rights Reserved.
Copyright © 2016 David B. Osborne. All Rights Reserved.

2019 - Revised and Published by David B. Osborne

ISBN 978-0-9951832-0-9

To:

Flying Officer Bill Bellingham   Killed in Action - Nov 19, 1944 (Age: 21)
Private Everard Connor   Killed in Action - Oct 28, 1944 (Age: 21)
Corporal Douglas McKnight   Killed in Action - Feb 26, 1945 (Age: 25)
Guardsman George Holden   Killed in Action - Aug 10, 1944 (Age: 29)

And

My Children; John, Robert, Margaret and David

"Remember, everyone has to die someday. I have had a very full and good life. I had hoped to have a few years to enjoy retirement but I guess such is not to be. I have preached the gospel of life after death and now I have the opportunity to "live" that gospel."
- Robert E Osborne - In a letter to his son David. November 22nd, 1985

"Now go, write it before them in a table, and note it in a book, that it may be for the time to come for ever and ever:"
- Bible (KJV) - Isaiah 30:8

[My father enjoyed reading the Peanuts (R) comic strip by Charles M Schulz, and Snoopy in particular so I have included various images throughout this book. He was very interested in WWI and flying in general.]

This is the original draft and requires a great deal of polish. However, in doing so, one must not eliminate the straightforward presentation in style deliberately set out by the author — as he would have lived it out as a young man entering, then facing the realities of war. Expressions, phrases, grammar and openness of the other ranks must be preserved or the essence of the document loses its full impact and flavour.

M Coleman
25 NOV 82

COMMENTARY - L. R. COLEMAN

This is essentially the soldier's story. It is one man's experience and yet it mirrors every man and woman who "joined up" as another rank during World War II. It is a profound memoire, profound in its simplicity, its honesty and its credibility. It tells of a soldier's pride in his Regiment - his passionate respect for those he would follow even unto death - his contempt for those who would use the system to their own advantage. It speaks of love in a time of hating. It is paradoxical, as its title suggests *Pax in Bello - Peace in War*. It is a compassionate and a heroic document which fills in the unwritten words, in letters home to Mum. The book should be considered a Canadian classic for it deals with the very soul of those young men and women who pitted their innocence against the evils of darkness. In turn, they speak through this true story, to the young people of today. This book is an enactment of the 23rd Psalm - the soldier's psalm - it is a reflection of Milton's Paradise Lost - and Regained. It is the sharing of a man's deepest inner feeling.

The author embraces death but is turned back, for the time is not yet, for the will of the creator. There is still work to be done and life to be lived. The sharing must go on - and is still going on.

"That you may tell your sons who see the light
High in the Heavens - their heritage to take: -
'I saw the Powers of Darkness put to flight!
I saw the Morning Break' "
- Sir Owen Seaman (1861-1936) - Between Midnight and Morning (1914)

Magog, Q.C., Canada

1939 – Bob Osborne and (Unknown)

PROLOGUE - [L. R. Coleman - unverified]

Bob Osborne came from Magog, Quebec. Prior to the war, he had distinguished himself in provincial high school track and field events, and as a cross country bicycle racer. He enlisted in the Canadian Grenadier Guards and went overseas as a Wireless Operator. This account is based partly on his personal story, told to me as we walked along a country road one summer night outside Wemyss, Ontario, and partly on the eyewitness account of George "Punch" Wright, who was in the same unit and was wounded in the same engagement.

In August 1944, the Guards were in action in the Falaise area. On those occasions when the commander of Bob's tank had to go to O-Group, Bob was put in temporary command. Later, with a switch of commanders, Bob became the commander of their tank, the GIRAFFE. In the fight for Hill 195, their tank was hit by a German Eighty-Eight shell, which exploded behind Bob and the tank driver (they sat side-by-side), wounding both. Bob's left ankle was severely fractured and he had shrapnel wounds in his buttocks. The tank then caught fire. The other members of the crew climbed out the conning tower, followed by Bob. However, he was so badly wounded that he fell back into the burning tank, and Punch Wright, who was watching this fearsome drama unfold, told me that he said to himself, "That's the end of Osborne." But it wasn't. Just as Bob fell back into the burning tank, the tank's supply of ammunition exploded and literally fired Bob out the conning tower! Bob told me he lay on the battle field "cursing God to His face and wanting to die". Then, in what sounded to me like an out-of-body experience, Bob said he heard a voice saying "You're not going to die. I have work for you to do." Bob now had burns on his face and neck and gunshot wounds in his leg. Another soldier carried him through the wheat field to a spot where the stretcher bearers would be able to reach him. He was flown to a hospital in England, where a Canadian doctor prepared to amputate his foot but fortunately, at the last minute in the operating room, the doctor decided to try to save the foot. The deep burns were treated with the new wonder drug, penicillin, to fight infection.

In November 1944, Bob was invalided home and spent the next nine months being shuttled for operations between Queen Mary's Veterans' Hospital (then known as the Montreal Military Hospital or M.M.H.) and the military hospital in Ste-Anne-de-Bellevue. In March 1945 he underwent a bone graft operation to build a new heel, given a 50/50 chance of success. The operation was an amazing success! In August 1945, Bob received his discharge from the army.

Bob initially decided to pursue a course in teaching, as he had a natural gift for it. Accordingly, in September 1945, he enrolled at McGill's School for Teachers at Macdonald College in Ste-Anne-de-Bellevue, Quebec. While there, he met and was greatly influenced by the local United Church minister, Rev. Francis Doxsee. He finished the course, taught school one year, and then decided to enter the Christian ministry. He obtained his B.A. at Sir George Williams College (now Concordia University), where he met our dear friend, Bill Steeper, of I.V.C.F. [InterVarsity Christian Fellowship]. He did his B.D. [Bachelor of Divinity] and S.T.M. [Latin: Sacrae Theologiae Magister; English: Master of Sacred Theology] at McGill and his Ph.D. at Edinburgh University. After his ordination, he received the rank of Captain and was put on the supplementary list of chaplains. He relieved several summers at C.F.B. [Canadian Forces Base] Borden and C.F.B. Gagetown. Bob told me that the young trainee soldiers at those camps devoured all he would tell them about what it was like "over there". But the C.O. had to ask him to stop because it was scaring the wits out of the young soldiers!

He served two pastorates in Canada before being appointed Associate Professor at Emmanuel College, Toronto. Following this, he was appointed Professor of New Testament at Carleton University, Ottawa, where he was twice voted one of the most popular professors on campus. He is one of a small handful of people who has greatly influenced my life.

PREFACE - Robert E. Osborne - Ottawa, Ontario (1983)

Many books have been written about the Canadian sailors who fought the war in ships and the airmen who flew against the enemy in the sky but, to my knowledge, there have not been many books written about the young Canadians who engaged the enemy in tanks. Apart from Regimental Histories, their brave story has never been told. This book is an attempt to remedy that omission. It is one man's story and therefore cannot be everyman's experience, but it is the author's hope that it will touch bases at enough places that many of those who read it will say - that's the way it was - I remember that!

The motto of the *OSBORNE* family is *Pax in Bello*. It seemed to me that *Peace in [the midst of] War* was what my book was about. The peaceful English countryside, the peace experienced in the little parish churches, but above all the peace that came when, for me, the fighting was over. That indescribable peace given to those who have looked death in the face and have been given a second chance to live and to love. The Osborne motto, which may sound paradoxical to some, is just what this member of the family felt in those days of the Second World War.

The book began from a packet of letters that my mother had kept. They were letters that I had written to her during the war. I did not keep a diary but I used my letters home to record my feelings and descriptions of places visited. Some of the letters have holes in them where the censor has snipped something out. Using the letters as a framework, I wrote the book from my memory of events. The book then is half my record of events and places at the time of writing and half my reminiscences. I hope it is autobiographical and nowhere to be considered fictional. In a few places I have changed names to avoid any embarrassment - "No names, no pack drill!" [Say nothing and avoid repercussions!] I have called the shots as I saw and remembered them and if sometimes they differ from those of others then my only plea is that this is the very stuff of which history is made.

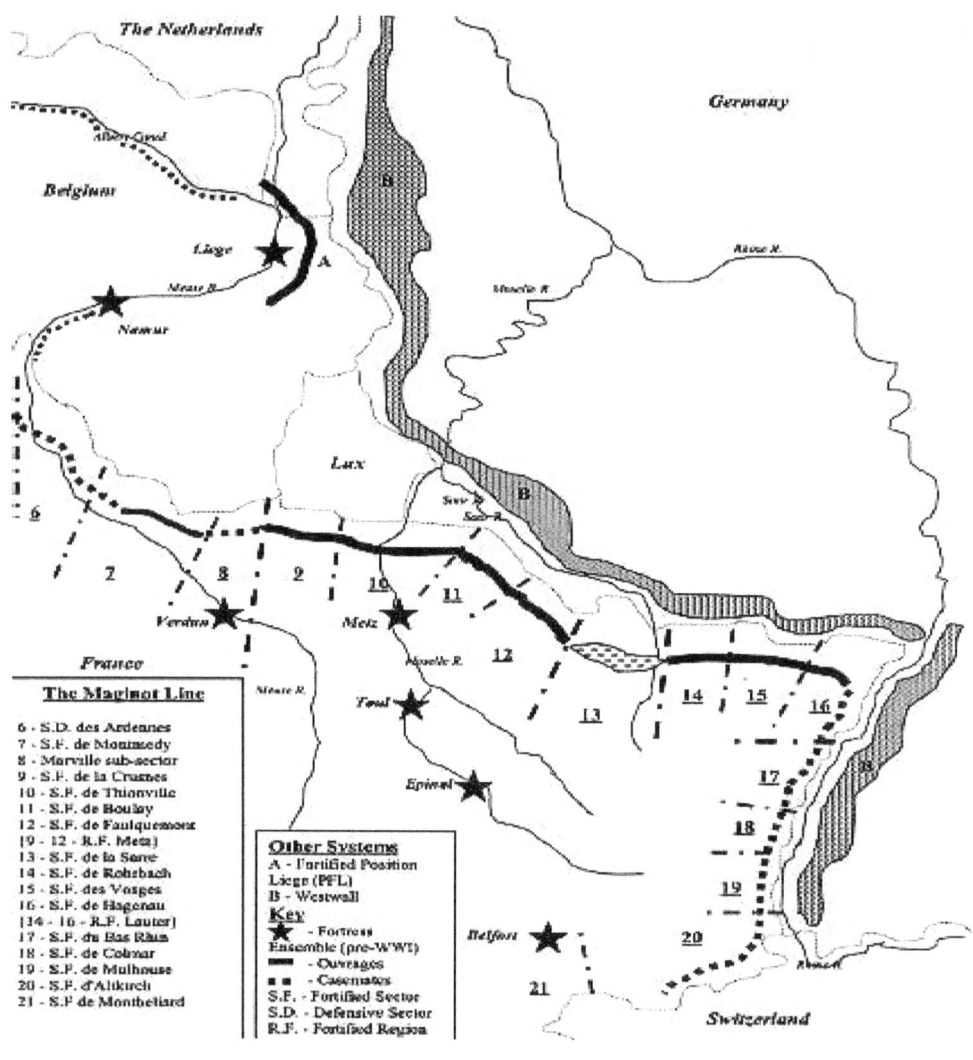

THE EMPIRE STRIKES BACK

"... until the curse of Hitler is lifted from the brows of men
... If we can stand up to him, all Europe will be free ..."
- Sir Winston Churchill (1874-1965) - Speech: Their Finest Hour (June 18th, 1940)

I had dropped out of High School in 1937 to work in the laboratory of the Dominion Textile plant in Magog, Quebec. I returned for my final school year in September, 1939, just after the outbreak of the Second World War. It was a small school and our graduating class had only seven students - four girls and three boys. The boys were Bill Bellingham, Everard Connor and myself. We were a very happy class and we had a wonderful principal who was also our English teacher, Miss Esther Magoon. She gave to us her own love for literature and poetry. Bill was a handsome boy with brown curly hair, an engaging smile and he was a first rate athlete. He played on our hockey team and was also our best pole-vaulter. Everard was a star on our hockey team. The three of us got along famously even though I was the oldest as I had been out in the work force for two years. Although I was senior in age, I never felt it and I learned a lot from the other two. From Everard, I learned to organize my material. His favourite saying was "You can't beat a man with a system." After graduation he hoped to enter university to study engineering. Bill used to help me with my Physics problems and on the very morning of the Physics exam he took me into an empty classroom before it started and explained a formula to me which later appeared on the paper. Without his help I would not have passed my Physics and would not have earned my High School Leaving Certificate. Bill and I often talked about the future and he planned to go into medicine.

As the year went on and the new year of 1940 advanced, we three naturally talked more and more about the War. This was the period of the "Phony War" when the R.A.F. [Royal Air Force] were dropping leaflets on Germany while the British and French troops were sitting cozily in the Maginot Line. It did not really upset our studies however, until May when the Nazi blitzkrieg broke through the "invincible" Maginot Line and rolled relentlessly toward Dunkirk. Early in June I knew I must enlist as soon as possible but my mother insisted that I write my final exams first. It was difficult to keep my mind on my studies during those days in June as I listened to the news on the radio and heard Winston Churchill's defiant words to Hitler and his gang of Nazis. Britain had her back to the wall and I felt that this was indeed going to be "her finest hour" and I wanted to be a part of it.

I recalled the words of Wordsworth as Miss Magoon had taught them to us:

"We must be free or die, who speak the tongue
That Shakespeare spoke: the faith and morals hold
Which Milton held.—In everything we are sprung
Of Earth's first blood, have titles manifold."
- William Wordsworth (1770–1850) - It Is Not to Be Thought Of (1807)

My alarm clock went off long before dawn was showing in the east. Mother made me a good breakfast and I walked down in the dark to the Canadian Pacific Railway [C.P.R.] station to catch the Maritime Express that stopped in Magog at about 5:30 a.m. I was going to Montreal to compete in the Dominion Interscholastic Track and Field Championships. I was also going to Montreal to apply for enlistment in the Royal Canadian Air Force [R.C.A.F.] - That, my mother did not know. The train pulled into Montreal's Windsor Station about 8 o'clock. I walked up to St. Catherine Street and turned west until I reached Bishop Street. Ever since I had been a small boy I had been fascinated by flying - though I had never been up in an aeroplane. Some of my friends, Norman Ball, Angus MacIntosh and Wilber Turner had already enlisted and had come home to Magog wearing their Air Force blue uniforms. How I envied them. I would learn

Dominion Track and Field Championships May 1940

**L/Cpl Arthur Frederick Cordy
87th Battalion - Canadian Grenadier Guards
Killed in Action 27 February 1917**

later that Ball and Turner were Killed in Action as bomber crewmembers. One of my boyhood heroes was Billy Bishop and in my youthful fantasies I saw myself in the cockpit of my Sopwith Camel glued to the tail of an enemy Albatross, stitching a seam up his fuselage with my twin Vickers. A large Air Force flag hung outside the Bishop Street building. I had to wait until almost 9 o'clock before I finally reached the desk and filled out an application form; and another three hours before I was called in for my medical. I finally left the Recruiting Office about one o'clock.

As I stepped out the door and turned north to walk up to McGill's Molson Stadium, a woman across the street screamed. A huge glass insulator smashed to the sidewalk a few feet in front of me. The woman had seen the insulator falling and figured it would hit me dead on. Her scream saved my life. I hurried on to the stadium propelled by shock and the fact that the afternoon events were about to begin. I arrived just in time to change into my track suit, pin on my number - it was 96 - and run out on to the field. They were calling my name and number for my first jump of the competition. I hadn't had a bite to eat or anything to drink since 5 o'clock in the morning so I was famished. The high jump crossbar was set at 5 feet [152.5cm]. The best I had ever jumped was 5' 1" [155cm]. I can't explain it but I cleared every jump without a fault. Perhaps I was undergoing some kind of delayed shock from the narrow escape from death. Anyway, my adrenalin must have been pumping and before I knew it I was in a jump-off with a lad from Glebe Collegiate in Ottawa. The bar was now resting at 5' 3" [160cm]. I could do no more. Monroe of Glebe went on to win at a measured height of 5' 3 and 5/8" [162cm] and I placed second. Dr. Errol Amaron, the principal of Stanstead College, came over to congratulate me.

I returned home that evening to begin my anxious wait for the letter from the R.C.A.F. They had warned me it would take some time because they had a great many applications to process. I had applied for Wireless Air Gunner and I could hardly wait to wear that blue uniform with the white flash of air crew on my cap.

A month went by during which I sat the Provincial High School Leaving Exams. The radio told us that Dunkirk had fallen and the Germans were getting ready to invade England. Winston Churchill spoke from a bomb shelter in London on June 4th, 1940. "We shall fight on the beaches... we shall fight in the fields and in the streets..." I could not wait for the R.C.A.F. any longer. An advertisement in the Montreal Star announced that the Canadian Grenadier Guards had been mobilized for Active Service and were now recruiting. June 26th marked my twentieth birthday. I wrote my last exam in the morning and hitchhiked to Montreal right after lunch. I was very lucky to get a lift in a police cruiser as a number of policemen from Sherbrooke were also going into the city to join up. We broke all the speed records with the red light flashing and the siren blowing. I booked in at the Y.M.C.A. on Drummond Street and the next morning I walked to the Guard's Armoury on Esplanade Avenue. A big sign outside depicted a Guardsman with the caption - CAN YOU MEASURE UP? The Guards had a minimum height standard of 5' 8" [173cm].

Along with Billy Bishop, my other hero was my Uncle Arthur, my mother's younger brother. He had gone overseas with the 87th Battalion of the Canadian Grenadier Guards and had been Killed in Action in 1917. I had never known him, because he died before I was born, but my mother often spoke of him and his picture was on the mantelpiece. The Guards' recruiting officer was a young lieutenant - Bernard Ghewy. I was impressed with his quiet and soldierly bearing. I told him that my uncle had been in the Guards and said I wanted to join up. Lieutenant Ghewy asked me about my education. I told him that I had just written my final exam the day before, but the results would not be out for six weeks. He said: "Somebody gave me the benefit of the doubt once so I will do the same for you, Osborne." I was sent down to the old Place Viger Hotel, which the military had taken over, where I was told to take off all my clothes and stand in line with hundreds of other men, all seeking enlistment in one of the various branches of the army. Finally, my turn came. A couple of doctors examined me and told me the results would be sent to the Guard's Armoury.

Lieutenant Bernard Ghewy
Camp Borden
Wearing the white arm band of the
Sigs Officer

Soldiers' pay

Where did Denise Harrington (*Citizen*, Oct. 19) get the idea that Canada's Second World War soldiers got paid $1.30 an hour? They were paid $1.30 a day. And, in theory at least (and often in practice) they worked 24 hours a day. This meant they got a little less than 5½ cents an hour.

Besides, a proportion of this pay was held back compulsorily so that on discharge the ex-serviceman would have enough money to get started in civilian life.

The inflationary outlook of today's young people leaves me gasping. Just think, Denise, those soldiers who were under fire for the nine hours the Dieppe Raid lasted got paid (if they survived) 49½ cents for the experience. Not very big money, perhaps. But what an experience! But then, you couldn't have everything in those days. However, there were compensations. Unemployment hardly existed.

Strome Galloway
Ottawa

The July 1st holiday, Dominion Day [now called Canada Day], was coming up and I couldn't afford to sit around the "Y" waiting for the medical results as it cost a dollar a night. I hitchhiked home and returned to Montreal on July the 2nd and went straight to the Armoury where Lieutenant Ghewy was on duty again. He remembered me and looked to see if my medical report had come in. It had. He opened a large brown envelope and said: "Osborne, you have an advanced case of tuberculosis. I advise you to see a doctor immediately." I protested as I was in excellent health and there must have been some mistake. I explained to him that I had undergone a medical just before the Track and Field Championships and then another for the R.C.A.F. Those doctors had found nothing wrong with my lungs. He agreed there must be some error so he sent me back to Place Viger with a memo to some doctor that he knew asking for a re-check. The doctor listened to my lungs and had some X-Rays taken and in a few minutes he came out and reported that my lungs were as clear as a bell. I hurried back to the Armoury. This was my first encounter with army mix-ups, they had put some other chap's X-Ray in my envelope! But now all was well. The next thing I knew Guardsman Johnny Forrest was typing up my documentation and then Lieutenant Ghewy swore me in. I laid my right hand on the Bible and promised to serve my King and Country wherever and for as long as my services were required. Then I went downstairs to collect my kit. A whole pile of things were signed over to me - army boots, battle dress, wedge caps, anklets, khaki shorts, underwear shorts, mess tins, knife, fork, spoon, trousers, socks, suspenders, belt, housewife [A small cloth bag which contained a needle, thread, buttons. thimble, wool for darning socks, etc] and kitbag. I was loaded on to a truck and, along with some other new recruits, was taken to the Motordrome on Sanguinet Street.

I was in the Army. The date was the 2nd of July, 1940. My regimental number was D-26348. "D" for Military District No. 4, "26" for our Regiment and "348" indicating that I was the 348th person to enlist. My pay was $1.30 a day. We were told that for a few days we would be Confined to Barracks and would stay that way until we had learned how to march, salute and wear a uniform properly. We were told that we were not "Privates", we were "Guardsmen"! How proud I was to put on my tunic with the red shoulder badge of the Canadian Grenadier Guards on it. The same regiment with which my Uncle Arthur had served.

Along with a dozen other recruits, I was assigned to come under the instruction of an old imperial soldier, Corporal Godsell. We nicknamed him "Crime Sheet Godsell" because his favourite ejaculation was - "I'll put you on a crime sheet!" My first night in the army was an unhappy one as the fellow in the bunk above mine came in drunk and vomited all over me. What a mess! Now I was certain I would start filling out my crime sheet. How could I ever get this mess cleaned up and be ready for inspection at 0800 hours? Corporal Godsell, however, was sympathetic to my plight. He "crimed" the fellow in the upper bunk and charged him with being drunk and disorderly. He sent me down to the Quartermaster's [Q.M.'s] stores to draw clean blankets. After forty-eight hours of learning to "Fall In", "Stand at Ease", at "Attention", "Easy", marching and saluting, we were considered to have graduated from the "awkward squad" and fit to be turned loose on the unsuspecting crowds along St. Catherine Street. It was a scorching hot night but we wore our winter battle dress proudly. The sidewalks were crowded with men in uniform - Black Watch in their kilt, Service Corps, Signal Corps, Hussars with their smart blue and white wedge caps, Royal Montreal Regiment, Artillerymen, and of course many Air Force and Navy people. Some new recruits would mistake bus drivers for Air Force officers and give them a snappy salute, much to the chagrin of the bus drivers.

Along with my kit I had been issued with a little blue coloured book with the title: "Canadian Grenadier Guards - Canadian Active Service Force - Regimental Notes for Warrant Officers, N.C.O.'s and Guardsmen." The first ten pages of this little book dealt with the history of the Regiment which went back to the time when the Army took possession of Montreal on September 8th, 1760. In 1912, H.M. King George V had conferred upon us the name "Canadian Grenadier Guards" raising us to the status of Household Troops (Maison du Roi) giving us the name of the unit which is not only the Senior Regiment of the Brigade of Guards, but of all British infantry. I read with pride the exploits of the 87th Battalion and the

February 1941 - Central Technical School – Toronto, ON
Lippincott St
Robert E. Osborne - Top Row Right - within the pillars
Wearing "Guards" Cap badge

splendid record they had with the Fourth Division in the Great War. I wondered in which battle my Uncle Arthur had been killed. My heart swelled with pride as I read that our Regiment had taken part in all the great battles, and that in four supreme and victorious engagements it had been selected to attack the most important and difficult part of the German defences - Regina Trench at the Somme, Hill 145 at Vimy, Dury Mill at Drocourt-Queant, and Bourlon Wood at Canal du Nord. These Battle Honours were emblazoned on our Colours [flag]. I wondered if we would be adding to that list. We were certainly an elite regiment - one cut above everybody else.

I read eagerly on. "Guardsmen should be distinguished by their smartness ... by their resolution to overcome obstacles ... by their exertion to do their duty as well as possible and in a manner which will bring greatest credit to the Regiment to which they have the honour to belong." The bugler sounded the "Lights Out." I had to put my book away but as I lay awake in the darkness, listening to the snores of the other men, I was sure my Uncle had been the kind of Guardsman the book told about. I fell asleep thinking of him. The next thing I knew Reveille was sounding.

I was assigned to No. 1 Company commanded by Major Hannen. This was the King's Company and every man in it was at least 6 feet [183cm] tall. Actually, I was only 5' 11" [180cm], but in my army boots I cleared the six foot [183cm] standard. Not only was I in the best Regiment in Canada but I was in the best Company!

I had only been in the Guards for about three weeks when the Regimental Sergeant Major [R.S.M.] "Timmy" Cloutte came in one noon hour and asked for any volunteers who could handle a rifle. I was hesitant about volunteering because I was already wise to such army tricks. There was that old chestnut - "How many of you chaps can play the piano?" The unsuspecting volunteer, thinking it would get him off Sanitary Detail and playing in the Officer's Mess, would discover that he had been duped into a detail to move a grand piano from the Officer's Mess to the Drill Hall for the upcoming concert. However, the R.S.M. assured us that he was sincere and that this was an urgent matter. I volunteered along with some others as I had grown up with rifles and shot guns, as had most boys in the Eastern Townships, and I was a good shot. We were issued with a .303-calibre Lee Enfield rifle, a bayonet, web equipment and a clip of five rounds of ammunition. It was all very exciting. It was our first real "active" detail. The other guys were looking at us with envy as we embussed and drove out of the city. We passed through St. John and debussed at a hotel beside the Richelieu River, opposite Île aux Noix. Our mysterious assignment now unfolded. A train carrying German prisoners of war was soon to arrive and our job was to guard the short route from the Railway station to the Ferry wharf. These prisoners were being taken to Fort Lennox on the island [Fort Lennox was designated a National Historic Site of Canada in 1920]. It was a beautiful July day. We waited as curious onlookers gathered to see what was going on. The War had suddenly come to the vacationers on the Richelieu. We waited all afternoon and it was dark when the prisoners finally arrived. They were still wearing their military uniforms. There were U-Boat captains, Luftwaffe pilots and men from the Afrika Korps [German expeditionary force in Africa]. They were arrogant and exuded an air of superiority. One swash-buckling U-Boat officer took one look at me, laughed in my face, and said in perfect English - "We'll be in Canada by Christmas!" And he meant it too. Another Afrika Korps type stopped in front of me and spat on me. I motioned with my bayonet but he just laughed. It was my first sight of the enemy and I soon realized that they were tough dedicated professionals. We were just kids out of school, as green as grass, and those Germans knew it. This was the super-race Hitler had been boasting about and they were going to be hard to beat. I wondered what I would do if one of them suddenly made a break for freedom. The American border was only a few miles downstream and America was a neutral nation. My orders were to shoot to kill but I am glad none of them put me to the test!

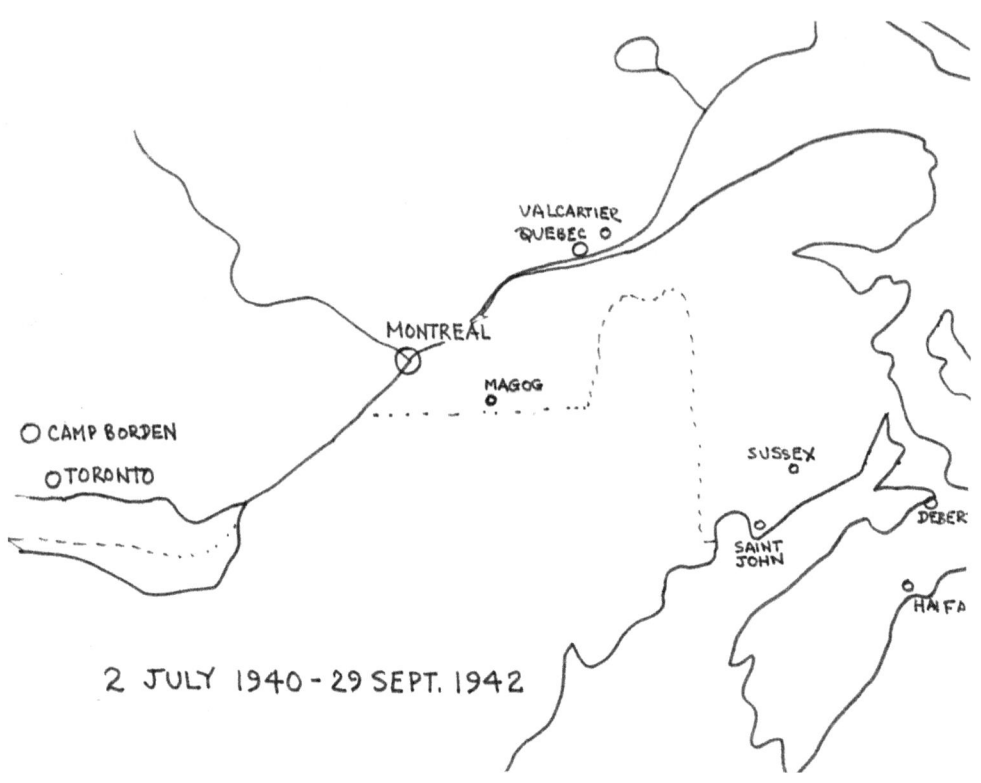

2 JULY 1940 - 29 SEPT. 1942

#1 Coy C.G.G. St Helenes Island 1940
Gdsm Robert E. Osborne
2nd row from top, extreme left
11th from left in same row Doug McKnight

SIGNAL PLATOON

I made a close friend of a lad called John Maffre. He had also written his High School exams and like me was awaiting the results. It was a warm afternoon in August and I was standing guard on St. Helen's Island near Montreal where the Regiment was camped. John, who was not on duty, came strolling along to where I was doing my guard. He had the Montreal Star in his hands and he waved it and said: "You passed, Bob!" I had an almost uncontrollable urge to throw away my rifle and go off with him to celebrate. Of course I did nothing of the kind, but simply smiled and kept on marching up and down like a good guardsman. John immediately put in for a transfer to the Air Force and before I knew it he was gone. John went on to distinguish himself in Malta. I was sorry to see him go. My application for Wireless Air Gunner came through about a week later but I did not seek a transfer. I was in the Guards now and I determined to make the best of it. I have since wondered though what would have happened if I had become a "Tail-End Charlie" [slang for the rear gunner in a bomber].

We were getting sorted out into different platoons. I had requested to be trained as a signaller since I knew the Morse code. Sergeant Stanton came to my tent one day and said, "I understand that you can read the Morse code". "That's correct", I replied. "Then stay here while I go over there". He pointed to a low hill. "I'm going to send you a message. See if you can read it." He walked to the top of the hill and raised his signal flag and sent the message - "If you can read this join me here." I did so. He said: "Osborne, you are now in the Signal Platoon." My old friend, Lieutenant Ghewy, was the Signal Officer and Johnny Forrest, who had typed up my documentation the day I joined up, was also in the platoon.

SERVICE MEN'S CLUBS

Clubs for service men sprang up all over the country. There was one on Phillips Square in Montreal that we used to frequent on those hot summer evenings. We would go in and write letters and then jive with the girls and listen to the hit songs like Vera Lynn singing - "There'll Be Blue Birds Over the White Cliffs of Dover". Other favourite dance tunes were - "Oh Johnny, Oh Johnny, Oh", "Ma, I Miss Your Apple Pie", "I'm In The Mood For Love", "'Till the Lights of London Shine Again", "We're Gonna Hang Out The Washing On The Siegfried Line " and "Wish Me Luck As You Wave Me Goodbye".

I MAKE MY WILL

As I walked down the line of tents on St. Helen's Island, Corporal Al Hubert came out of the Company Office tent and said - "Osborne, you haven't made your Will yet. We need that to complete your documentation". I ducked into the tent and made my will. I left everything to my mother. About all I owned was a bicycle and I couldn't imagine what good that would be to her! There was something sinister about making a will - as if you didn't expect to come out of this war alive.

"Let's choose executors and talk of wills;
And yet not so - for what can we bequeath
Save our deposed bodies to the ground?"
- William Shakespeare (1564-1616) - Richard II, Act III, Scene 2 (1595)

NEW YEAR, 1941

New Year's Eve, 1940, I spent in Camp Borden, Ontario. It was bitterly cold - well below zero [0 °F = -18 °C]. When I arrived back at the hut, after attending a show at the Camp Theatre, I found the place deserted. It was about 2230 hours and all the fires had gone out. I expected the hut orderly, who was detailed to look

Unit 'Missed' Hong Kong

Error in Guards' Order Discovered

> The complete list of Montreal service personnel arriving in Halifax on the Mauretania Monday, and scheduled to reach the city Wednesday, will be found on page 5.

A stenographer's mistake nearly led to the 1st Battalion of the Canadian Grenadier Guards packing up to go to Hong Kong, it was revealed last night by Lt.-Col. M. F. Peiler, O.B.E., at last night's dinner meeting of the 6087 and C.G.G. Overseas Association, in the Queen's Hotel.

Colonel Peiler, then commanding officer of the battalion, was proposing a vote of thanks to Major Angus Barwick, M.B.E., speaker, when he told the story of how, one morning at 6 o'clock when the unit was taking physical training at Debert Camp, N.S., a runner told him he was needed at Brigade Headquarters immediately.

On going to Brigade Headquarters Colonel Peiler said he was told that orders had come from Ottawa that the battalion was to be ready to move off at an hour's notice. Colonel Peiler went back and gave the necessary orders. Later, however, it was discovered that a stenographer had mistakenly typed Canadian Grenadier Guards for Winnipeg Grenadiers, and the order was then countermanded.

Major Barwick told of his experiences on the Canadian Military Mission which went to the Far East to assist in the repatriation of Canadians taken prisoner by the Japanese at Hong Kong.

He first served in the casualty branch of National Defence Headquarters, and after a tour of duty overseas was about to retire from the army when he was sent to Manila. On arrival there he found that "recovery teams" were already in the field. However, the Canadian Mission sent teams of men to Hong Kong and to Japan.

He outlined the arrangements made by the American forces to care for the repatriates, and said that the Canadian Red Ensign was hoisted above the Canadian's camp.

The Canadian prisoners, Major Barwick said, were generally in much better physical condition than those of other nationalities. They were sunburnt and healthy-looking, but it was difficult to make them realize they were at last free. Everything that could be done for them was carried out, however, and they had free issues of beer, cigarettes, chocolates and other delicacies.

Dr. Leslie Martin, president, presided. A brief address on his experiences as a prisoner of war in Germany was given by Flt. Lieut. T. Asselin.

Among those present were Col. G. S. Stairs, M.C., V.D., Brig. H. M. Elder, Lt.-Col. C. H. Hanson, Lt.-Col. D. H. Rolland and Lt.-Col. H. W. Rick.

after the fires, to return soon so I lay down on my bunk and pulled my greatcoat over me. I must have fallen asleep as I was awakened by a bunch of the boys arriving from the wet canteen - very drunk. The hut was like an iceberg now and I soon realized that if anybody was going to get those fires going it had to be me because I was the only sober soldier in the place. Some of the fellows just passed out and fell on their bunks without even removing their boots. I had a difficult time getting the three stoves going and it was long past midnight, about 0230 hours, when I finally got some heat coming from them. I noticed one fellow, down near the door, lying stark naked on his bunk - out cold! I wondered how long he had been lying like that as I had been so occupied trying to stoke up the fires that I hadn't noticed him. I threw some blankets over him and lay down myself knowing that I must awaken about 0530 hours to put some more coal on the fires. I awakened about 0630 hours to a howling gale blowing outside. The fires were still alight so I poured on more buckets of coal and then went over to look at the fellow I had covered with the blankets. At first I thought he was still drunk as he was babbling incoherently, but then I realized he was delirious. I placed my hand on his forehead and found he was burning up with fever. I put on my greatcoat and cap and went out into the gale and over to the Medical Office. Finally, I was able to get someone aroused. The corporal came back with me to the hut and took the man's temperature. It was 104 degrees [104 °F = 40 °C]. They came and carted him off on a stretcher to the Camp Hospital and I later heard that he had double pneumonia. I never saw him again. I will never forget my first New Years in the army. Where would we be in another twelve months? Happy New Year, 1941!

TYPIST'S ERROR

While we were stationed in Sussex, New Brunswick, Mel Graham and I were loaned to Brigade Headquarters to work at the Camp Telephone Exchange. The Exchange was located upstairs and we had two bunks in the room. The job was supposed to be handled by the Royal Canadian Corps of Signals [R.C.C.S] signallers, but the "Sigs" were short of trained men so we were asked to fill in until they could provide their own. It was really a cushy job once you got the hang of it. We had two days on duty and two days off. Unless things were terribly busy on the Exchange one of us could sleep or read. As soon as a call came in we would open the switch and say - "Camp Exchange, Number Please". When the subscriber gave the number we would reply - "One Moment Please" - then make the connection. There was no way of knowing when the conversation was finished without opening the switch and "listening in". If you heard no talking then you said - "Finished, Finished, Finished" - and disconnected the line. One night Lieutenant-General Eedson Louis Millard "Tommy" Burns, C.C. [Order of Canada], D.S.O. [Distinguished Service Order], O.B.E. [Order of the British Empire], M.C. [Military Cross], C.D. [Canadian Forces Decoration] called. I was on duty on the switchboard. "Hello, signaller", he said in his rather brusque voice, "Get me San Francisco". He gave me the number and told me to call him at the Mess as soon as I had got the call through. I had nightmares of trying to put the call through and old "Frosty Face" fuming and demanding to know what the blazes was wrong with those damned signallers. However, by a miracle, I got the call through immediately and asked the operator in San Francisco to connect my party, which she did pronto. I called the Mess and asked for the Brigadier. I don't think he even had time to order a drink. "Your party is on the line, sir", I said. I heard him begin to speak and I closed the switch and "listened out". He was so pleased that after he had completed his call he rang me back and complimented me on my efficiency. Little did he know that it was nothing to do with my efficiency but was sheer luck. Or did he know? Anyway, I thought he was a gentleman to ring me back.

Early one morning, about 0530 hours, a call came in to the Exchange for our Battalion. The message was simple - "1st Battalion Canadian Grenadier Guards prepare to move at one hour's notice". I rang the Adjutant and got him out of bed. I could imagine the feverish activity back at our lines. By the time Mel and I got off duty our boys were already packing. By noon we were ready and moving off to Saint John. Rumours were flying. We were going overseas. No, we were going to the West Coast. We were going to

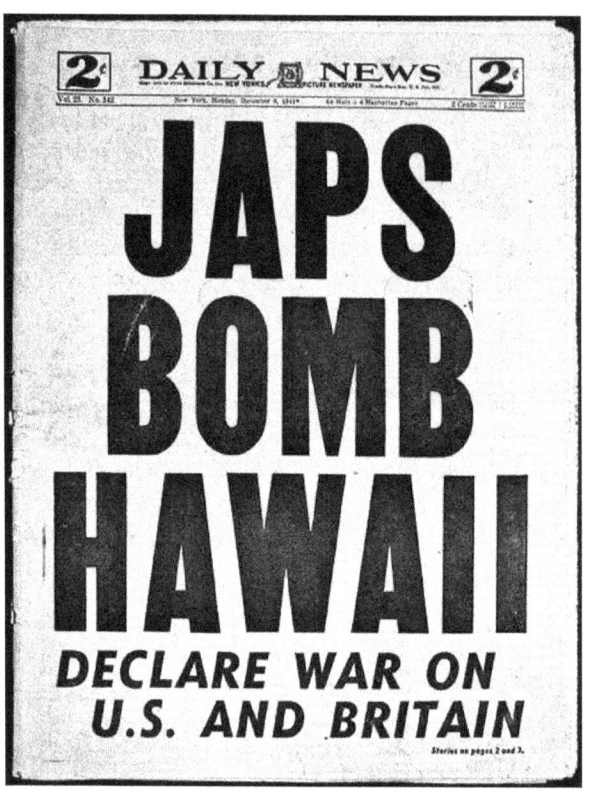

July 1961 - CFB Gagetown, NB
Robert E. Osborne and (Unknown)

Newfoundland - or Iceland. We were going to Bermuda. We were going to the Middle East - somebody had seen the tropical kit arriving in the Q.M. stores! The Adjutant was arguing with one of the Captains. How did he know we were going to Cairo? His batman had told him! The Colonel knew where we were going - but he wasn't telling. It was top secret. When we got to Saint John we debussed at Barrack Green. We took over duties from the Royal Rifles of Canada - they were going to Hong Kong, the lucky devils! I had a friend in "The Rifles", Billy Knapp, so I made some enquiries and soon found him. Billy was going overseas and here I was left behind to do boring garrison duty. It came out later that when Colonel Peiler got the message that morning at 0600 hours we were slated for Hong Kong too, then it was discovered that a stenographer in Ottawa had mistakenly typed "Canadian Grenadier Guards" for "Winnipeg Grenadiers". When the typist's error was discovered the order was promptly countermanded. In the meantime we had got as far as Saint John. I wonder if that call to San Francisco had any bearing on the situation. That was the last time I was to see Billy Knapp. The date was the 10th of October, 1941.

ATTACK ON PEARL HARBOUR

It was the 7th of December. I was lying on the top bunk in our hut at Barrack Green listening to the radio playing "Down East Music" when the program was interrupted for the news flash - "The Japanese have bombed Pearl Harbour". I was stunned but elated too. Now the Americans would be in it with us.

On the 8th of December the startling news - "Japanese attack Hong Kong. Our troops fighting valiantly". I wondered how Billy Knapp was making out. On Christmas Day came the sad news that Hong Kong had fallen after a heroic struggle. Billy Knapp later died in a Japanese Prison Camp. He was about twenty years old.

On the 29th of December we were relieved by the Governor General's Foot Guards and we moved back to Camp Sussex, N.B. It was a depressing New Year although I went home on leave. When I got back, winter had really set in and the snow was piled high. The temperature plummeted to 21 degrees below zero [-21 °F = -29 °C]. We ploughed through the snow drifts on our route marches and tried to lay telephone wire in the howling blizzards. I developed terrible sinus headaches which would disappear as soon as I got back to the warmth of the hut at night. I thought of Napoleon's retreat from Moscow and prayed that I would never have to fight in a winter campaign. In the evenings we would sit around the hot stove and tell yarns. One night I sensed something was up. As soon as we were comfortably settled Sergeant Higgins rose and made a nice little speech and presented me with a pipe. Then Corporal McNair got up and handed me a package of Bond Street pipe tobacco. He was followed by Art Hurd who handed me a box of wooden matches. Then they all shouted - "Now smoke it!" After using up nearly a box of matches I got the pipe going. I was now in full membership in the "Hot Stove Club".

KNIGHTS IN ARMOUR

Towards the end of the month rumours began to fly. We were going to be turned into an Armoured Regiment. On the 5th of February it became official. Those who did not want to go into tanks were given the option of transferring to some other outfit or branch of the service. Sergeant Higgins went to the Air Force and so did Art Hurd. Those who elected to stay with the Regiment were given tests and on the basis of these tests we were selected to be Driver-Mechanics, Gunners or Wireless Operators. Later, when the crews were made up, some would be selected as Crew Commanders. On the 13th of February, as I came in off parade and read the Orders, I was surprised to see that I had been promoted to Full Corporal. After dinner I went over to the Quarter Master's stores to draw my stripes. "Sign here, McKnight", said the quartermaster as he pushed the sheet in front of me. "I'm not McKnight", I said, "I'm Osborne". "What the hell difference does it make", he replied, "you two are always together, anyway". The next thing I knew I

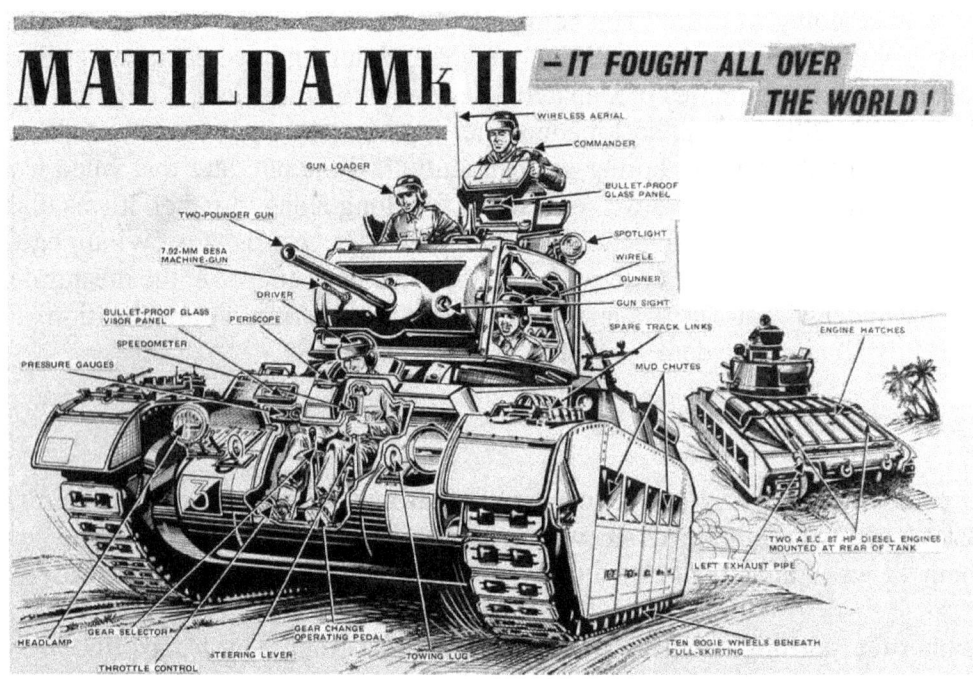

Valentine Tank

Morse Code "Key"

was posted to Camp Borden on a Wireless Instructor's Course. I was now a tank man with two hooks [A 2-bar chevron worn pointing down indicating a Corporal] on my sleeve. Things were looking up.

WIRELESS SCHOOL

My whole life in the Army now took on new meaning. Here was something challenging. The Wireless School had many rooms and one of the big rooms had little cubicles around the sides. We each entered a cubicle and put on headsets. The instructor sent Morse code to us and we wrote it down. This was done in two ways. The messages could be sent in running hand, that is, a straight forward message like "NO. 2 SQN RENDO AT 375 481 AT 0900 HRS" or if the message was in code it would look like "BXYDR LMEDC UYWAQ LIKEX". It was obviously much easier to read the running hand type of message because you could guess at a letter if you missed it but there was no way you could guess at a missed letter in code. We were warned that our final tests would be in code. The sending speed would be anywhere from 15 to 25 words per minute. To copy down code at that speed you had to read much faster than you could write. Every day we spent hours in the code practice room. Besides learning Morse at this speed we also had courses in Electricity where we learned about Ohm's Law, series and parallel circuits, voltage and amperage, super heterodynes and so on. In the tank it was the Wireless Operator's job to look after the battery, or accumulator as they called it, so we had to learn all about electrolytes and the care and maintenance of batteries. There were also lectures on Map Reading, Armoured Corps organization, Wireless Links between Tank Troops, Squadrons, Regimental Headquarters, Brigade and Divisional Headquarters. We were kept busy all day and on most nights we went back to the School to practice on the "key" [Hand-switch used to send Morse code]. We were told our final test would be not only on our ability to read Morse but to send it as well. There was a very good esprit de corps. Nobody was grousing and everyone was determined to pass those exams and earn the right to wear the coveted "wireless flash". Most of us had been regimental signallers and had won our "flags" [the badge depicts a set of signal flags]. This gave us a head start. Those who had to learn Morse code from scratch were really up against it. I was trying to help one fellow who was struggling so we would go down for an hour's practice every night. It was good for me too because one of the best ways to learn is by teaching and it also gave me valuable practice in "sending". I passed the test with flying colours - getting one perfect message at 23 words per minute. I was now a qualified wireless operator with an increase in trade's pay of 40 cents a day.

ARMOURED CORPS SCHOOL - C.F.B. BORDEN, 1942

Today I had my first ride in a tank. It was a Matilda, or more technically an Infantry Tank Mk II Matilda A12, the kind they used in the African desert. It had a 2-pounder L/50 40mm main gun in the turret and a No. 11 wireless set. I was impressed with the cleanliness of the turret; it was painted white and had the smell of oil and petrol. I sat in the gunner's seat and peered through the gun sight. Then I slipped over to the Loader/Operator's seat and tried to imagine operating the wireless and working the gun. We went for a ride and I was surprised at how smooth and comfortable it was. My first impression, and one that never left me, was that there was something about the inside of a tank turret that reminded me of a ship. Perhaps it was the clean white interior, or it may have been the smell. There was also something that reminded me of a bomber aircraft.

In many ways tank crews are like ship's crews or bomber crews. They have to learn to live and fight in very cramped quarters. We had to operate as a team but we also had to accept strict personal discipline. We did our job as a member of a crew. In my corner of the turret, on the left-side of the gun, I lived in a world of my own - "cabin'd, cribb'd, confin'd" - although I was in very close proximity to the others. If you didn't learn to live like this then little irritations could erupt into quarrels and endanger the lives of everyone. By a

Squadron	Armoured Recce Regiment	Senior Regiment in Brigade	Middle Regiment in Brigade	Junior Regiment in Brigade
"HQ"				
"A"				
"B"				
"C"				
1 Bde	nil	11th Canadian Armoured Regiment (The Ontario Regiment)	12th Canadian Armoured Regiment (The Three Rivers Regiment)	14th Canadian Armoured Regiment (The Calgary Regiment)
2 Bde	nil	6th Canadian Armoured Regiment (1st Hussars)	10th Canadian Armoured Regiment (Fort Garry Horse)	27th Canadian Armoured Regiment (The Sherbrooke Fusilier Regiment)
4 Div	29th Canadian Armoured Reconnaissance Regiment (The South Alberta Regiment)	21st Canadian Armoured Regiment (The Governor General's Foot Guards)	22nd Canadian Armoured Regiment (The Canadian Grenadier Guards)	28th Canadian Armoured Regiment (The British Columbia Regiment)
5 Div	3rd Canadian Armoured Reconnaissance Regiment (The Governor General's Horse Guards)	2nd Canadian Armoured Regiment (Lord Strathcona's Horse (Royal Canadians))	5th Canadian Armoured Regiment (8th Princess Louise's (New Brunswick) Hussars)	9th Canadian Armoured Regiment (The British Columbia Dragoons)

View inside a typical tank turret

sort of unspoken rule you respected the other fellow's privacy, such as it was, and got on with your job. It was an old fashioned rule, but it worked.

The tank driver didn't go throwing his tank around like the general public believed. People think tanks just go crashing through trees and buildings and over precipices! Unfortunately, this impression was reinforced by recruiting posters, bond drive advertisements and even postage stamps. The tank is usually shown with its front tracks poised high in the air about to crash down. If a tank driver did this he would probably break the suspension of his vehicle not to mention what he would do to his crew. A good tank driver is constantly driving with his crew in mind. He doesn't wait for the crew commander to tell him, but searches ahead for hull-down and turret-down positions. He also tries to give his gunner the best possible platform for shooting. I was always lucky in my drivers. Mike O'Donnell, "Shorty" Halladay, "Chick" Weir and Jack Kane were all first-class. They never let out their clutch too fast or mashed their gears. A good driver watches his R.P.M.'s and knows just when to shift up or down sweetly into the next gear.

Our tank had five forward speeds and one reverse. All my drivers gave me a ride as smooth as a Cadillac. They were always thinking of us crowded up there in the turret and did not bump us around. Jack Kane was especially thoughtful. He tried to give Gordie Hatch, our gunner, the steadiness of a billiard table when he was engaging a target at top speed - that's the mark of a good driver. What I have said of the driver of course applies equally to the co-driver. He must help the driver in every way and sometimes engage the enemy with his bow-gun when called upon by the crew commander to do so. If something happens to the Commander it is usually the co-driver who has to slip up into the turret and take the Loader/Operator's place on the gun, while he in turn takes over command of the tank.

The Wireless Operator lives in his own little world, curled up on his seat in the corner of the turret. His world at first seems extremely limited. The breech of the gun is inches from him. He loads the gun and must be very careful not to get his hand between the breech and the wireless set when the gun is fired or he will lose his hand. There may have been such accidents but I never heard of one. His main job is the wireless so he must maintain his radio in good running order. He is trained to make minor repairs. If a valve (tube) burns out he has a box of spares neatly packed in sponge rubber with which to replace it. If the fault is of a more serious order he will have to call the R.C.C.S. Instrument Mechanic who will take the set away and replace it with a serviceable one. Later on, the radio we used in the Sherman was a No. 19 set. Every day the Wireless Operator is given a frequency on which to net (tune) his set. This must be done very accurately or the set will go off net and the tank will be out of communication with the other tanks in the squadron and regiment. There is an "A" set which is used for communication within the squadron and regiment. Depending on atmospheric conditions, terrain, and length of aerial it has a range of 10 miles - that is using R/T [Radio Telephony or Voice Transmission]. The range would be greater if he was using W/T [Wireless Telegraphy or Morse-key]. The "B" set has a "visual range" - that is, if you can see the other tanks then you can communicate with them. Some strange things happened though with the "B" set. I have picked up tank battles in Russia and the Western Desert because of unusual atmospheric conditions. This phenomenon is explained as Skip-frequency. The signal went up like a rubber ball, bounced off the ionosphere, came back to earth bounced again, repeating the process. If you happened to be just at the spot where one of these "bounces" hit the ground you could pick up the signal. In addition to the "A" and "B" sets, there is an intercom (I/C) by which the Crew Commander talks to the members of his crew and they to him. The crew cannot, however, use the "A" or "B" sets. Located on the turret wall beside the Crew Commander is a switch-box which he uses to change from I/C to "A" or "B" sets as the situation dictates. One of the most frequent errors made by a Commander was to forget to switch off the "A" set when speaking to his crew or vice versa. I still have a vivid recollection of one of my former Crew Commanders during an exercise getting a severe reprimand from the Command Officer [C.O.] for some tactical error. He acknowledged the C.O.'s message with correct wireless procedure, then turned to speak to his crew, but

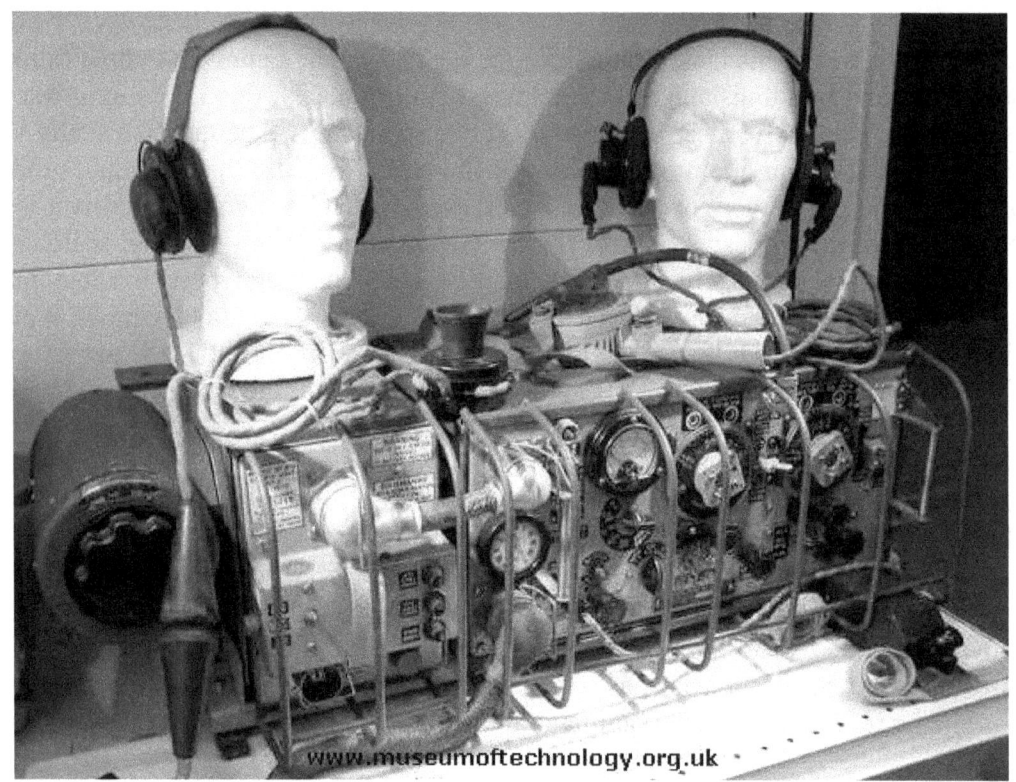

No. 19 Wireless Set

.30-calibre Browning machine gun and ammo belt / case

forgot to switch from the regimental channel. "To hell with you - you old bald-headed bastard!" The rest of the crew couldn't hear it but I did as Wireless Operator. I can still see the look on the Crew Commander's face when he realized what he had done. I'm sure he must have had to buy the drinks in the Officer's Mess for many a night after that classical boo-boo.

From the Crew Commander's position the Wireless Operator looks a bit weird. The red glow of the pilot lamp on the wireless set is reflected on his face giving him a look like some jolly elf as he sits crouched up on his seat in the corner on the far side of the gun.

As a tank crew member you knew you were "going to get it" sooner or later. The statistics were stacked against you. I know some fellows said that it always seemed that it was "the other fellow" who got hit but not you. I never felt that way. I lived to bury some of them. I don't want to give the impression that I had a death wish, but I knew from watching other tanks getting hit and brewing up [catching on fire] that unless we were exceptionally lucky our time would come too. The question was "When?" and would you be killed or wounded? We all faced the reality of death every minute we were in action. It's a valuable lesson in self-knowledge. I wrote a letter to my mother, which began - "Dear Mother: When you receive this you will already have received word from the War Office in Ottawa that I have been killed..." I sealed it and gave it to our Quartermaster with the instructions - "If I'm killed, wait a few days, and then send this to my next-of-kin. If I'm wounded - burn it!" We knew we were playing against the best team in the league and we were just up from the minors. These "boys" were real "Pros" - veterans of numerous tank battles on the Russian and African fronts. We were facing our first test. It could be murder. It was!

ON THE PORT SIDE OF THE GUN

The Wireless Operator lives in a little world of sound, not of sight. Shut up in a corner of the turret he is truly confined with just enough room to load the Browning machine gun and the main gun. He must constantly remember to keep clear of the recoil of the main gun or he could lose his arm or hand. He listens intently to the crackling on the air waves. Inside his earphones comes the babble of voices couched in the jargon of wireless procedure. "Hello, Charlie four, enemy 'ant' corner of hedgerow - figures two-one-four-eight-one-six. I say again two-one-four-eight-one-six. Over." The reply comes: "Hello, Charlie four, roger, out". [The message is to No. 4 Troop to warn him that there is an anti-tank gun sighted out of the corner of the hedge-row at the map co-ordinate given] The chatter on the "A" and "B" sets would drive the average person insane but to the trained ear of the Wireless Operator it is all intelligible and very important. He is the nerve cell of the tank crew, relaying intelligence to the Crew Commander, keeping him in touch with the command and troop situations. His world is one of semi-darkness. Through his periscope he has a very limited view of the world outside. The red pilot light on his wireless set gives a warm, friendly glow to the world inside. His knowledge of the action outside is based on wireless messages and bits and pieces of information pieced together from other members of the crew - especially the Commander. It is the crackling on the R/T with its steady background "mush" that he relies upon for his view of reality. Occasionally he may resort to the W/T and send a message from the Morse key strapped to his thigh, but only very rarely. If he does this, the message is to the distant tank or Brigade or Divisional Headquarters. His world is one of sound and his impressions of that world must be formed from scraps of information picked up from countless radio messages. He learns to rely on his wireless set, and often does not know in which direction the tank is moving, especially when the gunner is rotating the turret to engage targets.

He has two jobs, besides being the Radio Operator he is also the Loader/Operator. This means that he is also responsible for loading the main gun and keeping the .30-calibre Browning machine gun operating smoothly. He must remedy any stoppages and see that the belt of ammo is feeding properly. I used to spend many hours oiling the machine gun and checking every round in the belts of ammunition so there would be

July 26th, 1955 Robert E. Osborne

Captain William Avery "Billy" Bishop
Royal Aircraft Factory, S. E. 5a, No. A 8936
No. 60 Squadron, Royal Flying Corps (RFC)
72 Aerial Victories
1917

no stoppages. If the Crew Commander calls for an Armour Piercing or High Explosive round, the Loader/Operator must select the right shell from the rack. He must also set the delay fuse on the High Explosive shells if the Commander calls for it. In the heat of action the Loader/Operator can be a very busy boy!

If a shell in the gun fails to go off then a pre-arranged Misfire Drill is carried out. It goes like this. The Crew Commander says - "Stand by ten seconds!" Then - "Examine cap!" At this command the Loader/Operator quickly opens the breech and looks closely to see if there is a dent in the cap where the striker pin should hit it. If there is - providing it has not gone off in the next instant and blown him to kingdom come - he reports - "Cap struck!" The Commander then orders a delay and if possible the turret personnel would get out of the tank. If the cap does not show a dent, then the Commander gives the order - "Unload!" at which the Loader/Operator opens the breech again, extracts the shell and hands it quickly to the Crew Commander who tosses it overboard. I am thankful to say that I never had to go through this "drill" with a live round up the spout, though we often practiced it.

CAMP BORDEN ARMOURED SCHOOL

One of the subjects in our course was learning the wireless link-ups of an armoured regiment, brigade and division. We would draw little parallelograms to represent tank formations and then with coloured pencils sketch in the various wireless hook-ups. There would be the link between the Troop Leader and his four tanks on the "B" set, then the wider linkage on the "A" set to the Squadron and the Squadron rear-link to Regimental H.Q. and on to Brigade and Divisional H.Q.'s. There was also the Tactical Reconnaissance (Tac/R) with the Air Force and a hook-up to the Artillery. Later we were to install a phone at the rear of our tanks so the Infantry boys could speak to us. It must be remembered that a tank commander with his headsets on could not hear an infantry man trying to call him, especially when the tank motor was running and the guns firing. At this time a magazine appeared at Camp Borden called "The Tank". It did a lot to raise our enthusiasm for our new corps. There were articles in it by men who had actually fought in tanks during the B.E.F.'s [British Expeditionary Force] retreat to Dunkirk. Other articles told about the fighting against the Afrika Korps in the desert. The Tank ran a contest which offered a prize of $5.00 and year's subscription to the magazine for the best suggestion sent in each month. I sent in a suggestion that a sand-table be set up with little model tanks on it and coloured strings to represent the various wireless links. To my great surprise and delight it was announced in the next issue of The Tank that my suggestion had been judged worthy of that month's prize. I learned later that the suggestion was acted upon and a large sand-table was set up in the Armoured Corps School to teach wireless linkups.

BILLY BISHOP

Toward the end of February I got a weekend pass to go to Montreal to attend the Annual Boy Scout Patrol Leader's Banquet which was held at the Windsor Hotel. The guest speaker was Air Vice-Marshall William "Billy" Avery Bishop. It was a great thrill for me to see one who had been my boyhood hero. He was much stouter than I had imagined. It was the first time too that I had seen anyone wearing the Victoria Cross. I had never seen a man with so many decorations. Bishop was wearing the ribbons of the V.C. [Victoria Cross], D.S.O. [Distinguished Service Order], M.C. [Military Cross], D.F.C. [Distinguished Flying Cross], and many others. His eyes still had that keen blue gaze that had sought out the Hun over France.

THE LONELINESS OF THE EARLY MORNING

There is no feeling more desolate than the one experienced when one returns from leave. I had to get an early morning train - 0520 hours. My mother, of course, was up and cooked me a good breakfast. Then I

Returning from Leave - Goodbye to Mother - 1942

Above is shown a small section of one of Canada's huge military encampments, that at Debert, Nova Scotia. Constructed during the summer and fall months it houses thousands of men, members of the Third Division of the Canadian Active Service Force.

said, "Goodbye" - you never knew if it might be the last "Goodbye". I hitched my kit bag on to my shoulder and started off toward the station. The snow was deep and no snow plow had been through. I walked in the middle of the road, ploughing through the knee deep drifts. The houses were all in darkness. I am quoting to myself Wordsworth's lines - "Dear God! The very houses seem asleep." In one house a light is showing. Is it someone else, like me, going off leave? Or is it perhaps sickness? My watch says it is just going 0500 hours. I stop, put down my kit bag in the snow, and rest for a moment. The railway station looms ahead dark and deserted - no lights on the platform. I enter the waiting room. How is it that all railway waiting rooms smell the same? A combination of train smoke, tobacco smoke and whatever it is they use to clean the wash rooms. There is no one else here. I listen to the telegraph key in the office clicking away. "Come on," I reprove myself, "you can read Morse, you've got your 'wireless flash' now go on and read that stuff." I can make out some letters but there's no coherent message. The telegrapher, wearing his green eye shades, goes over and sits by the key. He swings round a telephone mouthpiece and speaks into it. I can't quite hear what he is saying. I go over to the ticket window. It's dark in the office except where the telegrapher is bathed in light under the green shade suspended from the ceiling. "She's on time," he says, "left Rock Forest twenty minutes ago." I hear the semaphore clatter outside. The stationmaster switches on the platform lights. Another serviceman opens the door letting in a swirl of snow. He stamps his boots. He's in the Air Force. He asks for a match to light his cigarette. I hear the train whistle. We pick up our kit bags and go out on to the platform. The headlights of the train glare at us as it comes panting and puffing into the station and then there is a screeching of brakes and an exhalation of steam as the monster comes to a grinding stop. We run down the platform to where the trainman is holding his lantern, grab the metal bar and swing ourselves up the steps. The car is fairly crowded with service people. A soldier and a C.W.A.C. [Canadian Women's Army Corps] are sleeping in each other's arms. She wakes and arranges her hair. I find an empty seat about two thirds of the way down the car. "All aboard!" sings out the trainman. I heave my kit bag up on to the luggage rack and settle back into the seat. Might as well have a snooze. I peer out the window. It's dark outside and the window is cold. We cross the bridge over Cherry River and I think of the good times I've had canoeing and skating on it. I remember the time that I fell through the ice and had to go into the Goyette's farmhouse to dry my clothes. The conductor looks at my ticket and I curl up next to the window again and fall asleep lulled by the rhythm of the wheels. Was it like this when Uncle Arthur returned from his last leave home in the First War?

DEBERT, NOVA SCOTIA

I arrived in Debert Camp to find the new Armoured Corps in full swing. It was really exciting. I was an N.C.O. [Non-Commissioned Officer] now and an instructor and I found that there were a lot of young men eager to learn how to become Wireless Operators. No longer did I have to go on rifle-drill, parade and route marches. I was an instructor in the new Wireless School and I loved every minute of it. The head of the school was Captain "Buck" Buchanan. Rumour had it that he had been a bush pilot. If he had I couldn't figure out why he wasn't training pilots. Anyway, "Buck" was our boss.

I came into the School Office one day after giving a lecture to my class. I overheard Captain Buchanan say to another officer - "That chap Osborne is the most unprepossessing fellow I have ever met." Then after a pause he continued, "But, his classes always come out tops in the exams. I can't understand it. He must be a damn good teacher." I had to go over to the Y.M.C.A. library and get a dictionary and look up the meaning of "unprepossessing" in Webster. "Not having a prepossessing or winning appearance", I read, "not attractive or engaging." Well, well, as the poet said:

"O wad some Pow'r the giftie gie us
To see oursels as ithers see us!"
- Robert Burns (1759-1796) - To a Louse (1786)

Major-General Frederick Franklin Worthington
(September 17, 1889–December 8, 1967), M.C., M.M., C.D.
Nicknames: "Worthy" and "Fighting Frank"

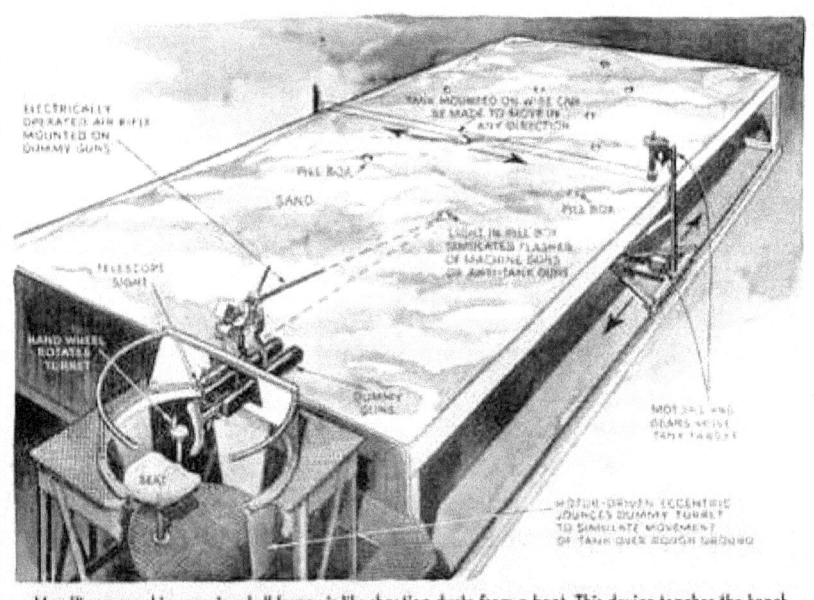

BOUNCING "RYPA" TRAINS CANADIAN TANK GUNNERS

For teaching gunnery at the Canadian tank school at Camp Borden, Ont., a training device called a "rypa" simulates the roll, yaw, pitch, and alternating oscillation of a tank in action. Looking through a telescopic sight, the gunner turns the revolving turret and aims a dummy machine gun at moving targets on a sand-pit range. An electrically operated air rifle, aimed with the machine gun, shoots lead pellets.

Handling a machine gun in a hell buggy is like shooting ducks from a boat. This device teaches the knack

That month of May in Debert must have been one of the most active in the Regiment's history. Everywhere "tanks" were being talked about and all sorts of new words were being added to our vocabulary - laager (not the beer!) - rendo - R.Y.P.A. - super heterodyne - hundred-hour check - L.A.D. - buffer and recoil system - command net - A.C.V. - "RAMS" - pressel switch - snatch-plugs - paralax - bogeys - Besa - Ohm's Law - power traverse - elevating gear - side-tone - Marco - Slidex - Solenoid ... In the messes at night all these new words were so bandied about that anyone visiting us from another corps must have thought we were speaking a foreign language. So we were - the language of "Tank Folk".

Although my job was that of a Wireless Instructor, I also had to learn about armament because I was a Loader/Operator and my task was to teach new Loader/Operators. In spare periods I sat in on the classes for tank gunners at the Gunnery School which was just next to ours. The R.Y.P.A. was fun. R.Y.P.A. was derived from the first letters of the words - Roll, Yaw, and Pitch Apparatus. It was a tank turret with a .22-calibre rifle instead of a 6-pdr gun. A sand table with miniature tanks, trucks, jeeps, etc., provided the targets. You sat in the gunner's seat, pressed your eye to the gunner's scope and the motor was started. It really did simulate a tank's movements.

The press had been playing up the career of our new General, Major-General Frederick Franklin Worthington, M.C. [Military Cross], M.M. [Military Medal], C.D. [Canadian Forces Decoration], nicknamed "Worthy" and "Fighting Frank". He had fought in the Great War and in the South American revolution against Pancho Villa. We were all anxious to see this new colourful leader of our armoured corps. He had already arrived in Canada from Britain but we had not seen him yet, apparently he was supervising the assembly line where his first "Ram" tanks were rolling off. The Ram was a cruiser tank designed and built in Montreal, Quebec, Canada, based on the U.S. M3 Medium tank but it was used exclusively for training. We had all seen the picture of General Worthington wearing his tank beret, his piercing black eyes and his row of medal ribbons.

At the end of March he arrived in Debert. I was teaching an afternoon class in Elementary Electricity and turned to the blackboard and wrote the formula for Ohm's Law - "I [current in amperes] equals V [voltage in volts] over R [resistance in ohms]". As I wrote I sensed an unusual stillness in the room and as I turned round to face the class, General Worthington was standing about a foot from my face, his hands on his hips, and his jaw thrust out. "What are you teaching, Corporal?" he brusquely snapped. "Eddy-Eddy, sir", I replied. [These were the code words used for letters of the alphabet. "E" was "Eddie" and "Eddy-Eddy" stood for "Elementary Electricity".] "Very good, carry on Corporal." he said as he turned and disappeared out the door. In order to recover from my state of shock, I gave the class a smoke break. A minute or so later, about a dozen officers came pouring into the room - red tabs everywhere. "Have you seen the General? Which way did he go?" "He went thataway," I said and pointed out the door. Apparently there was nothing "Worthy" liked better than to escape from his entourage and see things for himself, before anyone had a chance to put on a "show" for him. I could now say that I had seen the new General face to face.

A trooper would be lying on his back underneath a tank and look round to see the General lying under there beside him. A sleepy gunner dozing off during an outdoor lecture on the "Buffer and Recoil System" would be rudely awakened by a shot past his ear. "Worthy" posted marksmen for just such a purpose! He was a "fire-eater" and we loved him and called him "Fighting Frank".

"In peace there's nothing so becomes a man
As modest stillness and humility;
But when the blast of war blows in our ears,
Then imitate the action of the tiger:

Grenadier Guards Cap Badge and Proper Beret Placement

No. 11 and No. 19 Wireless Sets
Note the accumulators (batteries) on the floor

Stiffen the sinews, summon up the blood."
- William Shakespeare (1564-1616) - Henry V, Act III, Scene l (1599)

LEARNING TO DRIVE

As tank crews, we were encouraged to do every job in the tank. I had to learn to drive but when the Driving School was in progress I was kept busy teaching Drivers how to operate the radio. I had a further handicap - I had never learned to drive a car. A great many of us having grown up in the Depression could not drive when we joined up. My school friend Bill Bellingham joined the R.C.A.F. and had his pilot's wings but he had never driven a car. He came home on leave and asked his dad for use of the car and drove it right through the back of the garage! Before we could get into the tank driving course we had to pass our truck driving test, so it looked as though I was blocked. Corporal Jack Harper from the Motor Transport section realized my plight and came to my rescue. He requisitioned a truck and after supper he took me out to the driving ring and tried to teach me. We went out every night but no matter how hard I tried I couldn't get on to the "double clutch". Jack had great patience with me. Steering was no problem but I just couldn't get the hang of shifting gears. Jack knew that once I got into a tank I would be all right because the gears were synchromeshed and I would not have to double clutch. He recommended that I go on to the Tank Driving Course and once I got into the driver's seat of the Ram I had no problem at all moving up through all 5 gears and shifting down again. It was great fun even if I did have to use two hands on the shift stick.

MAJOR HENRY "GRIFF" GRIFFITH

At the beginning of May, the Colonel went overseas with a small draft of officers and other ranks. Major (later Lieutenant-Colonel) Henry Griffith took over command and had the unenviable task of whipping us into shape. No man could have been better suited for the task. "Griff" had served with the 87th Battalion in the First War as a senior N.C.O. and later as a Lieutenant. He knew what we were in for and he brought those lessons learned from the First War to us and saw to it that we learned them. Every morning, before we were dismissed to our training as tank crews, "Griff" held a Regimental parade at 0800 hours and woe betides the squadron that marched late on to the parade square. I can still hear him saying - "When I say parade is at 0800 hours I mean 0800 and not 0801." At this time the tank man's black beret became our official head-dress and "Griff" was determined that the Grenadiers would wear it properly. Each morning he would issue the command - "Check berets!" and we would all check to make sure that our berets were in a straight line across our foreheads and two fingers above the eyebrow. It was a small thing but it established the discipline and concern for correctness that became the hallmark of the Guards. He knew that the time would come when the battle was on, and we were in a tight corner, when discipline would save the Regiment from disaster.

NIGHT VISION

Today we had night vision tests. It was quite interesting. We were handed a clip-board with thumb tacks all down the left side of the board. Each tack represented a number - one, two, three, etc. Then we were taken into a darkened room and it was explained to us how the eye works at night. Physiological terms like "rods" and "cones" were used. We were told that it took a few minutes for the "visual purple" to build up. This failure to wait for the build-up of the visual purple for night vision was the cause of so many fatal accidents - especially with the D/R's [Despatch Rider] who were handed a message in a lighted room and then went out immediately into the blackout and ran smack into a parked tank with their motorbike. So many of them were getting killed on "schemes" that Lord Haw Haw [German radio propaganda broadcaster William Joyce] said: "We don't need to fight the Canadians, we just need to keep them well supplied with motorbikes." We were taught that if we kept one eye covered or closed when we came in out of the dark

Scar-faced William Joyce, whom Canadian servicemen overseas remember as "Lord Haw Haw," was executed as a British traitor in London on January 3, 1946. One of his nightly broadcasts from Germany gave me the creeps.

Seven war correspondents had been transported in hush-hush atmosphere to a heavily guarded field south of London, arriving about 14.30 hours. A bevy of brass, including three generals, surrounded three huge trucks from the backs of which were suspended rolls of steel mesh. We were then briefed in what was tagged "Operation Frontenac."

It was invasion stuff. The trucks left on a signal at about 20 mph, laying a wide carpet of steel mesh behind them. As they reached the far end of the field three Spitfires roared in, wing to wing, and touched down near us. The impact caused a wave action to result so that the mesh at the far end was flapping upward 15 feet. The Spits lifted sharply and flew off while halfway down the strip.

The brass had a hurried discussion. An officer came over to express apologies — censors would be instructed to accept nothing on the operation. It was a two-hour drive back to London.

We arrived just in time to hear "Jairmany Calling" and Lord Haw Haw leading off with: "The British again risked the lives of brave Canadian airmen this afternoon in a typical snafu called 'Operation Frontenac' at . . ."

He then went on to list all the classified information we had been given at the briefing. Who had been the spy supplying Lord Haw Haw? And how and where had the relay of all the information been done within the past two hours?

Canadian 4th Division Patch

into a lighted room then we would not lose our visual purple, the night vision would remain in the closed eye. It would also help to wear dark glasses before a night exercise. Vitamin A was reputed to help you see in the dark and some Night Fighter pilots were reported to have developed cat's eyes by eating quantities of carrots! During the actual test, objects were flashed on a screen and we were given a few seconds to write down what we thought we had seen. One trick for better night vision was not to look directly or stare at the object but to scan your eyes across from one side to another. This had something to do with the rods and cones. I scored very high on the test. Apparently a person might have very good day vision and poor night vision or vice-versa. However, I wondered if my high score was due to the fact that I might have a better imagination than the others and that I was a Wireless Operator and accustomed to writing legibly in semi-darkness! No doubt it was all duly recorded on my personal records. At any rate it would be a help when we got to England where we would have to operate in the blackout.

THE GREEN FIELDS BEYOND - DIVISIONAL DRUMHEAD SERVICE

The day was Sunday and the whole Division attended a Drumhead [Consecration of the Colours] service. It was very impressive with all the drums piled up and draped with flags. The chaplains from various units participated. We were proudly wearing our green Fourth Division "pool table" patch for the first time. We felt like real tank men now that we had our new patch on our sleeves. I was proud to think that my Uncle Arthur had also been in the Fourth Division in the first show. After "Worthy" inspected us, he had us all sit on the grass. It was a lovely day and many of the wives and families of the men had come from Debert and other nearby villages. The General told us that he had chosen the colour green for our divisional patch for two reasons - One, because it was the colour of the 4th Division in the last war and two, it was the tank man's symbol of victory. The motto of the Royal Armoured Corps was - "Through mud and blood to the green fields beyond." He went on to tell us straight that what we were going to experience in England was quite different from what we had experienced up to now. He said that we had done a phenomenal job in a few months of converting ourselves into an armoured division but we were now going to England where there would be a shortage of food and our stomachs would shrink to half their size. Eventually he said we would come to grips with a savage and skilful enemy who would soon discover that the 4th Division would "give no quarter - ask none - and many of you will not come back, falling in the mud and blood of the battlefield. But with the courage and determination of all, some will win through to the green fields beyond." His concluding remarks were: "Now I'm going to wish you good hunting, good killing of Nazis, and a great deal of luck - soldier's luck!" It was great stuff and we lapped it up. At last we were going to strike a real blow against Hitler and his Nazis and we had a blood and guts General to lead us. Some of the wives and older children who had assembled that day were pretty upset by the straightforwardness of "Worthy's" speech. The grim reality of this war was coming home to them for the first time and these may be the last days that some of them would ever spend with their husbands and fathers. But for those of us who were single this was what we had joined up for and we were raring to go.

WATCHMAN WHAT OF THE NIGHT?

Apparently some fellow wrote a letter home in which he announced that we would soon be sailing from Halifax for England. The letter was intercepted by the censor and there was a hell of a stink about it. Rumour has it that he is to be court-martialled and that General Worthington is furious and is going to make an example of this chap to remind us all that breaches of security will NOT be tolerated. There really was no excuse for this soldier's action because we've had it drilled into us about the dangers of giving information to listening ears. Every canteen has posters with the slogan - "CARELESS TALK COSTS LIVES" - with a picture of somebody telephoning, a seductive enemy agent listening, and a troop ship sinking. My mother and I had worked out an arrangement by which she would know when I had sailed for overseas. My last communication to her would be a postcard in the Cam Silhouette Series which bore the

Dear Mum:
Read about Arthur's wedding in the paper.
I did not know Tommy Baird had enlisted.
Love Bob

Bessie Sainsbury Osborne (Cordy): born 2 August 1891 in Capelton, Sherbrooke County, QC; died 31 December 1977 at Brockville, ON.

slogan - "Watchman what of the night?" She knew that when she received this postcard she would not hear from me again until I wrote to her from somewhere in England. I mailed that postcard to her and she kept it and after the war I checked the postmark. It read - Truro, Nova Scotia, September 23rd, 8:30 A.M. and she received it in Magog, Quebec, on September 25th. We sailed from Halifax, Nova Scotia, on September 29th. This is the way my mother and I communicated without giving anything away to the enemy. After all, I was a Signaller and Wireless Operator so I should have been able to work out a code.

THE LAST SUPPER

We knew we were leaving for Halifax the next morning, so Doug and I went into Truro and had the biggest steak dinner we could get. It cost us the earth - over a dollar! We topped it off with a delicious chocolate sundae. Remembering the General's words we knew it would be a long time, if ever, that we would eat like that again.

A LOT OF TRIPE

We set sail from Halifax in the afternoon of the 29th of September. Doug and I leaned over the stern rail watching the shore of Canada fade away on the horizon. Our ship was the Athlone Castle, of the Union-Castle Line. We were quartered below decks. It was like the black hole of Calcutta, the air was so foul. It was terribly overcrowded and we slept in hammocks. The food was awful. One day we had tripe and only one man of the fourteen at our table could stomach it. He just moved along from plate to plate and cleaned up the whole lot! When I met Doug on the deck and told him how much "Mac" had eaten, he said, "Bob, that sounds like a lot of tripe to me." I spent most of my time on deck where the air was clean and bracing. There were many gambling games going, one chap won so much that he hired two fellows to sleep on each side of him to guard his winnings. The Athlone Castle soon became a floating gambling casino. We had boat drill every morning and the guns were tested. I was in charge of an Oerlikon [20mm Light Anti-Aircraft] gun and this gave me a good excuse for spending most of my time on deck. Day after day we sailed with the convoy through the frothy seas and looked at the leaden sky and grey water. For the first couple of days we were shepherded by Catalina [Consolidated PBY Catalina multi-role flying boat] aircraft out of Halifax, but as we sailed farther out into the North Atlantic we had only our naval escort to protect us. One night there was great commotion and we all stood to for "Action Stations". The escorts dropped depth charges as an enemy U-Boat shadowed us for some time. The German submarines, operating in wolf packs, were at their height during this period of the war. I reckoned that a man would last about two minutes in that icy murky blackness. Every day it got colder as we passed close to Greenland, then Iceland. The convoy consisted of twenty transports with warships out in front and destroyers on the flanks.

CROSSING THE ATLANTIC

I never knew anything could be so dark and foreboding as the north Atlantic in October. It was a major crime to smoke or light a match on deck after dark as a U-Boat commander could spot that tiny light for miles. One very dark night as I was going my rounds checking up on my Oerlikon crew, a shutter blew off one of the windows. The light shot out like a searchlight over the water. Shouts of "Get that bloody light out!" came from different quarters. About midnight one of the naval officers invited me up to the bridge for a cup of Kye [Also known as Pusser's Kye] - a navy version of cocoa. Hard gritty chocolate scraped into thin flakes and boiled in evaporated milk. While we were standing there with our eyes screwed up peering into the sleety darkness, suddenly a great black shape veered up in front of us. There was a clanging of bells and hurried orders "Hard a starboard! Full steam Astern!" as our skipper took evasive action. "Damn that Dutchman!" he said, putting his pipe back into his mouth. Apparently the ship ahead had "zigged" when he should have "zagged" and we narrowly missed a collision. When things settled down and the

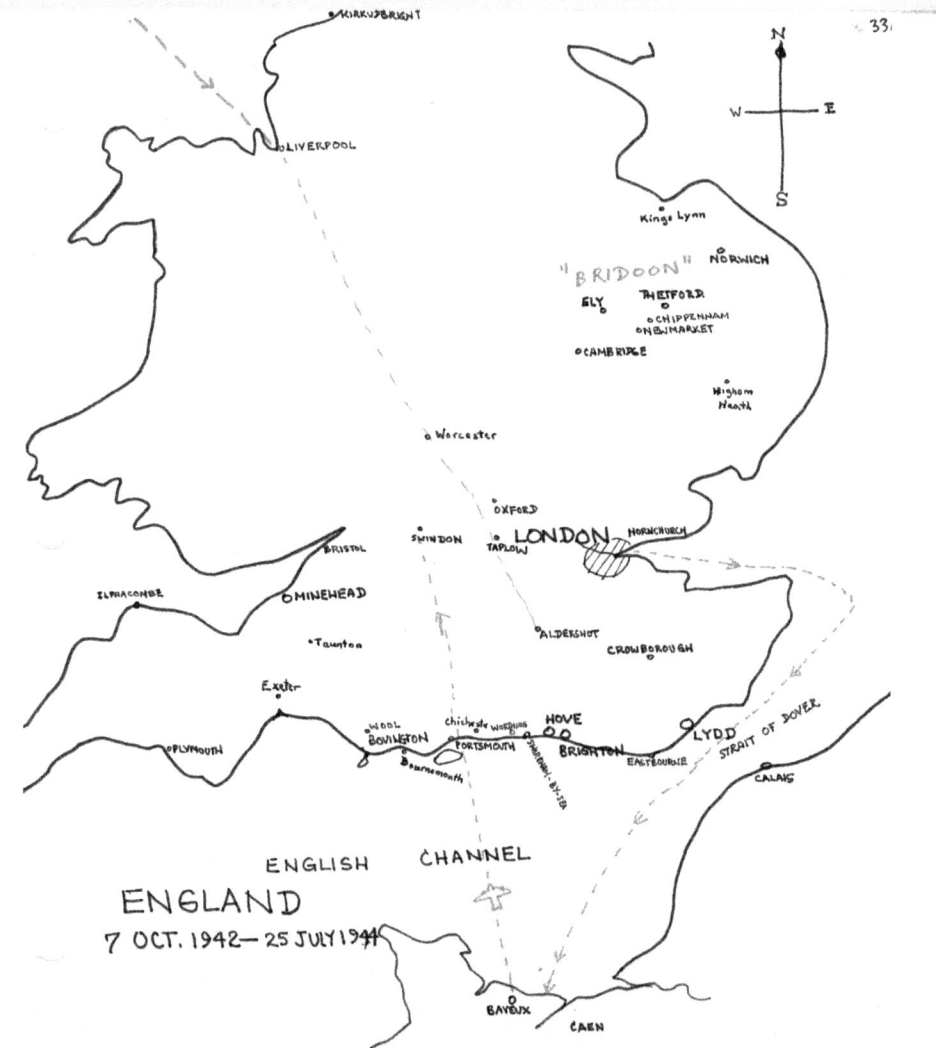

ENGLAND
7 OCT. 1942 — 25 JULY 1944

engines resumed their steady rhythm, we had another cup of Kye. Thousands of men were sleeping down below oblivious of how near a thing it had been. I can think of more pleasant deaths than going down in the murky waters of the North Atlantic as the result of a collision or a tin-fish [torpedo] in the belly of the ship.

As we neared the Irish coast we could see Rathlin Island on our starboard bow. Earlier that morning before dawn I had seen a light winking and one of the crew told me it was on the Isle of Skye. How good it was to see land again and know that the perilous voyage across the Atlantic had been made in safety. Spitfires came out to greet us, flying low over the ship and doing victory rolls. I had never seen a Spit before - what a beautiful machine - so sleek and graceful - like a ballerina. As we entered the Irish Sea the convoy split up. We turned south toward Liverpool, the other ships kept on toward the Clyde. I could see the signaller on one of the ships blinking out a message. It read: "Cheerio old chap." We reached Liverpool on the 7th of October and we sailed up the River Mersey, past a forest of sunken ships. The Atlantic crossing had taken eight days.

"OVER THERE" AT LAST

After we had come ashore by tender at Liverpool on the 7th of October, we found ourselves in a giant railway station. It was dark outside and very dimly lit inside. My first impression was the smell - fishy - then I looked up and noticed that most of the roof glass was blown out. I had an awful lot to carry. On my back was my large pack with a blanket and gas cape. At my side was my small haversack. On my chest was my respirator. To balance it on the other side was my water bottle. My Bren gun ammunition pouches were crammed full. In my hands I carried my kit bag and my rifle was slung over my shoulder. Altogether my kit must have weighed over 60 pounds [27kg] - half of my total weight! I was still wobbly from the sea voyage and I remember the steel cleats on my boots slipping on the wet cobblestones on the way up the road from the tender and the weight of my equipment pulled down and back so that I couldn't get up. If it hadn't been for the helping hand of some comrade I would have remained there sitting on the wet pavement, in the falling rain, with the darkness coming on, somewhere between the Liver building and the Liverpool railway station. Finally, we boarded the train. How small it looked - like the little Hornby trains I used to play with as a boy. After a while there was a banging of doors, a blowing of whistles, the guard waved his green flag and we puffed slowly out of the station. We missed the Canadian trainman's familiar "All aboard!" We were in England at last, somewhere "over there" and it was exciting. Soon the rhythmic clackety-clack, clackety-clack of the wheels lulled us to sleep. We awakened to the grey world of a dull English autumn day. It was the 8th of October. As we raced along past villages, under bridges, into tunnels and out again, accompanied by the shrill whistle of the little engine, we got our first glimpse of England. How neat and tidy everything looked with its chequered landscape and everything in miniature. Row upon row of identical looking houses with chimney pots belching coal smoke as housewives prepared breakfast. Now and again a woman in an apron would open the back door of her house and wave. We waved back. There were neat little gardens with hedges and in each a small Anderson shelter [Anderson Air-Raid shelters were designed to accommodate up to six people and were 6 feet (1.8 m) high, 4.5 feet (1.4 m) wide, and 6.5 feet (2.0 m) long]. We were told that our destination was Aldershot and that the Brass Band and Drums of the British Grenadier Guards would be there to welcome us and play us to our barracks. One couldn't help but wonder would we ever see Canada again? What great adventures lay ahead?

RELATIVES

Most Canadians had some relatives in the "Old Country." My mother had an aunt in Aldershot so I was able to visit her and her husband soon after my arrival. I remember walking through the blackout, stumbling over the curbs, trying to find "Northbrook Road", then "No. 18", then the gate and almost knocking myself senseless on the lamp-post just outside the gate. And I was supposed to have such good

Copyright Museum of English Rural Life, Reading University.

It could take half an hour for the water to heat up but following the invention of the geyser by Benjamin Waddy Maughan in 1868, scalding hot water could be had instantaneously. The geyser consisted of a copper cylinder in which finely divided streams of water were heated by the rising hot gasses from rows of gas jets in the base.

"Let's suppose you want a large can of tomato juice. You don't just come piling in here and yell for 't... but you bring what we call a ration book, ..."

night vision! I lifted the knocker - rat-tat-tat. After a considerable pause a male voice called from inside - "Who is it?" "It's Bob Osborne from Canada", I called out. I heard the male voice on the other side of the door repeat what I had said. Then a woman's voice - "Charles, for heaven's sake let him in - it's Bessie's boy!" Uncle Charles Wigley had retired from the British Army before the First World War. He and Aunt Fanny had known my Uncle Arthur when he had visited them in 1916 before he went off to France and was killed. Now, here I was, twenty-five years later wearing the shoulder flashes of his regiment, the Canadian Grenadier Guards. They observed, "Oh, you look just like Arthur." They meant my cousin Arthur who had come over with the First Division Artillery in December 1939 and had now returned to Canada as a Major, and instructor. I often went to visit them after that and found a home away from home. I would save something from my food parcels for them - a tin of salmon - a package of biscuits. It was hard for old folk to wait in long queues for food and I was glad to share these delicacies with them. A tin of salmon was a rare treat and worth a lot of points under their rationing scheme. Mother sent me a package of tea bags. I gave them to Aunt Fanny and she took them out to the kitchen. I walked out to see her cutting them open and emptying the contents into her tea caddy. "No, no, Auntie, just use them as they are." I said. "What? Leave them in that gauze you say? I declare, what will they think of next!" I took a snapshot of them in their back garden alongside a hedge clipped like a peacock and of course their Anderson shelter. In their garage they had a beautiful Austin Wolseley car which Auntie had won doing the "Fashions" contest in The News of the World. She had also won four tickets to Italy of which she sold two and gave the other two to her son for his honeymoon. This had happened just before the outbreak of war. Both of them were too old to learn to drive but they kept the car and when they wanted to go for a spin they hired a chauffeur!

THE ENGLISHMAN AND HIS BATH

One of the places we discovered was a serviceman's canteen. It was located in a lovely old house surrounded by a high hedge. The kind of house you read about in Victorian novels. It must have had a name like "The Grange". Jack Smith discovered it first and came back to the barracks exclaiming - "I've found a bath, man!" "A what?" I asked, not sure that I had heard him correctly. "A bath, man. A bath!" Only Jack pronounced it "bawth". Jack, who hailed from Jamaica, missed the lovely swimming he had enjoyed at home, so the next best thing was a warm "bawth". It really was a luxury. The only trouble was trying to figure out how to run the darn thing. It had a gadget called a geyser and you had to push levers and hope to Gawd the pilot lamp didn't blow out. I had visions of a terrible explosion and me rushing naked down the stairs to the hoots and hollers of the troops in the billiard room. We played chess here too and one evening I got into a game with an Englishman. Before I knew it there was quite a crowd gathered around watching. I checkmated him neatly. He stood up and shook hands. "By Jove Canada, it's the first time I've been beaten since coming to this club". I decided to quit while I was still ahead and studiously avoided his presence and only came to the club for a "bawth" after that. After all there was nothing patriotic in letting the side down.

ALDERSHOT - OCTOBER 18th, 1942

A "Tank Circus" came to Aldershot. This was made up of Afrika Korps tanks and Panzer PzKW's, Marks II, III, IV - all captured in the Western Desert. The idea, I suppose, was to let us have a close-up look at the enemy A.F.V.'s [Armoured Fighting Vehicle]. This would accomplish two things - help us in our A.F.V. recognition and give us confidence that these enemy tanks were actually knocked out by our gunners. It gave me a strange feeling crawling over and inside these tanks realizing that they had actually taken part in battles in the desert. I found I was asking myself questions like - I wonder who the commander of this tank was? Did he get killed or is he now a prisoner of war? In what battle did this tank get hit? Had Rommel ever stood on this tank or rapped its steel flank with his swagger stick? The neat hole in this one - was it made by a Crusader [British Light Cruiser Tank]? Was the driver killed? The shot seems to have passed

H.M.S. Victory

right through where his head must have been. The insignia too intrigued me. Here was one with a scorpion painted on it. Another, with a palm tree reminiscent of North Africa. Did these insignia represent Regiments, or Corps, or what? Here was one with its score of enemy tanks destroyed painted neatly on its side - seven. Maybe it wasn't "lucky seven" for its crew. Was it the eighth - a Crusader perhaps - that wrote "Kaput" to it? I wonder what battle this Mark III died in. For a few minutes the war in the desert became very real to me. In my imagination I could hear the sounds of battle - the rev of the engines, the shouts of the crew, the smell of cordite and the cries of the dying. There were Italian tanks too, as well as some British tanks and transporters.

DESERT VICTORY

In a letter dated November 15, I wrote to my mother:

"Today is a big day for England. The Church bells are ringing for the first time in 3 years - my but they sound good with a ring of hope in them. Hope for a complete victory soon ... The news is very good these days but I feel it is as Churchill says - 'It's not the beginning of the end but the end of the beginning.' However, I guess Hitler's elastic will soon break and fly back and hit him. I fancy he already feels the gloom surrounding defeat closing in on him."

The occasion which prompted the ringing of the bells was the news of victory at El Alamein in North Africa. The church bells, which had hung silent in their bell towers since June of 1940, now rang out joyously. The order had been that they were only to be rung in case of an enemy landing. The code word was "Cromwell" (conditions are ripe for invasion). Now at the request of Mr. Winston Churchill conditions were ripe for a victory celebration.

"In peace there's nothing so becomes a man
As modest stillness and humility;
But when the blast of war blows in our ears,
Then imitate the action of the tiger:
Stiffen the sinews, summon up the blood."
- William Shakespeare (1564-1616) - Henry V, Act III, Scene l (1599)

NOVEMBER 1942

It was Sunday morning. Portsmouth, or "Pompey" as the locals called it, was recovering from another night of bombing. I wandered toward the sea, detouring around the fire trucks and stepping over the hoses which twisted over the cobblestones like so many serpents. When I got to the harbour I could see the object of my quest plainly enough. There she was. H.M.S. Victory in all her splendour. Lord Nelson would have been proud of her. She had seen a lot of shot and shell in her time and she was seeing a lot now. I wonder if his ghost paced the quarter deck last night. My reverie ended as the naval sentry asked me my business. "I just want to have a look at the ship", I said, "I've heard about it ever since I was a small boy." "Go ahead, matey", he replied, "You're welcome to go aboard." Overjoyed, I marched up the gangway not forgetting to salute as I stepped onto the quarter deck. A Naval rating met me and conducted me over the ship. I was especially moved as he pointed out the brass plaque on the deck marking the spot where the hero of Trafalgar was cut down by a French sniper.

Winchester Cathedral

St. Swithin's day if thou dost rain
For forty days it will remain
St. Swithin's day if thou be fair
For forty days 'twill rain nae mair.'
St. Swithin's day if both rain and shine
Then thoust guess is as good as mine

Updated with an extra verse

DECEMBER 20th, 1942

At Winchester I visited the Cathedral and Castle and heard all about Saint Swithun (died c. 862), the good bishop who wanted to be buried outside his cathedral. But his successors thought differently and buried him inside. It began to rain, the legend says, and it rained for forty days until they dug up his body and buried it outside again. And so the story has it that if it rains on Saint Swithun's Day, July 15th, it will rain for the next forty days.

"St Swithun's day if thou dost rain
For forty days it will remain
St Swithun's day if thou be fair
For forty days 'twill rain nae mare"
- Saint Swithun's Day Proverb

In the north aisle of the Cathedral, I saw the grave of Jane Austen and my thoughts went back to the English Literature class at Magog High School and our teacher Miss Esther Magoon who had introduced us to Pride and Prejudice. I wondered where the other two boys who were in that class were now and what they were doing - Bill Bellingham and Everard Connor. Before I left Winchester I visited the Castle and saw the round table of the knights of King Arthur. It was raining hard as I walked to the railway station. Saint Swithun where are you?

CHRISTMAS PARCELS

I seemed to be hungry all the time during the first weeks in England. General Worthington had warned us that our stomachs would shrink to half their size. Christmas, with the arrival of food parcels from home, promised to help ease the hunger pains. There was great excitement when the cry went up - "The Christmas mail has arrived!" Alas, there must have been a fire aboard the ship that carried some of our food parcels because they had been spoiled by the Pyrene fire-extinguisher fluid (typically either carbon tetrachloride or sodium bicarbonate and concentrated sulphuric acid H_2SO_4). Had the ship been attacked and set on fire by enemy action? There was a beautiful box of Laura Secord chocolates sitting on the barrack room table on Christmas Eve and not a soul dared to eat them. All we could do was look and drool. It was torture as they looked so invitingly good. For a couple of the fellows the temptation became too great and they ate them in spite of the potential consequences. They spent Christmas Day in the Military Hospital having their stomachs pumped out. We always knew when the overseas mail had arrived because we had liver for dinner the day before. This invariably was the sequence - liver one day, mail the next. The ships that brought the mail must also have brought the liver. The one item of English food that none of us will ever forget is Brussels sprouts. I had never tasted them before going overseas. They were like a very, very, tiny cabbage and invariably they seemed to have sand in them. When I would complain, Doug would remind me - "You've got to eat a peck of sand before you die." My reply, "Then I can go anytime!"

FIRST CHRISTMAS IN ENGLAND

Christmas 1942 was a memorable one because it was my first wartime Christmas in England. It was also memorable for another reason. Before our regiment left Canada it had built up a sizable canteen fund. These profits from the dry and wet canteens had been earmarked to provide us with a real Christmas dinner with all the trimmings for our first Christmas overseas. On Christmas Day, 1942, we sat down in our mess hall in Aldershot, ready for the feast. Nothing had been forgotten. After the turkey came the plum pudding. To make the occasion even more memorable the High Commissioner for Canada in Britain, Mr. Vincent Massey, had come down from London, along with a C.B.C. [Canadian Broadcasting Company] crew to

record the festivities for the listeners back home. As is the tradition on Christmas Day the officers served the other ranks. I had just put my spoon into a good helping of the pudding and raised it to my lips in anticipation when the "brass" descended on me and enquired for the listening public back home how the pudding tasted. Well I hadn't got my first mouthful yet, so I put the spoon into my mouth, smacking my lips to savour the rich delicacy. It is a good thing that the film crew hadn't come up to our table at the same time because if they had I'm sure the expression on my face would have set all of Canada laughing. I'm also sure that the C.B.C. sound engineer edited out the expression that passed my lips. Somewhere there had been a S.N.A.F.U. (Army slang for "Situation Normal - All Fouled Up") in the cook house and instead of sauce, our puddings had been generously ladled with mayonnaise!

Doug and I got up early and before breakfast we walked into the town and found a little Anglican church and went forward for Holy Communion. There weren't many people present but we felt we had begun Christmas right. *Pax in Bello.*

THOSE POLISH ALLIES

There was one thing Doug and I could never understand. When we went on leave to Scotland, all the lovely Scottish lassies would be walking arm in arm with the Polish soldiers. Here we were good Canadians, speaking their language - or something like it! - bearing Scottish surnames. But we didn't have a chance with these Scots girls. "What's wrong with us?" Doug would say as we walked home from a dance. "My name is McKnight, you'd think that would cut more ice with these lassies than some unpronounceable Polish name." "I'm darned if I know chum, but if you find out let me know. Maybe we've got halitosis or something!" Not all the Scots girls felt that way of course and hundreds fell in love with and married Canadian servicemen. Sergeant "Sandy" Forsyth found a beautiful bride in Edinburgh. But an awful lot seemed to prefer the Poles. This puzzled me. It hurt our pride. Somebody tried to explain to us that it was the glamour of the foreign accent. I don't know. Perhaps it was their more glamorous uniforms. No doubt the English servicemen felt much the same way about us when they saw us with a W.R.N.S. [Women's Royal Naval Service, W.R.N.S. pronounced WRENS], A.T.S. [Auxiliary Territorial Service], or a W.A.A.F. [Women's Auxiliary Air Force] on our arm.

THE DAY I BECAME AN AIR GUNNER - ALMOST!

On your embarkation leave, people at home would give you a slip of paper with the name and address of some relative in the Old Country that they hoped you would visit. Armed with just such a name and address I took the train from Glasgow westward along the Clyde to the beautiful town of Helensburgh. As we left Glasgow the great dockyards of the Clydebank slipped past the train window. A sailor in the compartment with me said - "There's the Queen!" I kept staring out the window but I couldn't see any royalty. Then suddenly it all came into focus and I saw her - the great Queen Mary ocean liner, cleverly camouflaged, stretching along the skyline.

When I reached my destination, I found my way to Mrs. Macmillan's home. I was just in time for a delicious Scottish high tea. My hostess said - "Now if you will just walk down to the High Street, Alex will be glad to entertain you." I caught on to the fact that the good lady owned some kind of establishment and not wishing to offend, I took myself off to the High Street as instructed. I discovered that Mrs. Macmillan was the proprietress of a very high class public house [pub]. Alex was the bar tender. I entered and introduced myself. Alex said - "Mrs. Macmillan just phoned to tell me that you are to have anything in the house. Now what will you have to drink?" I'm sure I must have staggered the good man - "Thank you, but I do not drink spirits. Could I have a mineral please?" When I got back to the Regiment a week later and we were swapping stories about our leave, I was the envy of them all when I told my story about Mrs.

The Short S.25 Sunderland was a British flying boat patrol bomber developed for the Royal Air Force (RAF) by Short Brothers. It took its service name from the town (latterly, city) and port of Sunderland in northeast England.

Macmillan and her pub. "It would happen to you Ossie, the only non-drinker in the whole goddam squadron and you get an opportunity like that! Geez you might at least have brought us back a bottle of Johnny Walker." I suppose I might - frankly it just never occurred to me.

"For in my youth I never did apply
Hot and rebellious liquors in my blood."
- William Shakespeare (1564-1616) - As You Like It, Act II, Scene 3 (1599)

If the boys in the squadron were disappointed by my insensitivity to their needs it was nothing compared to a disappointment I experienced on the same leave. Mrs. Macmillan's son-in-law, Angus, was in the R.A.F. and stationed on the Sunderland Flying Boat base about a mile along the road from her house. He lived at home with his wife and mother-in-law. After supper we were sitting by the fire chatting and he asked, "How many more days leave have you got?" "I must leave day after tomorrow," I replied. "Look," he said, "we have to take a kite out tomorrow to do an instrument check. If you would like a flight in a Sunderland, I can fix it up. We have to have all the guns manned just in case and since you are a tank gunner I guess you know how to aim and fire a Browning." What an opportunity! I could hardly sleep that night with the excitement of anticipation. I was going to get my chance to be an Air Gunner after all. He had to be down at the base about 0600 hours but it was agreed that if he did not telephone before 0730 hours then flying was washed out. I ate my breakfast of eggs, fried tomatoes, toast, marmalade and tea and waited. 0730 hours came and no phone calls. 0735 - 0740 hours and still no phone ringing. I assumed that it was off. However, since it was a beautiful morning I decided to walk down to the base and have a look at the flying boats. I got down there just as one of the big birds was taxing out for takeoff. It was an inspiring sight. When I got back to the house Mrs. Macmillan said that her son-in-law had phoned just after I had gone. She had called to me but I had not heard her. The Sunderland that I saw taking off was the one I could have been aboard! Imagine my further disappointment when Angus arrived for supper that night to tell me that they had flown a triangular course - north to Scappa Flow - west to Ireland and back to Helensburgh. They had had a good dinner on board as well. Wouldn't it have been great to see Scotland and Ireland from the air with the mountains all snow covered? The only consolation was that they had not seen a single enemy aircraft so I would not have had the opportunity I had dreamed of - firing my Browning at a Jerry fighter. What I really needed was a good Scotch to drown my sorrow. Mrs. Macmillan, what time does your establishment close?

HEADLEY DOWN - JANUARY, 1943

On the 24th of January we began an exercise called - NIGHT INTO DAY. The idea behind it was to teach us how to operate in the dark. Reveille sounded about 1750 hours and then we had breakfast just as it was getting dark. At 1830 hours we went on parade. During this period we had a number of Harbouring [encampment] schemes. As Squadron Wireless N.C.O. my job was to see that the communications were in order. Most of my operators had just graduated from using a radio in a jeep and now suddenly to be thrust into a tank in the dark was asking a little too much of their ability. I nearly went crackers and so did our Squadron Wireless Officer - Lieutenant "Pinky" Tomlinson. Our biggest headache was the officers, and the higher the rank, the bigger the headache. A few officers appreciated the delicate mechanism of a wireless set and realized they were dealing with a fine instrument. Far too many, however, when it failed to operate as efficiently and easily as a telephone, either began to curse the poor Loader/Operator or abuse the radio set. One officer actually kicked it in my presence. So here we were in the total darkness with an awful SNAFU, commanding officers and squadron leaders hopelessly lost on Headley Common. To cover up for their own inept map reading and inefficiency they would blame the wireless set or the P.B.O. [In the First World War the two-seater aircraft carried a pilot and observer. If the pilot was killed, as was often the case, the Poor Bloody Observer (P.B.O.) didn't stand much of a chance of making it safely back to the ground].

MAJOR GARNER O. CURRIE,
Canadian Grenadier Guards.

Captain Garner Ormsby Currie,
Canadian Grenadier Guards. C.A.S.F
Son of the late General Sir Arthur Currie.
G.C.M.G, K.C.B, VJJ, and of Lady Currie.

Montreal Star November 23rd, 1944

Son of Great War Commander, Major G. Currie, Battling Huns

MAJOR G. O. CURRIE, of Montreal, son of the late General Sir Arthur Currie, commander of the Canadian Corps in the Great War, has fought in France, Belgium and Holland with the British Columbia Regiment, a tank unit from Vancouver.

He has been serving with this regiment in the field, and without any relief led a squadron in its fighting advance from Abbeville, where he joined the regiment, to Bergen Op Zoom and Steenbergen in southwest Holland. Recently he had his first leave—48 hours—at the Canadian Officers Leave Centre in Brussels.

Major Currie was originally a member of the Canadian Grenadier Guards, of Montreal, but he did not fight with this regiment. When a vacancy for a major occurred in the B.C.R.'s he was given command of "A" squadron and he led it skilfully and daringly. He and the squadron have been in all major engagements since the crossing of the Somme at Abbeville and one of the most spectacular actions was in the advance north of Antwerp which began Oct. 20.

The first major objective was the town of Esschen and although two infantry battalions were fighting forward to get into the town it actually was tanks led by Currie which entered the place first.

Along with a squadron led by Major John Toogood, of Vancouver, Major Currie and his tanks got to the outskirts of Esschen just at dawn and right on schedule. Infantry had been delayed south of the town but Currie led his squadron right into Esschen.

There were some Germans in the town but they did not fire on the tanks, who put up such a show of strength that 10 Germans surrendered without a fight.

"We simply stood up in our turrets and they waved a white sheet to us," said Currie.

After scouting around Esschen, Currie took his squadron on to other tasks northwest of Esschen and up towards Bergen, where there were some fiery actions. Meanwhile, infantry had overcome all opposition south of Esschen and entered the town to occupy it in strength and hold it firm.

Some of my operators wanted to quit and re-train as gunners who at this point in our training had nothing to do but sit in the gunner's seat and sleep, quite unmolested by higher ranks. I had to run around on foot, in total darkness, trying to find "D" for "Dog" or "N" for "Nuts" who were in trouble and straighten out the problem. It was usually some simple mistake. I recall climbing into a Troop Leader's tank while he was cursing a blue stream, leaning down into the turret, working upside down, and quickly realized that the Band Selector Switch was in the wrong position. A flick of the wrist and I had him back on the Squadron net. He calmed down immediately, thought I was an electronic wizard, and began talking rationally again. In a case like this it was really the fault of the P.B.O. but the lad got so rattled by his Commander's impatience and vituperation that he got all flustered and forgot to do his "drill", which would have sorted out the trouble in a minute. I realized that my operators must get their "netting drill" down thoroughly. They had to know it cold. In a moment of crisis it must be as automatic as driving a car. I made up my mind that the next time I taught in a Wireless School I'd make them do it blindfolded. All this flak plus the unconventional meal hours took its toll on me and I developed stomach pains that became chronic for the duration. Years later a Medical Board determined that this was when my stomach ulcers began.

HEADLEY TO HOVE

On the morning of the 19th of February, 1943, we moved from our camp on Headley Down to Hove on the Channel coast. I was Major Garner Currie's Loader/Operator. He was our Squadron Leader and a very good one. Johnny O'Donnell was our driver. I was sitting in my Loader/Operator seat and watching the road unwind through my periscope. We were the lead tank and the Major was reading the map. I think we must have been somewhere between Midhurst and Pulborough. The road ran along beside the Rother River. There was a steep bank on our left and across the road to the right the land slipped away to the river. I could see a narrow bridge coming up. I hoped somebody had Recce'd [performed reconnaissance on] this road to determine if this bridge was wide enough for a Ram tank. It was one of those old stone bridges that arched over a tributary stream running into the Rother and had probably been there since the Middle Ages. The present road, however, had been resurfaced recently and was somewhat wider than the bridge. We were leading the Regiment so nobody had been over it before us. O'Donnell didn't slacken speed. He was a good driver and I had absolute confidence in his ability, but I still closed my eyes. We shot through the narrow gap between the stone sides of the little bridge. There couldn't have been more than inches to spare. We were over it and on to the paved road again. I opened my eyes. Whew! That was close, but Johnny was a good driver. Major Currie's voice came on the intercom - "Nice driving, O'Donnell!" Johnny picked up his mike and replied, "Thank you, sir". In doing this he had to let go of one of his tiller bars [steering control] and the left track wandered ever so slightly, but just enough to grab into the soft turf on the left bank. With the speed we were travelling it was only split seconds before we were racing up the bank at a precipitous angle. I thought for a moment that we might go right over the top, but we lost momentum, the tank slowed, toppled off, and rolled down the bank landing with a smash in the middle of the road. The Major had managed to drop into the turret. He was a tall man, well over 6 feet [183cm], and his quick reaction saved his life because the tank came down hard on the road and snapped off one of the turret flaps. It was a miracle Major Currie wasn't decapitated. The other turret flap remained intact and GREYHOUND - all thirty tons of her - was balanced precariously on that one little steel flap. Silence. Dirt, papers, battery acid, every movable thing was falling down on us. Quick thinking O'Donnell had switched off the ignition when he saw her going over. He had taken some flying lessons at Cartierville before the war so no doubt it had been drilled into him "Before a crash landing always switch off to avoid risk of fire."

We had been led to believe that you couldn't roll a tank over without its going on fire. So the immediate thing to do was to bail out. I thought "What happens if that one little flap breaks off under the weight as we crawl out?" It would be curtains. Imagine being pinned across the back under all that weight of steel! Major Currie went first and made it safely. I followed. What a relief to stand up safely outside. It was a near thing

JUNE 1942

"RAM" Tanks
Pictures taken in Debert, N.S. in June of 1942

and not one of us was hurt. GREYHOUND was straddling the road, upside down, blocking the whole convoy - like a giant beetle rolled over and helpless on its back. Soon some big "Macs" [armoured heavy utility vehicle] with winches arrived. They manoeuvred into position, fastened strong cables on to our tank, and rolled her over again where she landed off the road right side up on her tracks. Major Currie had to leave us to lead the rest of the Squadron and Regiment into Hove. O'Donnell and I were left with the tank. We watched the whole Regiment go by, gawking curiously at us and making rude gestures. At last they had all passed and the road was silent. "Well," said Mike, who had been looking at our tank, "I don't think there is much wrong with her tracks and the suspension looks O.K." We inspected GREYHOUND carefully, apart from a few dints and gouges, a sheared aerial, and one missing turret flap, she looked pretty good. "Ossie," Mike said, "you get the fire extinguisher and cover me. I'm going to start her up." "No, Mike," I protested, "she's drenched with gas and oil - she'll likely explode and go up in a sheet of flame - don't be a fool!" "Just cover me with extinguisher, Ossie." Mike said steadily, "I think she'll be O.K." He jumped in and switched on. The engine fired up and for a few seconds I couldn't see Mike, or the tank, as they were enveloped in a white cloud. Then it cleared and there was Mike, grinning and GREYHOUND ticking over as if she had just come from an Ordinance check. I climbed up into the turret, put on the headsets and switched on the radio. The intercom was still working: "Driver, advance!" We drove her to Hove. When we arrived it was dark. The other crews had arrived hours before, had parked their tanks, and were comfortably settled into their new billets. I enquired where I could find the Squadron Leader. "He's in the Officer's Mess," we were told. "Driver, start up!" I said over the intercom to Mike, "To the Officer's Mess!" The Officer's Mess was on the second floor of a building facing the street. As we drove alongside I could see that there was a party in progress and Major Currie was being good naturedly roasted for losing his tank. From where I stood in the turret of GREYHOUND, I could reach the window so I swung it open and called out - "One Ram tank for Major Currie!" There was a sudden hush inside the smoke filled room and the Major came over to the open window. "Here's your tank, sir!" I said. Currie looked at me in wonderment, then leaned out the window and looked down at O'Donnell who was smiling like a Cheshire cat. The Squadron Leader let one whoop out of him and as far as I know he didn't have to buy another round of drinks that night. We proved one thing, you CAN roll a Ram tank over and it will not brew up [catch on fire]. I hope somebody reported this to General Worthington.

SUSSEX BY THE SEA - HOVE - SPRING, 1943

Some officers just did not know how to handle men. As a Troop we had been together for over a year. One day we received a new Troop leader, just over from Canada. If these officers had any sense they would call the Troop together and say something like this: "Look here, you chaps, my name is Lieutenant So-and-So. I'm your new Troop leader. I know you're a good Troop and that you've been at this game a lot longer than I have. You know a hell of a lot more about tanks than I do so I will need all your help and cooperation. If you play ball with me, I'll play ball with you and this Troop will be the best in the whole Squadron." When an officer took that attitude we'd follow him anywhere and help him to learn the game. Unfortunately, we got a stuffed shirt today who thought he knew it all and began throwing his weight around. He came along to our tank and addressed me as follows: "Corporal - where do we keep the master-switch for the Troop leader's tank?" I figured Johnny O'Donnell was behind this so I went right along with it. Any damn fool knows that each tank has its own master-switch. "The master-switch sir?" I repeated, "Oh, yes, sir, lately we've been keeping it in Sergeant Wells' tank, sir". I said all this without batting an eyelash and pointed to the tank next in line ahead of ours. "From now on, Corporal, I want that switch kept in my tank. Is that clear?" "Yes, sir", I replied and tried hard to keep from laughing. A dumb officer like that would be ruined by his men if he didn't learn to change his ways pretty fast and I saw it happen to more than one. In the army you are under discipline and have to obey orders, but if a Troop decided to ride an officer they could literally run him out of the Regiment. Fortunately most of our officers were good types.

"Monty", my pet kitten, became a mascot for our crew.

Location: Huron County
A static memorial featuring a Sherman Tank, along with a plaque dedicated to those who served in World War II in the famous tank.

Marker text: SHERMAN TANK
This Sherman Tank stands as a tribute to the valour of the Tanks Crews of all allied armies who used Shermans in every theatre of World War II. It commemorates also, all those men and women who worked in the Arsenal of Democracy producing some 40,000 of these American weapons.

Crew Members: 5, 1-76mm Cannon, 3 Machine Guns, Range: 120 Miles, Weight: 35 Tons, Top Speed: 24 MPH.

Oct. 1942 - The Sherman Tank received its baptism of fire with the British Eighth Army in the Battle of El Alamein, Egypt. June 6, 1944 - The British upgunned six hundred Shermans with their famous seventeen pounder anti-tank gun for the D-Day invasion of Normandy. This, the Firefly Sherman was the most successful tank used by the British and Canadian armies.

SHERMANS IN THE CANADIAN ARMY
Fourteen Canadian Armoured Regiments of Sherman Tanks fought in Sicily, Italy, Northwest Europe and Korea. One of the most famous exploits of the Sherman Tank was that of Major David Currie, commanding "C" Squadron, the South Alberta Regiment, who won the Victoria Cross August 20, 1944, in the battle of the Falaise Gap, France. The Insignia on Sherman 78-901 commemorates Major Currie's command tank.

SUPERSTITIONS

I guess we were all superstitious though we never talked about it. I don't suppose anybody would have wanted to have a tank with a number 13 painted on it or any combination thereof. For me, 13 was lucky and it was on February 13th that I had been promoted to Corporal. I had my own way of climbing aboard the tank and if for some reason that usual route up GIRAFFE's slippery side was thwarted, I was upset. One officer I knew always put his steel helmet on a certain way - with the white Guards painted plume on the right side just as if he was going on parade. If by any chance he happened to put it on backwards, which was an easy thing to do with a steel helmet, he felt very uneasy. One of our tank drivers had got some yellow clay on the hull of the tank as we landed in Normandy and with dire threats he forbade anyone to wash it off as he felt it was a good luck talisman. A gunner I knew used to stretch a single strand of a woman's pubic hair to align his sights. A co-driver always peed on the right front track before climbing aboard. And of course nearly everyone had their good-luck talisman - teddy bears, St. Christopher medals, four leaf clovers, and so-on. I carefully preserved a threepenny bit that I had received in a piece of Christmas cake. I don't suppose there was any crewman that didn't have his own secret superstition.

BRIGHTON

When I came into the billet today there was Doug waiting for me. "Come on," he said, "get those tank clothes off and put on your best uniform, we've got a date." "What do you mean, 'We've got a date?'" I asked. While I was changing, Doug explained that he had met a W.A.A.F. and she had promised to bring her friend along next time. We rushed out of the billet and headed for Brighton. "We're meeting them at the Clock Tower", Doug explained. "What time?" I asked. "They're stationed at Shoreham," Doug said, "and I told them we'd be there between 1600 and 1630 hours." When we got to the Clock Tower our two dates were already there. Mine was called Mary and she seemed to be a very pleasant girl. She was brought up on a farm in Gloucestershire. The girls explained that they had to be back in their billets by 2200 hours. Just enough time for some dancing at the Dome. We had a pleasant evening and my partner was an excellent dancer. We saw the girls onto their train and made a date to go to dinner and a show at the Regent on Saturday.

On Saturday afternoon we met our two W.A.A.F.s and took them to dinner. As we were sitting at the table waiting to be served, I asked my partner "Why do you English girls like to go out with Canadians?" Her reply surprised me. "Because you're so polite to us," she replied, "you treat us as if were something special." "Well you are." I said. Then I watched as two English men in uniform sat down with two A.T.S. girls at the next table. The two men slouched into their chairs and never gave a thought for their partners. "See what I mean." said Mary. Doug and I had held the chairs for our partners to be seated before we sat down ourselves. "Yes, I think I do." I replied. This was a revelation to me because I had been brought up on Lord Chesterfield's Letters to His Son and I had just assumed that all Englishmen were models of manners.

THE BIG SMOKE

Most of the fellows never got beyond London on their leaves. The reason for this was because London was the hub of the British railway system and you went there first to catch your train from King's Cross Station for Edinburgh or Euston Station for Glasgow. If you were headed for the West Country (Devon and Cornwall) you boarded the train at Waterloo and if it was Norwich you were headed for then you got on at Liverpool Street Station. For the Midlands (Nottingham and Sheffield) the train left from St. Pancras. Paddington was the station if you were going to Oxford - Stratford-upon-Avon - Worcester. Victoria Station, for Canterbury or Brighton. The reason why so few ever got beyond "The Big Smoke", as we called London, was because when they got to the city, with their money belts full of pound notes and their

THE CHURCH OF ST. MARY DE HAURA, NEW SHOREHAM

14-day passes, they found they had to wait for the next train out to whichever point of the compass they were heading. This inevitably led them to wait in a pub and that lengthened into a 14-day pub crawl in London. The different branches of the service, and even the various regiments and Air Force squadrons, had their own favourite pubs. Many of our lads would head for The Bunch of Grapes as soon as they set foot on the station platform at Victoria. Since I did not drink, I rarely went into a pub but sometimes I would go in with a bunch of the lads if we were all going up to The Big Smoke together. I remember one time when I was in a pub with Doug and it seemed to be the favourite watering hole of a British regiment, The Green Howards. They resented our intrusion and after a few drinks one of them made a snide remark about "these bloody Colonials", referring to us of course. In no time a fight started which soon developed into a donnybrook. I didn't mind fighting in the ring, but one thing I didn't relish was a fractured skull from some drunk hitting me from behind with a bottle. Doug knew exactly what to do. "Grab a chair, Bob, and get into a corner", he shouted. It was the right tactic. In the corner nobody could get behind you and all you had to do was fend off the opponent in front. Eventually the Military Police arrived but not before "the bloody Colonials" had wrecked the pub and Doug and I had made a strategic withdrawal in the face of the enemy.

ST. MARY DE HAURA

It was after tea time on a Sunday night in Shoreham-by-Sea. Mary and I were walking together wondering what we could do for the evening. "Let's go to church." she suddenly suggested. "O.K." I replied, "But remember, I'm not used to the Anglican form of service so you'll have to help me find my way around in the Book of Common Prayer". The parish church of St. Mary de Haura (Latin: St. Mary by the harbour) looked like a little cathedral. The Normans had built "New" Shoreham and the harbour around the year 1100 and this little church dated from 1100 to 1225. It had an impressive tower 81 feet [24.7m] high. I was thinking what a dandy O-Pip [Observation Post] it would make as we entered and took a pew in the north aisle from which we could see the pulpit. The setting sun was throwing long shafts of light on the stone pillars. There was something very peaceful about this little church and this service of Evensong. The musty smell of the Prayer Books and the stale odour of incense and candle smoke all added up to an atmosphere of serenity. I had the feeling that long after this war was over and Hitler was a name almost forgotten, people would be gathering under this roof and singing and praying and listening to the Bible being read, just as they had been doing since Norman times. I thought of the Osborne motto *Pax in Bello - Peace in War*. I experienced it there, worshipping in that ancient parish church. As we walked out I looked back up the aisle, through the pillared arches to the dimly lit altar and the cross bathed in the blood-red gleam of the setting sun.

"Lord, now lettest thy servant depart in peace, according to thy word."
- Bible (KJV) - Luke 2:29

We strolled down toward the harbour in the fading light. I thought of those lines of Thomas Hardy:

"Yonder a maid and her wight
come whispering by;
War's annals will fade into night
Ere their story die."
- Thomas Hardy (1840-1928) - In Time of 'The Breaking of Nations' (1916)

**Corporal Robert E. Osborne
22nd Canadian Armoured Regiment
Canadian Grenadier Guards
Hove - Sussex - England 1943**

GAMES PEOPLE PLAY

I was out walking with an English W.A.A.F. one evening when we came across a bunch of Canadians playing softball on the village green. In typical Canadian fashion, the boys were talking up the game. "Come on fellas, whadya say there - let's go, eh?" "That's lookin' 'em over Shorty". "Hey, ump, did you see that?" "Get the ump a pair of glasses." We stopped to watch as she had never seen softball being played. Above the yelling and the antics of my fellow countrymen, I tried to explain the rudiments of the game to her. As we strolled away, and the raucous voices of the players faded across the common, she remarked - "Sound like a lot of magpies, don't they." A week later, on a Saturday afternoon, I wandered into the Hove cricket grounds which were just behind our billets. There wasn't a sound until the batsman hit it for six, and then there was a polite round of applause and a few "well dones". They say you can tell a lot about people by the games they play. I never felt that so eloquently as the difference between the two games I saw this week - the doves and the magpies.

SUSSEX

"In a fair ground - in a fair ground - Yea, Sussex by the Sea!"
- Rudyard Kipling (1865-1936) - Sussex (1902)

"The great hills of the South Country
They stand along the sea:
And it's there walking in the high woods
That I could wish to be..."
- Hilaire Belloc (1870-1953) - The South Country (1920)

HOVE

Lieutenant Freddie Hill is our new Crew Commander and Troop Leader. He is a good chap. We like him and work hard to be a good crew and give him a break. Today we were in the middle of an exercise on the South Downs. I was sitting in my corner of the turret trying to picture the scene outside when suddenly I heard Lieutenant Hill's voice on the "A" set. He thought he was on the I/C talking to us in the tank - instead, his transmission was going out to the whole regiment. "That old baldheaded bastard", I heard Freddie saying as I monitored the "A" set, "doesn't have enough brains to blow his beret off!" "Ooh no!" I screamed at Fred, tugging violently on his pants leg and pointing frantically at the switch box behind him. But it was too late of course, the words had gone out and could not be recalled. Through my periscope I could see the C.O.'s jeep abruptly change direction and head straight across the field toward us. It was an easy mistake for Lieutenant Hill to have made and there wasn't a thing I could do to help our new Crew Commander. He jumped out of the tank and took his bawling out like a man. I was to make the same mistake myself during the battle at Hill 195, only that time I was on the I/C when I should have been switched to the "A" set. So what I said for Regimental ears was heard only by my crew who must have thought it was damn stupid, which it was!

AIR RAIDS - HOVE - MARCH, 1943

Air raids could be really nerve-wracking if you got them night after night. You would just get through your supper and the warning sirens would go off. If you were in London on leave it was especially aggravating. In Brighton, when the enemy aircraft were directly overhead, they sounded what they called the "pips". I huddled in a brick doorway with a civilian. We could hear the enemy raiders in the sky above us. They dropped no bombs so they were probably returning from a raid on London. It's an eerie feeling - perhaps

that's the origin of the saying - "It gives me the pips" [The actual origin (c. 1425) is attributed to the Latin word: pituita. Later (c. 1881), the general meaning became: To become annoyed or irritated.].

In March of 1943 we were stationed in the Brighton-Hove area and experienced a series of air raids. Sometimes these would be lone raiders, coming in low over the Channel to avoid detection by our radar and then up over the sea wall before our Ack/Ack gunners could engage them. Then they would drop their bombs and scoot for home. The whole thing wouldn't take much more than a minute but that minute could leave a wake of death and destruction. On one of these hit-and-run raids they hit a butcher shop. We went to help clear away the rubble and search for survivors. The local inhabitants were standing around watching silently. It was about eleven o'clock in the morning. We came across a small child's arm - like a doll's. Then, a teddy bear. Then, what ten minutes before, had been a lively four year old. As we gently passed the little twisted body up to the waiting hands above, a woman in overalls came over and stood looking at it for a long time. Then she turned and walked away. Not a sign of emotion. Not a word. Not an anguished sob. Nothing. After the grim work was over we repaired to a nearby cafe for some coffee. "Did you see that woman?" I said, "It was her child you know." "God, these bloody English women are cold," somebody said, "not a tear, not a cry, not a damn thing!" "Hang on a minute," one of the other lads put in, "don't kid yourself, I watched her face as she turned and walked away. I've never seen such determination." "The old stiff upper lip, eh?" someone else remarked. "No," said the first speaker, "She'll go back to her aircraft factory or wherever it is she works and she'll work twice as hard as any other girl in the shop."

In a lighter vein, I was coming out of the Squadron Office on Wilbury Road at about 1600 hours one beautiful spring day just as a Focke-Wulf [German fighter aircraft FW190] came whistling down the street hotly pursued by two Spitfires that were hammering away at it for dear life. The cannon fire from the Spits was flying all over the place. There was a young woman coming toward me pushing a large pram. At the same moment and with instinctive reflex action we both dove under an army truck parked at the curb. Here we were, flat on our bellies under the truck, staring into each other's eyes. The din going on above us was terrific as the coastal guns joined in. She had left her pram in the middle of the sidewalk. As soon as the planes had passed we picked ourselves up off the road, dusted ourselves off and there was the baby sleeping as peacefully as you please in his blankets. The two Spits nailed the Jerry raider and we were up on our feet in time to see it go down into the sea at the foot of the street just beyond the sea wall. Nice shooting, boys!

One night at supper, the cook had produced a beautiful cake with thick chocolate icing. I can see it now - a drooling masterpiece - in the centre of the table. He had just cut it and we were about to dig in when the raid came. There was a whirlwind scramble of arms and legs as we dove under the table. A minute later when it was all over we scrambled out and back on our benches only to discover Corporal Jack Smith sitting serenely with a look on his face like the cat that swallowed the canary. While we were cringing in terror under the table, Jack had polished off a few good pieces of chocolate cake! "May we all die happy," he chortled with his face full of cake, "what a way to go!" What a way indeed. As the French Queen said - "Give them cake."

The Sussex Daily News of Tuesday March 30th, 1943, reproduced a picture of the bombed houses with the caption - "The Homes of People Suffered - Clinic and Church Demolished." The article ran:

"TWO SOUTH COAST TOWNS BOMBED AND GUNNED. Sixteen people - 10 at one and six at the other - including three children, are known to have been killed when four F.W. fighter-bombers raided two South Coast towns at midday yesterday.... One of the raiders was shot down into the sea when fighters took up the chase..."

The paper also carried another news item from the German News Agency. It ran:

"The German News Agency claimed last night that fast German fighter-bombers carried out a low level attack on Brighton at noon today.... A British fighter plane of the Typhoon type was shot down after a short air duel by one of our F.W. 19O's."

A SOUND OF REVELRY BY NIGHT

Most cities and towns had a club for servicemen. Churches often provided them too. These clubs had a canteen and often in the evening had dancing. If the club was located near a camp then it became the rendezvous for servicemen. Local girls volunteered to help in the canteen and acted as dancing partners although I'm sure many girls had bruised toes because, of course, we danced in our heavy army boots. Favourite dances were the Jive and the Palais Glide. We also danced the Boomps-a-Daisy, the Hokey Cokey and the Lambeth Walk. The tunes that we danced to were - "Roll out the Barrel", "I'll See You Again", "The Beer Barrel Polka", "Moonlight Becomes You", "A Nightingale Sang in Berkley Square", "Waltzing Matilda", "Wish Me Luck As You Wave Me Goodbye", "I'm In The Mood For Love", "Dance With A Dolly", "Rose of England", "We'll Meet Again" and many more. When we were stationed in Hove, somebody, I think it was our Padre, had the marvellous idea that we should have a Regimental dance in the Royal Pavilion in Brighton. It was a magnificent place built by the Prince Regent in the style of an Indian Palace. Our Regimental Band supplied the music and it was the nearest thing to a "Ball" that I had ever experienced. What a setting for a Strauss waltz! I had an interesting experience that night. I was dancing with a W.R.N.S. and she asked me my name. When I told her she turned quite huffy and said I was being fresh. I couldn't figure out what was wrong. As the dance ended she returned quickly to the other side of the ballroom obviously much annoyed. Fortunately for me her friend, another W.R.N.S., had been dancing with Doug, so I asked him to try to find out why she had suddenly turned so frosty. During the next dance he put the question to her friend and in a moment they were both coming across the floor to where I was sitting it out. By coincidence the W.R.N.S. that I had been dancing with had the surname "Osborne"! When she had asked my name and I replied with hers she thought that I had somehow discovered her surname and that I was making fun of her. I then crossed the floor with Doug and her friend and it was all explained. She was full of apologies and during the next dance asked me if I was related to the Lincolnshire Osborne's'. I said no, that my branch of the family came from Cornwall. What was that old joke about the two Englishmen marooned on a desert island who couldn't speak to one another because they hadn't been introduced? One thing that I will never forget about that palace were the chandeliers. They were very beautiful and must have weighed about a ton each - who would want to polish all the glass prisms?

"There was a sound of revelry by night ...
The lamps shone o'er fair women and brave men ...
On with the dance! let joy be unconfined;
No sleep till morn, when youth and pleasure meet
To chase the glowing hours with flying feet -"
- Lord Byron (1788-1824) - Childe Harold, The Eve of Waterloo (1816)

NIGHT FIGHTER

One starlit night on the South Downs just north of Brighton, I picked up an interesting conversation on my tank wireless. I knew there was a raid on and I could hear the enemy aircraft streaming in from the coast on their way to London. I could also hear our night fighters circling and diving among them. It was a beautifully clear night with a new moon rising. I saw a plane go down and end up in a bright yellow splash.

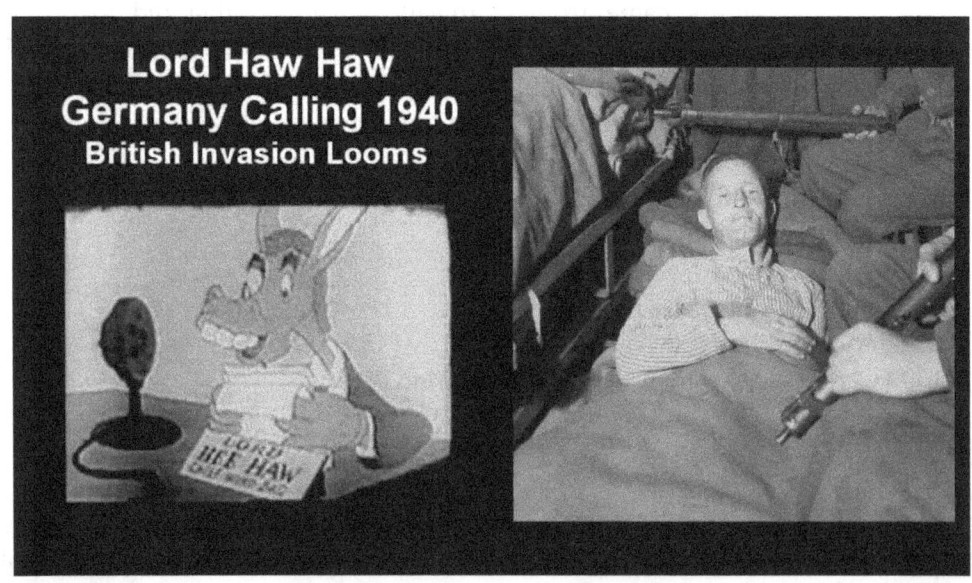

I hoped it was one of theirs and not one of ours. Then I overheard a conversation that went something like this:

"Hello, Bad Hat, One Five. Biggin Control calling. We have a customer for you. Vector [Steer] one eight zero. Buster [Speed Up]."
"Hello Starlight. One Five calling. No contact."
"Flash your weapon [Use your Air Interception Apparatus]" came the Controller's reply over the radio.
"Weapon flashing."
"Hello One Five. Any joy?"
"No. Listening out."
"He's right in front of you!" the Controller warned excitedly.
"Can't see anything."
"Hello One Five. Any joy?"
"No."

Sitting on top of my tank with my legs dangling inside, I imagined a pretty W.A.A.F. controller sitting in an Operation's room at Biggin Hill with earphones on her blonde head deftly pushing aircraft markers around on a huge map. I pictured the night fighter pilot in his cosy cabin squinting into the dark sky in front of his plexiglass while his assistant fiddled with the detection instrument. I pushed the earphone off one ear. I could hear an aircraft directly overhead. Then the W.A.A.F.'s voice again - urgently:

"Bandit! Straight ahead of you!"
"Damned if I can see him!"
"Fire your guns!"

As I gazed upward I could see the red sparks from the guns though I could not see the plane. Then the sound of cannon fire reached my ears. The enemy bandit exploded in mid-air. It was thrilling to have front row centre at the destruction of an enemy aircraft. I couldn't help but think that the W.A.A.F. should get at least half a credit for one Dornier destroyed. Some of these girls must have been aces before the war ended.

BATH - BRIGHTON

One of the worst features about being the member of a tank crew was that you sometimes got covered in dust. We would come in from a day's driving on the South Downs looking like we had been working all day in a flour mill - only instead of being covered in white we were covered in grey dust. Again it was Jamaica "Jack" Smith who discovered the "bawths". For a shilling you could rent a towel and a private bath. A woman attendant would draw the water - no fussing with a geyser here. You could just lie there and luxuriate in the warm water up to your neck. It was the next best thing to heaven after a day of riding in a tank on the chalky, dusty, South Downs, north of Brighton. I had heard of the Englishman and his bath and how he took it with him wherever he went throughout the "Empah". Jolly good, wot?

APRIL FOOL

Lord Haw-Haw announced in his Berlin radio broadcast that the Luftwaffe would bomb the Worthington Circus - the 4th Armoured Division, out of existence. He said this devastating raid would take place on the 2nd of April. The day came and went and not a single bomber arrived.

Wild Plover

DINING OUT

It wasn't easy to get a good meal in Britain during the war. I never saw a glass of milk but once, all the time I was there. Things like bananas and grapes were unheard of. I went to the Pantomime and the children were being regaled by a comic singing a song about bananas. Some of these youngsters had never seen or tasted a banana. When we went on leave and stayed with relatives or friends we always took our Ration Book with its precious coupons along. Everything was based on points. You could spend all your points on one tinned delicacy or distribute them on staples. When I visited my relatives in Hornchurch, they said that it was the first time they had been able to get a roast for two years. Before we left Canada, in Debert Camp, General Worthington had warned us that our stomachs would shrink when we got to England. He was right and it was a painful process. One night when we were stationed in Hove, I decided to go into Brighton and splurge. I discovered a very nice upstairs restaurant on a quiet backstreet. In the days before the War it must have been quite an exclusive place because even now, after four years of war, it didn't look too shabby. The decor was "Old World" and the waiters were formally dressed. What really surprised me was that it was not crowded. The maitre d'hôtel seated me at a cosy table in the corner and the waiter approached and presented me with the menu. As he did so, he whispered confidentially - "May I recommend the plover, sir?" Plover? What was that? I'd never heard of it, but suspecting that this was all they had anyway, and not wishing to spoil the fantasy, I said, "Yes, why not? I think I shall have the plover, please." It turned out to be delicious and the best meal I had in England. All I needed was an orchestra playing, some good white wine, and a beautiful female companion to make the evening complete. I was alone. There was no string quartet. I didn't drink. The plover was superb.

THE CHOCOLATE SOLDIER

Corporal Jack Smith and I were billeted in the same room in the hotel in Hove. The room was totally bare of furniture and we slept on the floor without a mattress. Jack was not only fond of his "bawth", he also loved good music. Tonight he came back from an evening in Brighton and announced - "Osborne, you can't miss it; Richard Tauber is giving a concert tomorrow night." Not wishing to reveal my ignorance I refrained from asking - "And who is Richard Tauber?" Instead I accepted Jack's invitation to go to Brighton and hear Richard Tauber sing at the Theatre Royal the following night. I had the pleasure of hearing one of the world's great tenors sing one of my favourite songs, My Hero from The Chocolate Soldier. Walking home in the blackout Jack and I were singing:

"I have a true and noble lover
He is my sweetheart, all my own
His like on Earth, who shall discover?
My heart is his and his alone ...
Come, come, naught can efface you
My arms are aching now to embrace you
You are divine
Come, come, I love you only
Come, hero mine"
- Oscar Strauss (1870-1954) - The Chocolate Soldier (1908)
- English Lyrics (1909) by Stanislaus Stange (1862-1917)

I loved chocolate but it was rationed so we didn't get it very often. One day I arrived back from the tank park in Hove to hear that the chocolate ration had arrived. I hurried out of my tank coveralls and ran down to the canteen where the chocolate was being dished out. I went up to the counter where the Auxiliary Service Officer was distributing the chocolate. "Your name?" he asked. "Corporal Osborne," I replied. His

German Messerschmitt Me410

finger ran down the list of names. "Osborne - yes - Osborne - you've already had your ration." "What?" I blurted, "I certainly have not." "Somebody came in here not ten minutes ago and said his name was Osborne and I have crossed it off the list." "Can you describe him to me - do you remember what he looked like?" "Yes - I think I can - not as tall as you - about five foot eight I'd say and with dark hair." "Moustache?" I asked. "Yes, a neat one." "I think I know who it was" I replied, and took off on the run. I entered the quarters and bounded up the stairs. The fellow was standing by the fireplace. "Look here. Did you collect my chocolate ration?" I demanded. "No, Corporal, I didn't touch it." "You're lying," I said, "and if you don't hand it over right now I'll beat the hell out of you." He knew I was on the boxing team. Actually I don't think I would have laid a finger on him but the threat worked. "Don't hit me! I'll get it," he pleaded and went over to his kit bag and pulled out my chocolate ration. "If I ever catch you doing that again," I warned, "I'll charge you with theft." Later he WAS charged with the theft of some wrist watches and sent away from the Regiment.

COUNSEL FOR THE DEFENCE

While we were stationed at Hove, I was detailed to be an escort for a prisoner to be tried by Court Martial. This was my first experience with the execution of military justice. As an escort I had to fall in on one side of the prisoner while another escort fell in on the other. We formed up outside the room where the trial was to take place. At the command of the R.S.M. "Escort and Prisoner - Fall in!" we took our places on each side of the accused. The R.S.M. opened the door and we marched in, in double time - "left, right, left, right, left, Prisoner and Escort - Halt!" The trial, I thought, was conducted fairly. The accused was charged with being A.W.O.L. [Absent With Out Leave] for nine months, from the time of his leave soon after our arrival in England, until his arrest. He was found living with a woman in Birmingham. There was no question of course of his guilt. In spite of this the defence counsel put up a brilliant argument and confounded the witnesses for the Crown. As far as I could judge, he discredited their evidence altogether. In cross-examining them he got them all mixed-up. Somebody told me afterward that the counsel for the defence had been a brilliant criminal lawyer on civvy street. I guess he was just having a great time keeping his hand in. Of course when the verdict was handed down, it was "Guilty as charged", even though as far as I could see the defence counsel had "won". Probably in a civilian court, with a twelve man jury, he would have gotten his client off. The accused got two years in the detention camp so I imagine he "missed" the war altogether. A case where perhaps crime did pay because if he had stayed clean, he would most certainly have been killed or wounded. But who would want to go back to civvy street with a Dishonourable Discharge?

ELEVEN O'CLOCK FRITZIE

One week at Hove, in the spring of 1943, a pattern of hit-and-run raids occurred. Every morning at precisely the same time - eleven o'clock - a lone [German Messerschmitt] Me410 came in low over the sea wall at Hove, dropped his bombs and scooted away. The gunners on the coast signalled his arrival by their firing, but by the time they were in action he was up and over them and away into the town. He must have been after our tanks which were deployed in a park just north of the town. This hit-and-run raider got away with the same tactics for a week. I called him Eleven O'clock Fritzie. I decided that the next morning I'd be ready for this bold raider and I mounted the [M2] .50-Calibre Browning on its Ack/Ack mounting and fed a belt of the big ammo into it. I kept a close eye on my watch and just before eleven o'clock, when all the crews were getting ready for their "elevenses" tea break, I got up in the turret and waited. Sure enough, right on the dot of eleven, our visitor arrived. The guns down on the sea coast began barking away announcing his arrival. I didn't hear any bombs but a minute later the plane came into sight. Apparently I wasn't the only one who had decided that Fritzie had pushed his luck just a wee bit too far and had decided to give him a warm reception. Guns began firing all over the park and some bigger guns behind me were

de Havilland DH-98 Mosquito

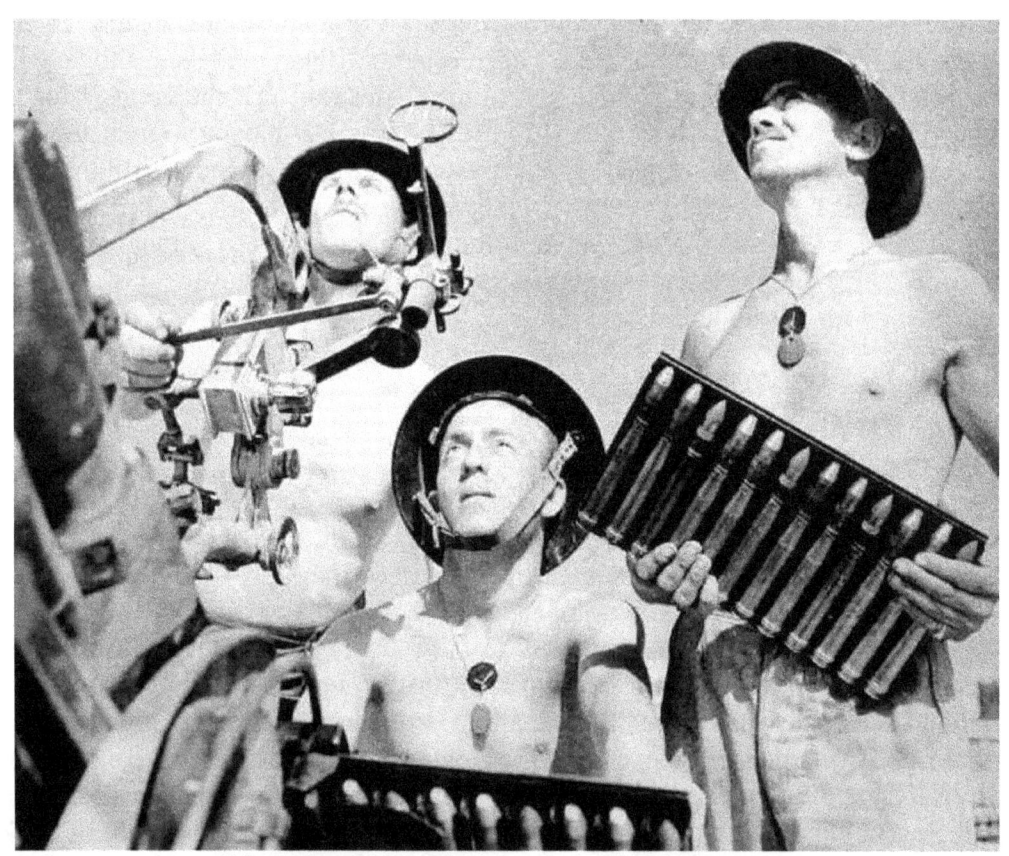
Manning the anti-aircraft (Ack-Ack) gun.

firing too - must have been a mobile Ack/Ack battery which had moved in to support us. There was a terrific din. Jerry was getting one hell of a hot reception. The plane was coming right into my line of fire now and it seemed to be hit. Tracer was going into it from all directions. Just then it veered, almost stalled and was dead in front of my gun. I shouted at the top of my voice - "That's not a Jerry!" But of course nobody could hear me in that crashing melee. I could see that one engine was glowing red as it was on fire. Then the aircraft went down and crashed behind some trees near the railway line that ran behind the tank park. The terrific din of all the guns ceased as quickly as it had begun. I jumped down from the tank and joined a bunch of others who were running over to see the downed aircraft. It was lying across the tracks in the railway cutting like a giant wounded bird. To our horror we recognized it as a [de Havilland DH98] Mosquito aircraft - one of our own! The pilot was dead and wearing the blue and white ribbon of the D.F.C. [Distinguished Flying Cross] under his Aviator Wings. The navigator was badly wounded and had lost a leg. They had been on a low level sweep over France and had got shot-up over there. The pilot had been killed and the Navigator had taken over control of the aircraft and was trying to bring it home. Our aircraft weren't supposed to come in over Brighton, or Hove. It was fair game for our Ack/Ack to shoot them down if they did. There was a recognized point of entry for fighters returning from sweeps over the enemy coast. Anything approaching our coast not through the recognized entry area was meat for our gunners, so naturally the boys gave it a hot reception. They were more eager than ever because of the lone enemy raider who had been making a monkey of them all week. The Navigator of the Mosquito undoubtedly knew better than to approach the coast at this sector, but with a dead pilot and a badly damaged aircraft, he was struggling to make a landfall - anywhere. He counted on our gunners knowing their aircraft recognition. He probably would have gotten away with it too had it not been for the pattern Eleven O'clock Fritzie had been establishing all week. It was sad to think that the Enemy had lured us into shooting down one of our own planes. But this kind of thing happens in wartime. I think there was a Mosquito flying around over Brighton and Hove for a week after that to make sure the Ack/Ack boys knew what it looked like and to make sure there were no more ugly incidents of this kind. With only a split second to make a recognition, a Mosquito could easily be mistaken for a Me410. We were getting a bit trigger happy and following the rule of shoot first and ask questions afterwards. It is interesting that Eleven O'clock Fritzie never showed up again. I often wondered if our Mosquito had intercepted him on his way over to bomb us and had shot him down, but in doing so had got shot up himself.

I always had a dreadful fear of killing one of our own after that. It was inevitable of course. It happened all the time in war, but it would haunt me. That is why I held my fire when the robot tanks were launched against us on Hill 195, held it until I was sure. The white flags fluttering from their aerials made me think that they might be Bren Gun Carriers with some of our boys crouching in them. I knew the Argyle and Sutherland Highlanders had tried to hold the position on the Hill during the night and I thought a carrier had ventured too far or they had been taken prisoner and were escaping back to our lines. That's why I held my fire, and the remembrance of Eleven O'clock Fritzie.

TRACK AND FIELD

In a letter to Mother written on May 23rd, 1943, I said:

"I have had an exceptionally busy week. We had a Track and Field Meet yesterday (May 22). I tied for top honours with 14 points. I still have a little left in me yet I really thought my track days were finished. If I can do well in the big meet next Friday I may earn a two weeks trip to a sports camp where I can get good coaching and good food (milk and eggs). They are stressing the sports angle and I even have a nice white track suit and new spike shoes."

Dunster Castle

MINEHEAD - JUNE 26th, 1943

We finished the day's work at Minehead about 0700 hours! The reason for this was that the range that we were using extended out into the Bristol Channel and was closed to firing after this hour in order to allow shipping a safe passage. We got up in the middle of the night, went out to the range in the dark and began shooting at first light. At seven, we stopped firing, cleaned our guns, maintenanced our tanks and caught the lorry back to our billets for breakfast. After breakfast we were free for the whole day. What could be better in mid-summer! I discovered a beautiful outdoor swimming pool. This was gracious living - after your swim you could lie on the lawn or sit at a table and drink tea and eat cakes. You'd never know that there was a war on!

One day I walked along the coast road toward Porlock. It was a superb day and I was thinking about Coleridge and trying to remember the opening lines of Kubla Khan:

"In Xanadu did Kubla Khan
A stately pleasure-dome decree:
Where Alph, the sacred river, ran
Through caverns measureless to man
Down to a sunless sea."
- Samuel Taylor Coleridge (1772-1834) - Kubla Khan (1797)

It must have been just such a day as this that the poet, dozing in his garden not far from here, had the vision which upon awakening he hastily wrote down. He had just got about fifty lines written when the visitor from Porlock knocked at his door and when he returned to his seat in the garden, an hour later, the memory of the line had gone. Like Coleridge, I could not recall the lines and as I was now perspiring with my walking, I scudded down the steep bank to the sea shore. There was no one about so I took off my uniform and went into the sea. The tide was at the full. After my swim I had a lovely sun bathe in the shelter of some big rocks. On my way back I stopped at a tea-room and the people there told me that I had gone swimming in a very dangerous spot, where strong tides and currents could have carried me to my death.

"Fools rush in where angels fear to tread."
-Alexander Pope (1688-1744) - Poem: An Essay on Criticism (1711)

On my birthday, Saturday afternoon, Padre Sinnamon arranged for some of us to visit Dunster Castle. Without, of course, mentioning the name of the Castle, this is what I wrote in a letter to my mother dated June 30th, 1943:

"The castle was built in 1088 and has been occupied by the same family ever since. It was a very interesting place - the Lord of the castle showed us around himself. There were I guess hundreds of portraits of former inhabitants painted in the garb of Elizabethan times and Cavaliers too. There was one thing, a Spanish tapestry painted on leather that was outstanding. An original Rembrandt also caught my fancy as did a hand carved staircase depicting a 'hunt'. There were also some original Chippendale chairs, etc. The bed chamber where Charles I slept while at a hunting party is still in good order with a four poster bed and brass warming pan. There was a Priest Hole behind the bed and I got in just to see what it was like - very dark! - and that's about enough for the castle. The village church was interesting too. We climbed the belfry by a circular staircase with 101 steps (like Casa Loma). We saw the Bell Ringing Chamber. There are 8 bell ropes and to ring a 'change' it takes about 4 hours - it's quite an art and interesting to learn about. There was also an old Mill by the stream which was mentioned in the Domesday Book - reminds me of Kipling's verse

Balliol College - Oxford

- 'see you the little mill that clacks so busy by the brook - she's ground her corn and paid her tax ever since Domesday Book.'

After all this we went for tea in the gardens of the Vicarage and had a lovely time - the Vicar's wife, assisted by two other ladies, served tea, sandwiches and cakes. We did enjoy it. So you see I did have a Birthday party after all."

The Lord of the castle, whose family name I could not mention for security reasons, was Luttrell. This afternoon tour of Dunster was a most welcome change of pace from the daily rough and ready life in an armoured regiment. In the midst of war you got a glimpse, if even for a brief period, of that England of more peaceful days and the England that we were fighting for.

"Stands the Church clock at ten to three?
And is there honey still for tea?"
- Rupert Brooke (1897-1915) - The Old Vicarage, Grantchester (1912)

OXFORD

The Army Educational Services could arrange for a limited number of servicemen to spend a week of their leave at Oxford. Jack Kane and I decided that this would be a most enlightening way to spend part of a leave so we made our application through the Educational Officer. When the great day of our leave arrived, Jack and I caught the train for London and then changed to the train for Oxford. No two undergraduates going up to the university for the first time were more excited than we were. We alighted at the station and emerged into the High Street to see for the first time "That sweet city with her dreaming spires" as Matthew Arnold had written. We had been told to report to Balliol College, so that is what we did. As we entered the gate and the porter showed us where to go and warned us not to walk on the grass - only Dons were permitted to do that - we entered the dining hall. Here we were met by two professors who saw to it that we all had a tankard of ale, and then when we were seated, gave us an informal talk on the different colleges that went to make up the University of Oxford. We were told that for the remainder of our stay at Oxford all ranks would be abolished. That evening after dinner I saw a British Brigadier and an American G.I. shooting craps! Alas our dream of a week at Oxford dematerialized in the cold light of day. The next morning we were informed that our registrations had not arrived. The Educational Officer had never sent them on or they had somehow gone astray. They were sorry but without the admission forms.... It was two very disappointed Grenadiers, who said good-bye to Oxford the next morning and, as the train puffed out of the station, took one last wistful look at the city with the dreaming spires. "Never mind, Bob." Jack said as the train gathered speed, "We can always truthfully say that we went through Oxford." "You're right, Jack," I replied, "you truly were 'A Yank at Oxford'." And so the two old Oxonians alighted at Paddington Station wondering how they would spend their leave now that they had been "sent down"!

THE HOME OF THE ROYAL ARMOURED CORPS

I received word that I was to be sent on a Desert Navigation Course that would be held at Bovington in Dorset. Bovington is the home of the Royal Armoured Corps and a Mecca for all tank men. It is to the Armoured Corps what Cranwell is to the R.A.F. I was very excited about going, especially since I was the only one from the Regiment. My orders were to alight at Wool Station where transport would meet me and take me to Bovington Camp. Everything went as planned. After a long train journey I arrived at Wool Station where a British army car and a driver were there to meet me. "Was I Corporal Osborne?" "Yes." I was surprised to find that I was the only Canadian being met. On arrival at the Camp I reported to the Orderly Room and was shown to my billet. At tea time I went round to the Mess Hall and queued up with

Training at Bovington

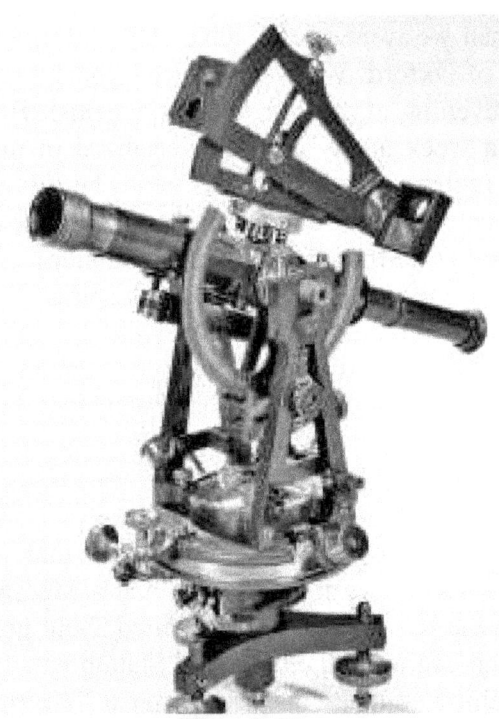
Theodolite

the other lads. They were all Limeys. It wasn't long before a sergeant came up to me and asked - "Corporal, what are you doing in this line? This is the Men's mess. You must dine in the Corporal's mess." This was a new one to me. In the Canadian Army we had a Sergeant's Mess but ranks below that all ate together. I dutifully took myself off to the Corporal's Mess. I could see that the class distinction in England had not disappeared!

The course proved to be very interesting as most of the instructors had been in the Western Desert and could speak with some authority on their subject. One in particular had served with the Long Range Desert Group under Major Stirling. We learned how to use a sun compass and a theodolite [more accurate and complex than a sextant]. I particularly enjoyed the interception problems where we had to work out the compass bearing, and speed, in order to intercept and ambush an enemy column. We learned how to navigate at night by use of the Air Almanac [astronavigation charts] and the stars. "The mean point of Aries" became a watchword. When the weekend came, I discovered that I was one of the few left in camp as all the others had gone home on weekend pass. This came as a kind of revelation to me to discover that the English soldier could go home on leave - something that we could never hope to do until "this bloomin' war was over". An English corporal and I borrowed a theodolite from the Stores and went down to Lulworth Cove and spent the best part of Saturday practising with it. We became close friends and it soon became apparent that we were the keenest men on the course. I felt an added responsibility as the only Canadian among all the Limeys and was determined not to let my side down. One weekend, when the English corporal and I returned to our quarters after a day of practising compass-adjusting, he came over to my bunk and said: "Somebody's been at my kit - is yours all right?" "Yes, mine's O.K." I replied, "But, you'd better report what's happened about yours!" He went off at once to find the Orderly Sergeant. The story he came back with was an eye-opener for me. He sat down on the side of my bunk and told me what had happened. Apparently it was Scotland Yard that had investigated his kit. He explained to me that he was a member of the Communist party and before enlisting he had worked in a factory in Birmingham. At noon hour he would get up on a soap box and harangue his fellow workers with the communist line. I was so naive that I thought all communists were "Russians"! It was a real shocker to me to discover that I had been close friends with a real live "commie" and that he was an Englishman. He was also the keenest man on the course along with myself. His greatest ambition, he told me, was to spearhead a tank column into Berlin and meet up with his Russian comrades. I never did find out the actual results of the course except that he and I topped the class. Whether we were tied for top marks I do not know. We were the only two really dedicated men on the course. Over a year later, when I was in hospital, I met a chap from his unit. When I asked him if he knew my Communist friend, he said that he did and went on to tell me that he had been killed while commanding his tank on the way to Berlin. So perhaps he achieved his ambition after all. I hope so. He was a very intelligent fellow, and a gentleman.

A couple of other things happened at Bovington Camp. The first concerns something that occurred one day when we were out with the tanks learning how to adjust the compass. In a tank, a compass needs to be adjusted fairly often because the amount of ammunition used changes the magnetic field and this affects the accuracy of the compass. This compass adjusting was done out in the middle of a large tarmac - like an airfield - where lines were painted on the tarmac so that we could point our tanks to the required point of the compass. I was lying under the tank examining something when I suddenly realized that it was strangely quiet. I crawled out from under the tank to discover that I was alone. The others had all disappeared. I walked the quarter of a mile to the N.A.A.F.I. [Navy, Army & Air Force Institutes - Store] to find them all having tea and rock cakes [small, hard fruit cake]. They had assumed that I, like them, would pause for four o'clock tea. They seemed to have a built-in time mechanism that signalled coffee at eleven and tea a four.

Daily Mail

ONE PENNY · FOR KING AND EMPIRE · FRIDAY, MAY 4, 1945 · 4 A.M. EDITION

taken with a HOVIS slice

CELL READY FOR LORD HAW-HAW AT THE TOWER

■ **Reports of traitor's capture in Germany**

■ **His date with the hangman draws near**

A CELL is ready in the Tower of London for Lord Haw-Haw, William Joyce, the radio traitor who fled to Germany in 1939 and broadcast propaganda in English to audiences in this country on behalf of his Nazi masters.

Introducing his radio programme with the words 'Germany calling, Germany calling', Haw-Haw spent five years trying — and dismally failing — to indoctrinate British families with the Fuhrer's vile creed.

Reports from Europe last night told of his capture, although there was confusion as to his whereabouts and no confirmation in London.

Even if he remains at large, at

BY **WILSON BROADBENT**
DIPLOMATIC CORRESPONDENT

the Tower all is prepared for him and the guard is standing by.

It is expected he will be held in the cell once occupied by another traitor, Norman Baillie-Stewart — known as the Officer in the Tower and imprisoned for five years in 1933 for betraying military secrets — passing 'Traitors' Gate and the Bloody Tower on his way in.

After his release, Baillie-Stewart went to Germany with the Nazi girl to whom he disclosed the secrets and, like Haw-Haw, broadcast German propaganda.

Some say that talk of the Tower for Lord Haw-Haw is a diversion, and he could go instead to Wormwood Scrubs or to Wandsworth Prison.

Whatever the truth, his fate is sealed — and he knows it.

When he made his last broadcast this week, Lord Haw-Haw was very drunk.

His understudy, Edward Dietze, took over for him last night, addressing England glumly on the Wilhelmshaven emergency

TURN TO NEXT PAGE

Traitor: Joyce wearing Nazi uniform and Hitler moustache

Now the Nazis are fighting each other

BY **DAILY MAIL REPORTER**

AS BRITISH tanks stormed into Denmark and the German government took refuge in Copenhagen, the Prime Minister was at his desk until the early hours this morning.

Cabinet ministers, who met yesterday evening to review the latest developments in Germany and Denmark, are standing by for any sudden summons.

News that Montgomery's armour had entered Denmark came as Albert Speer, once Hitler's Armaments minister, admitted on the Danish radio that Germany is defeated. He stated that all future German broadcasts will come from Copenhagen.

Throughout yesterday, telegrams recording the progress of the Allied Armies across Germany were coming in. But just how this rout of the once proud German army is going to end is a matter of conjecture.

A declaration that Germany has been defeated — arrived at by consultation between Britain, Soviet Russia and the United States — is not expected until there has been a triumphal march through Berlin by the Allied Armies, headed by the Russians.

Meanwhile in Denmark, German garrisons have begun to wage war among themselves. Some want to fight on, but the great majority clearly wish to surrender.

Regular troops are fighting small but fanatical S.S. formations.

The other incident concerns a guard detail. On this course we were free from all duties except that once during the course we had to stand a night guard. The area that I had to patrol was on the top of a very high cliff overlooking the sea. The guard house was inland at the foot of a steep hill. It was a beautiful still moonlight night in late July. I could see the ribbon of moonlight on the sea far below the cliff and it lit up the headland. The N.C.O. in charge of our guard sent up word that he expected the duty officer to make a surprise visit to see if he could catch us "off guard". I decided to surprise him instead. Running at right angles to the cliff and my guard beat were some ancient tumuli [mound of earth or stones raised over a grave] or long mounds about 4 feet [1.2m] high. My sentry "go" ran through them but I could hide behind them easily, concealed from anyone approaching along the path. About 0200 hours, I heard the Orderly Officer leave the guard house and begin the climb up the hill to the top of the cliff. He had the guard sergeant with him. I fixed my bayonet and crouched behind the grassy mound and waited. It seemed a long time before the two emerged at the top, but I could see the two of them clearly silhouetted on the path. They were walking straight toward me. I heard the officer say - "Sergeant, where is the sentry? It looks as though this post is unguarded." I heard the sergeant reply - "He should be here somewhere, sir." "Probably sleeping" the officer said. I waited until they were almost upon me as I wanted to time this perfectly. I could hear the sergeant puffing and blowing from the steep climb. Suddenly I sprang out and challenged in my best French - "Qui va là? Avancez et être reconnu!" ["Who goes there? Advance and be recognized!"]. My sudden appearance and my French took them completely by surprise. I thought for a moment that the sergeant would topple off the cliff. The officer, who had his hand on his pistol, recovered first. "My God, Corporal, you gave me a fright." When I arrived back at the guard room after my tour of duty the sergeant of the guard was still chuckling over it. "You sure scared hell out of old so-and-so," he said. "'ees been pullin that sneaky inspection for a long time. 'as 'is batman wake 'im at 0130 'e does, just so 'e can catch some pore bloke a nappin'. 'E tol me wot scared 'im most was your French! Be blow'd if 'e didn't think for a moment we'd been overrun by some enemy commando. Scar 'd the livin' 'ell out of 'im you did Corp. Serves the blighter right, it does!" "Well," I replied in my most patronizing Canadian-English, "I don't think you'll have any more trouble with old major so-and-so and his sneaky inspections, Sergeant!"

In a letter written to my Mother and dated August 7th, 1943, I said:

"I've just had a letter from my old chum John Maffre who transferred to the R.C.A.F. when we were in Montreal - perhaps you remember me speaking of him. He has seen a lot of action as a Spitfire pilot over in Malta but is now back in "Blighty". His brother got shot down - too bad. I often wonder if the next generation will appreciate just what these boys are doing for them. I guess it will soon be forgotten after the Victory Parades are over."

John and I planned to get together but it never did come off.

HOVE TO WORTHING

In August, we moved from Hove to Worthing. When we were in Aldershot, we were listening to William Joyce, Lord Haw Haw, on the radio when he announced that the town clock in Aldershot was two minutes slow. Some of our chaps went off to check on it and sure enough, he was correct. There was a spy in our midst but how was he, or she, getting this information so quickly to Berlin? On the 15th of August, we moved along the coast road to Worthing. It was a beautiful day and as we listened to the tank wireless, Lord Haw Haw said - "We know you are moving to Worthing, 22nd Canadian Armoured Regiment. We'll be round to stage a little welcoming party for you". Sure enough, that night, the Luftwaffe dropped some bombs which narrowly missed our billets in the Hotels Palace Court, Rivington, Shakespeare, Eden Hall and Berkley.

Junker Ju86P

Only when the tide goes out do you discover who's been swimming naked.
Warren Buffett

On another night, I was on guard duty and carried my Bren gun. A raider must have come in pretty high up and then after he got inland a way, he turned off his engines and began a long low gliding dive which brought him out at the coast just over our billets. I could hear his dive coming and then I saw the big black bird swooping over the roof of our hotel. I let go with the Bren, firing from the shoulder. I don't know if I scored any hits. His bombs dropped harmlessly out in the sea just beyond the beach and he disappeared into the darkness over the Channel.

WORTHING - AUGUST, 1943

One morning, just after breakfast, I came out of the mess to see a number of our fellows looking up at some little white puffs in the sky. It was one of those rare August mornings - not a cloud to be seen. There was a long vapour trail like a thin streak of chalk across the blue sky with a tiny glint of silver at its head like a comet. The plane was so high we couldn't hear it. The little puffs of white kept appearing way, way, up. "What are they shooting at?" somebody asked. Then the little white puffs ceased. Someone yelled, "There he is!" Sure enough, about half way between where the shells had been bursting and the sea horizon, a plane was plummeting straight down. We didn't see it actually crash into the sea because we were screened by buildings and the sea wall. The next day we read in the newspapers that for the first time the Allies had developed a shell that could reach the Junker [Ju] 86P-2 [High altitude photo reconnaissance aircraft with pressurized cabin] which could fly at 50,000 feet [15,240m]. Every morning, with typical German punctuality, this spy-plane had come over taking pictures of the coast. The Allies had been helpless to stop it because it was beyond the ceiling of our fighters and our Ack/Ack fire. Now at last our boffins [slang for scientist or engineer] had produced an answer to the enemy's high flying reconnaissance aircraft. Imagine, a Ju86P shot down from nine miles up in the sky!

ILFRACOMBE - AUGUST, 1943

Corporal Jack Smith and I decided we would take our leave in Devon. We chose the north coast and arrived in Ilfracombe on the August Bank Holiday to find everything booked solid. We did, however, get accommodation for the remainder of our leave in a private home, but where were we to sleep the first night of our leave? In desperation we went to the police. They said we could sleep in a jail cell, the only problem being that they had to lock us in. This was no problem for us and we had a good night's rest in the Ilfracombe jail that night. The same day, after getting fixed up with digs for the night, we headed for the beach as it was real hot August Bank Holiday weather. As we had no bathing trunks we selected a secluded spot behind some large rocks to change from our battle dress into our altogether. Jack was Jamaican and loved swimming in the sea. We had a wonderful time swimming and sunning, but when we went to get our clothes they were nowhere to be found. The tide had come in and almost covered the big rock behind which we had hidden them. What to do? Like Adam in the Garden of Eden, we were afraid because we were naked and didn't know where to hide. I said to Jack: "Now we are really going to get charged by the police for indecent exposure!" He replied: "We'll be sleeping in jail, and no mistaking it, man." What could we put on? I remembered those cartoons that we used to laugh at in the Funny Papers where people in our predicament always managed to find a convenient barrel somewhere. I gazed around for a barrel - there was none. "What about seaweed?" Jack suggested. "Then we'd look like Father Neptune", I replied and quoted Wordsworth:

"... Great God! I'd rather be
A Pagan suckled in a creed outworn;
So might I, standing on this pleasant lea,
Have glimpses that would make me less forlorn;
Have sight of Proteus rising from the sea;

Or hear old Triton blow his wreathed horn."
- William Wordsworth (1770-1850) - The World Is Too Much With Us (c. 1802)

"Damn you and your poetry! This is no time for levity, man." said Jack. "Hang on a minute - that may not be Triton blowing his wreathed horn, but isn't that woman up near the tea wagon signalling to us?" Jack peered over the tip of the rock which was now almost totally submerged by the incoming tide. "By George, you're right, Osborne." Jack always called me by my surname when he thought I had said something profound! Standing naked in the water and gripping the tip of the rock to prevent the waves from washing us away, we fixed our eyes on the woman. By arm signals she made us to understand that she had seen us go behind the rocks to undress, had noticed the tide coming in and our apparent ignorance of the fact, and had removed our precious uniforms to a place of safety farther up the beach. Saved! Using our best infantry tactics we swam and crawled from one rock to another until we reached our clothes. We offered to buy her a cup of tea from the tea wagon but she declined. No doubt she was too embarrassed to look us straight in the eye. "Whatever you do," Jack cautioned, "don't tell her where we're going to sleep tonight."

It was on this same leave that I had another embarrassing time. As I said we were living in this private home and a very beautiful home it was. Jack went out one evening and came back very drunk. He had been mixing Jamaican rum and Devonshire cider. He managed to get into the house without causing a disturbance, but once up the stairs and through the door of our room he insisted that I knock him out! He kept dancing up to me and throwing punches which I had to duck. He seemed to know that he was "stinko" and kept taunting me to hit him and knock him out. I calculated the odds. He was getting more rambunctious every second. What if I couldn't get in a solid punch the first try? What if I missed and he decked me? Jack was a black Jamaican and a superb athlete. I could not afford to muff this one. The frightening thought crossed my mind - what if I slugged him and he fell, and hit his head, and died? I had read of such things. Would any jury believe my story when I look the witness stand and said that he had pleaded with me to hit him? "Go on, Man." he kept repeating, "Go on and hit me. Hit me Osborne." He begged me to put him away. I feinted a punch and when he clumsily pawed the air I pushed him with all my strength and he fell on to the bed. He passed out cold. That was far worse than any experience I had in the boxing ring. As I expected the next morning he remembered nothing of the episode, but I made him swear never to mix rum and cider again. Which, I may add, he was pleased to do.

EXERCISE BRIDOON - NOVEMBER, 1943

On the 17th of September we moved by rail to Higham Heath in Suffolk. From here we drove our Ram tanks to our training area. A week later we moved to harbour in Chippenham Park, near Newmarket, Cambridgeshire. At this place we had some valuable training with our infantry - the Lake Superior and the Algonquin regiments. [The Lake Superior Regiment (Motor) - L.S.R.(M.) - renamed to Lake Superior Scottish Regiment after the war, bore the nickname Lake Sups (pronounced "Soups")]. We also learned to work with our Artillery batteries. In the middle of October we moved to harbour near Bury St. Edmunds in Suffolk. Here we took part in a large combined exercise called GRIZZLY II in which the 12th Manitoba Dragoons played the role of the enemy. We advanced north and captured Frog Hill north of Holt and close to the sea. In this exercise we worked in close support of the Algonquins. The area north of Bury St. Edmunds is known as Breckland. It is a wooded and heathland area and ideal for military exercises on a large scale.

All this training at the Divisional level was to prepare us for the big test that was coming up. We were excited to learn that we were to be pitted against a British Armoured Division - the famous Panda Division. They would have an advantage over us because they were equipped with Crusader tanks which were much faster than our Rams. The exercise was called BRIDOON and the rumour was that the Division that lost the

4th Canadian Armoured Division

mock battle would be turned into Flail tanks. We did not want any of that nonsense. We hadn't come all the way across the Atlantic to spend our time beating up the back areas setting off mines or clearing the verges of roads. We were hungry for a crack at the German panzers! So we were all keyed up when we went into "battle" against the Brits. The scheme began at midnight on the 1st of November. The game plan was that we (4th Canadian Division) known as "Southland" was to try to smash through Heathland defended by "Northland" (9th British Division) and capture a hill known as Eagle Tower, on top of which was a chrome mine. We were to seize and hold this objective for twelve hours, long enough for the Engineers to hypothetically extract the ore and blow up the mine. Then we were to make a tactical withdrawal to our start point in the South. Lieutenant "Freddie" Hill was our Crew Commander for the first two days.

On the previous scheme, GRIZZLY II, he and I had worked out a system of dead reckoning map reading so that we knew where we were all the time and could give the coordinates if needed. This was no small achievement on the dirty wet nights of dark November. The system worked like this. I sat curled up in my corner of the turret with the map open on my knees. Freddie would say to me over the I/C - "Just passing crossroad." I would then pin point it on my map and look ahead for the next salient feature. Then I would say to him - "Bridge - one quarter mile." As soon as we reached the bridge he would call out "Bridge" and I would give him the next feature to look for. In this way we always knew where we were on the map. The system worked - even on the darkest, dirtiest nights, and England in November can be pretty dark and dismal. On this exercise we also had to keep a sharp look out for "enemy" aircraft who were instructed to bomb us with flour bags. If you were hit it was only a short time before an umpire appeared in his jeep and ruled your tank and crew knocked out. You had to just sit there until the scheme was over. After hours of dodging low flying aircraft and trying to find fords across rivers, we found ourselves on the afternoon of the 3rd of November in a position covering the left flank at Bagmore Farm, just west of Frog Hill where we had enticed the British armour into a trap. I had been switched to a higher ranking officer's tank and I could hear our Recce reporting the advancing positions of the "enemy" as they moved deeper and deeper into our ambush. "Twelve hundred yards - one thousand yards - eight hundred yards - six hundred". Nearer and nearer the Crusaders came and still they hadn't seen us! "Shouldn't we open fire, sir?" I asked. I could see that the officer was in a near state of panic. He jumped down from the tank and ran back somewhere - to consult the Colonel, I suppose. We began to fire and soon the whole squadron and regiment was blasting away at Panda Division. It was great fun letting off all that blank ammo. When the smoke cleared, umpires were driving around waving white flags and declaring the Brits annihilated - which indeed they would have been if we had had real ammo up the spout. We were jubilant. I never saw that officer again. A scheme like this could be a test of how somebody was going to react when the real pressure was on. The "Cease Fire" came at 2200 hours but the battle was over in the middle of the afternoon. The Brits were mad - they accused us of playing dirty pool. Apparently our infantry had really foxed them too. Even one of our padres was credited with capturing an "enemy" tank and parading it before the General! "Northland" accused us of Red Indian tactics, but the truth was we were taking this whole thing very seriously, and they were thinking more about their next weekend pass. For them it was just another exercise, for us it was life or death - we weren't going to be turned into flails! General Worthington was overjoyed. His young 4th Armoured Division had just wiped out the prestigious British Panda Division. The weather turned beastly cold and we were given a rum ration in our tea. It was the first time I had tasted rum and I can't say I liked it, but it did seem to warm you up. The next day Brigadier J. D. B. Smith came to speak to us. "Well done, lads," he said, "After all you can't kill a man more than three times." We, "Southland", had gained our objective and held it for twelve hours after which we had withdrawn with "Northland" hotly in pursuit. We had drawn them in and blasted them to pieces. So much for the British 9th Armoured Division. They had been "written off".

That night we moved into a little harbour area not far from an airfield. The whole of East Anglia was dotted with airfields. We were dead on our feet as we had had little sleep for a week. My orders were to set the

boys to digging slit trenches before we hit the sack, so I told the crew to get the shovels out and start digging. They were cursing me roundly. It was near midnight - the ground was hard - this was carrying the realism of the exercise too far - we'd won, hadn't we? Nevertheless they all began to dig. All, that is, except "Chick" Weir our driver. He dug down about one foot then just said, "To hell with it - the scheme is over and I'm going to bed." He threw down his shovel, unrolled his sleeping bag and crawled into the sack. Chick was a wonderful driver and I didn't have the heart to insist that he carry out the orders After about an hour of exhausting digging, the rest of us had completed our slit trenches and snuggled into our blankets under the tarpaulin lean-to beside the tank where our driver was snoring loudly. We had just dropped off to sleep ourselves when we were awakened by the "crump!", "crump!", "crump!" of exploding bombs. An enemy night fighter had sneaked in behind one of our bombers and when our boys had gone in to land their kite he had laid a stick of bombs right across the little wood where we were harboured. He was aiming at the airstrip not far away. "Quick!" I shouted, "Into your slit trenches!" Everyone jumped up and dove into their newly dug pits. Chick, who was still three-quarters asleep, managed to crawl out from under the tarp and jumped into his trench. There he stood, like some ancient martyr, about ankle deep while the Jerry aircraft laid another stick of bombs not far away. Chick presented a comic picture standing there in the bright moonlight with the bombs going off - completely unprotected. We all had a good laugh and it broke the tension. "Damn good thing those weren't flour bags", somebody said. In the distance, illuminated by the chandelier flares, I could see the tall spire of Norwich cathedral.

Another story about this same raid was told to me by Colonel Harry Griffiths. Apparently, one of our officers, who was a bit upset by all these "real" bombs falling out of the sky, sent a message back to Regimental H.Q. asking what he should do. The signal promptly came back - "Dig your slit trenches a little deeper!"

After we had theoretically annihilated the British 9th Armoured Division in exercise BRIDOON we were whisked off to a little place near Chippenham, not far from the famous horse-racing track at Newmarket. It was an ideal spot for tanks, in a little wood with paved parking places, just outside the Nissen huts [prefabricated half-cylindrical corrugated steel structure]. It was early November and in the evening the orange light peeking out from behind the blackout screen and the lingering wood smoke gave a cosy atmosphere to the place. I hoped this was where we were going to settle down for the winter. Such was not to be our good fortune. One morning our Captain said - "Let's have a race. We'll run round the camp site. I've been looking at the map and I reckon it's about three and a half to four miles. Bottle of scotch for the first man back. Off you go!" It was a brisk morning, but I felt good. I decided to go after that prize - especially since I didn't drink! I arrived back at the start point about three minutes ahead of my nearest competitor to find some American Signal Corps men working up on the poles. "You fellas moving in here?" I asked. "Yeah, but not yet", he replied chewing on a cigar. "Whaddya mean, not yet?" "This place ain't fit for men to live in. The Limeys have bin in here. We gotta fix it up first before our boys can come in." I couldn't believe what I was hearing. Here I was hoping that we would be lucky enough to be left here to spend the winter and this G.I. Joe was telling me it wasn't fit for men to live in. "When our boys come in here," he went on, "they'll get 'roughing it pay'." Roughing it pay? I'd never heard of such a thing. What was this, an army, or a bloody ballet troupe? I began to wonder what the Yanks would do when they got into action. No doubt their Service Corps would see to it that all the comforts of home would be supplied! I was beginning to think that I might need that bottle of scotch after all.

WARCOP RANGES – KIRKCUDBRIGHT, SCOTLAND

When General Montgomery [Field Marshal Bernard Law Montgomery, 1st Viscount Montgomery of Alamein, K.G. [Knight of the Order of the Garter], G.C.B. [Knight Grand Cross of the Order of Bath], D.S.O. [Distinguished Service Order], P.C. [Privy Council of the United Kingdom]; nicknamed "Monty"

British Sherman "Firefly" Tank

Warcop Firing Range

and the "Spartan General"] took over command of the 21st Army Group he ordered that a more powerful gun be mounted on the American [M4A4] Sherman Mk V tank. He had realized from the warfare in the desert and in Sicily and Italy, that our tank armament was no match for the German Panther [Medium Tank; Panzerkampfwagen V Panther] and Tiger [Heavy Tank; Panzerkampfwagen Tiger Ausf. B] tanks. Monty wanted the French 75 mm M3 L/40 gun replaced by the British QF 17-pounder (76.2 mm) anti-tank gun. The Americans said that this couldn't be done. They argued that the Sherman was designed for the 75mm and if a more powerful gun, like the 17-pounder, was mounted in it, then it would break the suspension, or something worse, when firing a broadside.

A small detachment was sent to Warcop Ranges to prove one or the other wrong! The countryside around Kirkcudbright [pronounced ker-coo-bree] in Scotland is isolated and beautiful even in November. The ranges faced into the Solway Firth and it was into this arm of the sea that our shells were to land. "Love swells like the Solway, but ebbs like its tide". The area is noted for its beautiful sunsets and in peacetime was the haunt of artists. We were billeted in an old farm not far from Castle Douglas. We slept in the hay on the barn floor and were awakened in the morning by the rooster. We went out to the range, climbed into the turret and put a giant 17-pounder shell up the spout. There was an anxious moment as we all wondered what would happen. The order came to "Fire!" There was a terrific bang and a sheet of flame as the Sherman rocked on her tracks. She had stood the test. Monty was right - as usual. Now at last we had a gun to match the German Tigers. We called the Shermans that were fitted with the 17-pounder "Fireflies".

DECEMBER LEAVE

At the beginning of December I got a 4-day pass and I decided to spend it in Brighton. I wrote to Mary, the girl I knew in the W.R.N.S, and suggested that we might meet there. She was stationed in Shoreham, which was not far away from Brighton. She wrote back to say that she had wangled a week-end pass. As the time drew near I looked forward to the weekend with mounting anticipation. I caught the train for Brighton and arrived before noon. As I strolled down the street from the station I noticed a little hostelry called Emery's Hotel. It looked like the kind of little hotel that would just suit us for our weekend. I entered and engaged two rooms. It was a quiet, homey little place of three storeys.

I met Mary at the train station about 5 o'clock and we walked to the hotel. It felt kind of funny going up the stairs together - as if we were on our honeymoon. I was a bit embarrassed. Her room was on the top floor and mine was on the second - located at the foot of a short staircase leading down from her room. Once we had got settled, we set off for the evening. It was dark and raining as we came out of the hotel. I had made a reconnaissance in the afternoon and I knew where there was a good place to eat and theatre nearby where we could see a show. It was just as well that I had, because the night was pitch dark and we would have had a hard time locating anything in the blackout. We had a good dinner then we went next door to Sherry's to take in the vaudeville show. It was typical English music hall with songs and ribald jokes and a strip-tease. When we came out of the show we walked toward the sea front and strolled along the promenade. The wind almost blew us off our feet. The night was black and the sleeting rain was blowing off the Channel. We stopped and peered out into the stygian darkness. Out there - over there - was France and the enemy. "What a night for a commando raid!" I observed as I stared into the driving sleet that stung my eyes and I wondered what Jerry was doing on the other side of the Channel on a night like this. We held hands and walked eastward along the Prom trying to avoid the puddles. We put our arms around each other and snuggled our greatcoats together. It was not easy to walk this way but it was fun. We tried to kiss as we walked but every ten steps we'd slop into a great puddle of water. Mary was getting her feet wet so we turned back. The gale was more on our backs now so we pulled up our greatcoat collars and braved the storm. When we reached what I judged to be the centre of Brighton, we turned into the city toward the hotel. As soon as we got off the Prom, the wind slackened as we were then sheltered by the buildings.

The pubs were just closing and we could smell a fish and chip shop. People were coming out of it with their supper wrapped in newsprint. I asked Mary if she wanted some but she said she didn't. We groped our way along to where the hotel was supposed to be. After a couple of false stops we found it and were glad to enter its cosy precincts. A small light was burning on the desk but we were relieved that the landlord was not there to see us in our dishevelled state creeping quietly up the stairs. We kissed goodnight outside my room and agreed that Mary would give a little tap on my door when she came down to breakfast in the morning. I went inside, drew the blackout curtains and then switched on the light. A naked light bulb only seemed to add to the frigidity of the sparsely furnished room. I took off my wet greatcoat and hung it up in the wardrobe. Just then the sirens went signalling an air raid. I thought of poor Mary alone up there next to the roof. I decided I would go up and see if she wanted company. She had been through a lot of air raids so I am sure she did not feel any more scared than I did. Perhaps I was the one that needed company! I ascended the short flight and tapped gently on her door which she opened with a chuckle. "I rather hoped you would come up." she whispered. She had not put the blackout curtain up and the storm had passed revealing a cold moon which was shining right into the room, casting a beam of silver across the bed. "How sweet the moonlight sleeps upon this bank! Here will we sit, and let the sounds of music creep in our ears ... or at least the sounds of war!" "Mercy, where did you get all that?" she said as I sat down beside her. "Your bard of Avon. I do fear, my dear, that your education has been sadly lacking." "Shakespeare? I don't remember reading anything like that?" "Well, not the last sentence, but it's from the Merchant. You probably had to run to the air raid shelter that day and missed the line." "I did write my final exams in the shelter."

The next morning I was awakened by a tapping on my door. "I'll be ready for breakfast in 10 minutes." she announced. I could smell bacon cooking downstairs. As we entered the dining room there were two Warrant Officers from the Regiment sitting there, Adcock and Cunningham, who eyed us as we walked in.

A RUM STORY

Christmas 1943 found us stationed in Crowborough - between London and the white cliffs of Dover. It was a cold Christmas Eve, but no snow. After supper I decided I would go up to the Squadron Office and pick up the Christmas mail - which I had heard had just arrived - for our troop. When I got there, I could see that I would need a jeep to carry it all, so Corporal Pachal got one for me. We piled it high with parcels and I started off. I hadn't gone far before I hit a bump in the road and a couple of parcels bounced off. I threw them back on top of the heap and started off again. By the time I reached the hut the news of Santa's arrival had reached the boys and they were all out to greet me. I picked up each parcel and read out the name. It was like a Sunday School Christmas Party. "Jack Kane". "Here, Ossie!" Then I'd lift it up to my ear and shake it, or squeeze it, and make some asinine remark. "It feels like a pair of silk pyjamas, Jack." Then they would all hoot and holler. Everything went fine until I came to the parcel for Corporal Smith. Jack came from Kingston, Jamaica, and the firm he used to work for before the War always sent him a bottle of real Jamaican rum. Jack looked forward to this every year. As I picked up the parcel I feared the worst. I could smell it! "Something rotten in Denmark here." I chortled. Sure enough, the one fragile parcel in the whole jeep load had to be Jack's bottle of Jamaican rum - the one I had bounced off the jeep onto the road. I can still hear him cursing me. "You ought to be court-martialed Osborne! This parcel came over two-thousand miles, man, across the Atlantic, survived the attacks of U-Boats and the rough handling of stevedores, but you, you idiot, you dropped it on the last one hundred yards of its journey!" The beautiful aroma of that over proof Jamaican rum filled the room. I agreed, I ought to be court-martialled. If Corporal Smith had had the authority to do so, I would have been. Even today I can't eat a rum and butter toffee without thinking of that Christmas!

**The Parish Church of St John the Evangelist,
Crowborough, East Sussex.**

SECOND CHRISTMAS IN ENGLAND

My second wartime Christmas in England was a memorable one. Jack Kane got the idea that we should do something to make Christmas a little happier for the poor families in Crowborough. He spoke to our Padre and the project was launched. We decorated empty Petrol tins and placed them round the huts where the troops could place toys or extras from their Christmas parcels from home. Those who wished could also donate money. It was a good project and we got a great response from the lads. On Christmas Eve we loaded up some jeeps and set off for the town. What a thrill to knock at the door of some poor English family who weren't expecting a thing and call out in a cheery voice - "The Canadian Santa Claus has just arrived!" All our parcels contained a five pound note as well as the treats of food and toys and every one was delivered to a family whose father was serving in the desert army. I lugged a big parcel to one house. It was a shabby looking place. A woman opened the door holding a baby in her arms. She told me she was thirty-three years old. Her seven children crowded round. I could hardly keep the tears from my cheeks as I looked into the excited faces of those kiddies. The woman said that her husband was with the Eighth Army and that she hadn't heard from him for some time. She hadn't known how she was going to make Christmas for her children. She had prayed to God that something would happen to help her. My knock on the door was a Christmas miracle. I knew there were toys for all her kids in that big parcel as well as good Canadian food and five pounds. I stepped out of that house into the cold starry night with a glow in my heart. Thank God for Christmas - "Merry Christmas!" I felt like old Scrooge - "I am as merry as a school boy. I am as giddy as a drunken man." In a letter of thanks, the girl of ten drew a flag with "CANADA" on it, she didn't know that we didn't have a flag of our own. The little boy of three made a wavy line to say - "God Bless Us Every One."

CHRISTMAS MIDNIGHT AND DAY

On Christmas Eve, about 2115 hours we walked to the little Anglican Church across the road from the camp. It was a very clear cold night. The words of Christina Rossetti came to my mind [In the Bleak Midwinter (c.1872)] - "Earth stood hard as iron, water like a stone." Unlike her next line the snow had not fallen "snow on snow." As we entered St. John's Church the candles glowed warmly. We sang the old familiar carols and heard the Gospel story. "God rest you merry, Gentlemen, Let nothing you dismay." Our thoughts were far away, across the dark storm-tossed Atlantic. I thought of the seamen out there tonight in the sleet and cold peering into the dark waters for the Enemy. Where would we be next Christmas Eve? Who knows? Jack Smith whispered - "I hope you said that prayer of confession for my rum you broke, you miserable sinner." "I said it, Jack, I said it." I whispered back in my most penitent voice as the Padre pronounced the Absolution. As the holy hour arrived we went forward and knelt for the Holy Sacrament. *Peace in War*, I knew it there in little St. John's Church at Christmas midnight.

BOXING MATCH

After dinner on Christmas Day we had boxing matches in the N.A.A.F.I. They were only exhibition bouts so we didn't really go at it too hard. I went three rounds with Jack Kane, our tank driver. He is a wonderful guy. Jack comes from Brooklyn, New York. One of those Americans who couldn't wait for his country to get into the fight against Hitler and came up north of the border and joined the Guards. He has seen all the great boxers - Tony Canzonari, Barney Ross, Max Baer, Joe Louis, Jack Dempsey, all the greats. Jack held me in a clinch in the second round and whispered in my ear - "Hey, Ossie, take it easy, remember this is Christmas Day not Boxing Day!" After supper we attended an E.N.S.A. [Entertainments National Service Association] show. It wasn't bad. There was a blind actor that was really good. "And so to bed" as Samuel Pepys would say in his diary.

Volunteer Service Medal

- The Canadian Volunteer Service Medal is granted to persons of any rank in the Naval, Military or Air Forces of Canada who voluntarily served on Active Service and have honourably completed eighteen months total voluntary service from September 1939 to March, 1947.

Bars
A silver bar (often called a clasp), a maple leaf at its centre, was awarded for 60 days service outside Canada. A silver maple leaf is worn on the ribbon in undress.

Description
A circular, silver medal (.925 fine silver), 1.42 inches in diameter.

Obverse
Seven marching figures are depicted, representing men and women of the army, air force, navy and nursing service; and around the rim, the inscription 1939 CANADA 1945 VOLUNTARY SERVICE VOLONTAIRE.

Reverse
The reverse shows the coat of arms of Canada.

Mounting
The medal is linked to a straight suspender by a small ring passing through a small fixed ring at the top of the medal.

Ribbon
The ribbon is 1.25 inches wide with a royal blue centre (0.5 inches) flanked by two equal stripes of scarlet and dark green, the dark green being on the edges. The ribbon was issued during the war; the medal after the war.

Dates
The medal was established on 22 October 1943.

FROM A LETTER TO MY MOTHER - JANUARY 24th, 1944

"I guess you've heard about the medal ribbon we now wear for a year and a half of service. They look very pretty on our tunics, but most of us are rather disgusted at getting them for only 1-1/2 years of service because that makes them worthless. Most of us are completing 4 years of service and practically any trainee or conscript will be able to be eligible for this ribbon. If we are overseas though, we can wear a little maple leaf superimposed on the ribbon. The boys are calling it 'The Mackenzie King' or the 'Spam' medal!"

NEW YEAR - 1944

"I will lay odds that, ere this year expire,
We bear our civil swords and native fire
As far as France: I heard a bird so sing,
Whose music, to my thinking, pleased the King."
- William Shakespeare (1564-1616) - Henry IV, Act V, Scene 5 (1597)

BRISTOL ON LEAVE

My maternal grandparents came from Bristol so I persuaded Doug to go there on leave with me. "This is where John Cabot sailed from," I said to Doug, showing off my knowledge of history. "Did he now," Doug replied with a twinkle in his eye, "I thought he played goal for Toronto Maple Leafs". "That was Lorne, John's younger brother!" We had plenty of money so we thought we'd live it up for a night or two and book into a hotel instead of the usual leave hostel which really wasn't much different from sleeping in barracks. In these hostels you had to be up and out by 0800 hours and you were liable to be awakened by the M.P.s [Military Police] in the middle of the night and asked to show your Pass because they were looking for deserters and people who had gone A.W.O.L. We went into this hotel where we had noticed some serviceman coming out. We were told politely at the desk that they were "full up." We tried five or six others and it was always the same story. We were getting pretty fed-up and beginning to think that there was some prejudice against Canadians. Just as we walked out of the hotel an American G.I. walked in with the most beautiful blonde you'd ever seen. She had that flaxen hair of the true Saxon and the peaches and cream complexion to go with it. Doug and I stopped right there on the hotel steps and took a double take because this Yank was as black as the ace of spades. "Well I'll be damned!" Doug exclaimed, "What's he got that we ain't got. Will you tell me that?" "Yes, I'll tell you," I replied, "he's got one of the most beautiful girls in England, that's what he's got my friend, and what's more he's got a room in this hotel!" As we walked across the street nursing our jealousy we met a friendly corporal. We asked him about the situation we had just witnessed with the black boy and the beautiful blonde. "I can't figure it out either," he confided, "but I've experienced the same thing. For some unaccountable reason these English girls really go for our black troops. And the funny thing is that the more beautiful the girl, the more she seems to be attracted." "They do say that opposites attract," Doug put in. When we said goodbye to our American corporal we saw another couple walking arm in arm - the same thing. "Say," Doug said, "do you suppose if we got some black shoe polish...?" "Aw, shut up", I replied.

SHOREHAM-BY-SEA - SPRING, 1944

Doug and I went on leave together today. We took the train to Brighton, and then transferred to the line that ran west along the coast through Hove - Portslade - Altringham Halt - Southwick to Shoreham-by-Sea. We know a couple of W.A.A.F.s who are stationed here. It is a beautiful day. Is there anything more beautiful than a day in the early springtime along the Sussex coast when you've got a 48-hour pass in your pocket?

If you need directions, just ask a policeman

"Oh, to be in England
 Now that April's there...."
- Robert Browning (1812-1889) - Home Thoughts from Abroad (1845)

It was still early as we strolled along the High Street enjoying the sun and looking at the shoppers of whom there seemed to be more than usual today. We knew that the girls wouldn't be off duty until tea time so we thought it might be a good idea to find some digs. I had put up at a little inn down on the sea coast once before so I suggested we go around and book a room there. I remembered it particularly because there had been an Ack/Ack gun on a nearby roof-top that made a terrible racket during the night. When we enquired after a room the proprietor looked at us as if we were asking for the moon. "Didn't we know that the ban was off?" No, we didn't. "Were we not aware that this short period was the only time in the whole year when civilians could visit their relatives on the south coast?" No, we weren't. I thought he was going to ask us next - "Didn't we know there was a war on!" Now we began to understand why the High Street had been so crowded. I said to Doug, "You know the old saying, 'If you want to know the way, ask a policeman'. Here's a bobby coming along now, let's stop him ask him if he knows where we might find some digs." The policeman pushed his helmet back on his head and scrutinized us keenly. "We were wondering," I ventured, "if you might know where we might get a place to stay overnight?" "You see we didn't realize that the ban was off," put in Doug. The bobby scratched his head. "Well, lads, everything's filled up right enough. I don't know of a single vacancy anywhere." We thanked the copper and began to wonder whether we might be sleeping outside all night. The crowds on the street thickened. "Let's find a cuppa coffee," suggested Doug. About an hour later, as we strolled in the lovely warm sunshine, we met the same policeman again. He stopped us and asked, "Any luck, lads?" "Not a hope," we both replied. "I thought as much." He looked us over keenly and said, "Say what kind of lads are you anyway?" We were taken aback by that question and before either of us could answer he went on, "Are you going to get drunk and smash things up?" "Not us", we both replied at once. "We're not that kind," I said. "I don't drink at all and my pal here drinks very little and knows how to behave when he does." He knew, of course, from our speech and our shoulder flashes that we were Canadians. Some of our countrymen had been stationed in this area and had established quite a reputation as rowdy men. "Those wild Canadians!" the locals called them. "Well, then," said the bobby, "you're welcome to come to my home. I'm going off duty now and I'll take you along to meet my missus." We walked with the bobby to a tidy little house where his wife welcomed us and made us a cup of tea. It turned out that they had an only son, about our age, who was overseas with the Eighth Army. We slept in his room. We were careful to come in quietly that night. The next morning we were awakened by our host as he got ready to go on duty. "Here's a cup of char for you," he said, slipping two steaming hot cups of tea through the door. We had a song about the sergeant-major bringing "round a nice hot cup of tea" but we never expected it from a policeman. There's something mighty fine about the English bobby. I hope his boy survived the war. Oh, yes, we had a lot of fun with the W.A.A.F.s.

CROWBOROUCH - MAY, 1944

In some respects there is a similarity between a tank crew and a bomber crew. A strong bond of friendship grew up between the members. You get to know each other very well as you live in close quarters for long periods of time. Many of the skills are similar. Both Air Crews and Tank Crews have Wireless Operators, Gunners and Crew Commanders. In spite of these similarities there are some glaring differences. The ranks of Air Crews are invariably higher. In a Tank Crew, the Wireless Operator is usually a trooper (or in our regiment, a guardsman) and never a commissioned officer. Yet our Wireless Operators are every bit as well qualified as his opposite number in Bomber Command. The same could be said for our gunners, except where the Air Crew gunner was also qualified in wireless (W.A.G. - Wireless Air Gunner). Another big difference between us and the Boys in Blue is that when we come to the end of a training scheme or a battle we don't walk away from our tank and leave it to a "ground crew" to repair and maintenance. We have to be

both "fighting crew" and "ground crew". This means doing all our own routine maintenance and in the field it often means cooking our own meals and digging our own slit trenches as well as maintaining a guard on our tank. How we envy the Bomber Boys with their cocoa and buns and nice clean beds with a hot-water bottle after a raid. We also have to defend ourselves from attack at night which means that a watch must be constantly maintained by each crew. After we have cooked and eaten our supper, we have to take turns to keep a sharp lookout while the others sleep, which means you can never get a full night's uninterrupted sleep. Yet not many of us would trade our life for theirs, which reminds me of the week that the Typhoon pilots came to live with us. The plan was that they would stay with us for a week and drive our tanks and share our life and in this way they would get an appreciation for our difficulties and limitations. Then we would go and live with them for a week. Since they were to be our close support we needed to know something about each other. The two Typhie pilots attached to our crew had a smashing time driving our tank! They were rough with it and I saw Jack and George wince at the abuse GIRAFFE was taking. Hal and Jim, the two pilots, drove our tank like a couple of cowboys, banging and bumping it all over the place. We never did get our chance to fly in their aircraft because "Stand to" for the invasion interrupted all further exchanges. One of the surprising observations made by Hal as he climbed out of the driver's seat was - "You have a far greater sense of speed in these tanks than we have in our Typhoons." It seemed incredible that our top speed of 35-40 M.P.H. could even be compared with their 400 M.P.H. but I suppose when you are up there, there is nothing to compare your speed with whereas on the ground, trees and other objects flash by relatively quickly.

We have a new fellow by the name of Gordon Hatch in our crew. He is from Sherbrooke, Quebec, and gets The Sherbrooke Daily Record sent to him. Gordie is our new Gunner. I read in the Record, that he received today (17 Feb.), where David Bindman, from Thetford Mines, had been killed on active service in Italy. I was grieved to read this because Dave was a very fine person. We used to be keen competitors at the Eastern Township track and field meets held every May at Stanstead College. I shall always remember David Bindman as being a splendid athlete and a very special person. Why does war always take the best men?

I always enjoyed Sunday in the Army. The Sundays that I remember best were the ones during the time we were stationed at Crowborough. Breakfast was always an hour later on Sunday and that meant that Reveille was an hour later too. So, I had a chance to sleep in for an hour. Church parade was at 1100 hours. First, there would be the Troop inspection by our Sergeant. After that we would march on to the markers for the Squadron Parade. Finally, we would march to the Regimental Parade. After Church parade we would be dismissed and we'd all head for the N.A.A.F.I. I'd buy a cup of tea, a rock cake if they had any, and a Mars bar. Then I'd get hold of a copy of the Daily Mirror and look at the Comic Strip - "Jane". She had this little dog, a pet dachshund named Fritz. If the Eighth Army was advancing, Jane would be depicted in a state of deshabille. Everybody enjoyed Jane, especially when the Desert Rats were shoving the Afrika Korps back across the desert! General Montgomery got the credit for the desert victory but I think the creator of Jane, artist Norman Pett [1891-1960], should at least have had a M.I.D. [Mentioned in Dispatches] or an "Africa Star." Jane was great for morale. When the great V-E [Victory in Europe] day finally came, Jane was completely out of uniform!

BUTTERFLY BOMB?

One night, as I was corporal of the guard on the tank park, there was a fair amount of air activity - both ours and theirs. I had been up to check on the sentries in the tank park and just as I was returning, and nearing the guard house, I heard something falling out of the sky. I hit the ground instinctively. Nothing happened. What was it that had come down? I searched cautiously in the rhododendron bushes but couldn't see a thing. I thought it might have been a Butterfly Bomb [cluster bomblets dropped by aircraft] - one of Jerry's

DANGER

DO NOT TOUCH
NOT ONLY WILL THIS KILL YOU, IT WILL HURT THE WHOLE TIME YOU ARE DYING

DANGER

Small (Butterfly) Bombs lie hidden here.

They are likely to explode with deadly effect at the least disturbance.

KEEP AWAY

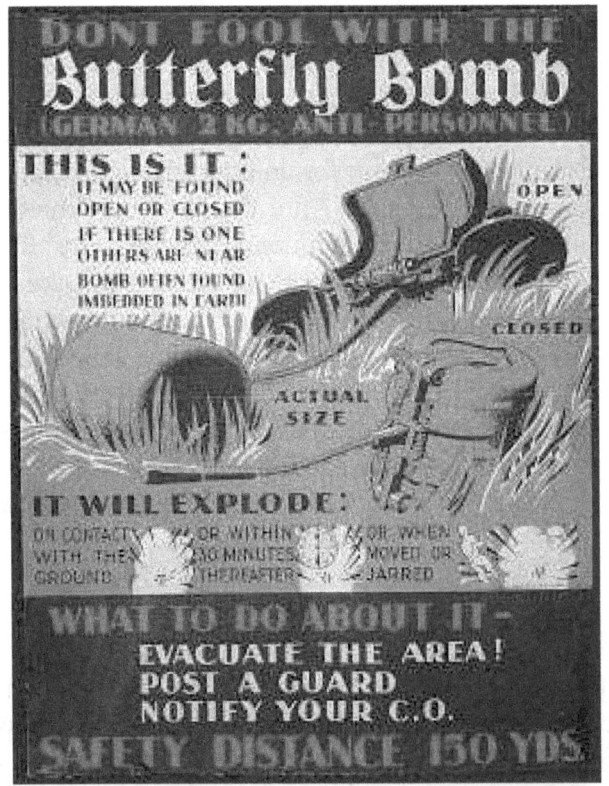

DONT FOOL WITH THE
Butterfly Bomb
(GERMAN 2 KG. ANTI-PERSONNEL)

THIS IS IT:
IT MAY BE FOUND OPEN OR CLOSED
IF THERE IS ONE OTHERS ARE NEAR
BOMB OFTEN FOUND IMBEDDED IN EARTH

OPEN
CLOSED
ACTUAL SIZE

IT WILL EXPLODE:
ON CONTACT WITH THE GROUND — OR WITHIN 30 MINUTES THEREAFTER — OR WHEN MOVED OR JARRED

WHAT TO DO ABOUT IT —
EVACUATE THE AREA!
POST A GUARD
NOTIFY YOUR C.O.

SAFETY DISTANCE 150 YDS.

nice little gadgets that could kill you at 25 yards [23 metres] and injure you within 150 [137 metres]. I decided that if the diabolical thing was in the bushes I'd better not look for it in the dark. I went into the guard house and wrote up my report and hoped they got a bomb disposal squad to deal with it the next day. We called them Butterfly Bombs because they came down with a fluttering sound and had metal "wings" that made them look like a butterfly. They were called Devil's Eggs by the Germans, due to the look of the munitions cluster.

GOOD ADVICE FROM A DESERT RAT

One Sunday, as we were sitting in the N.A.A.F.I. after Church Parade drinking coffee and reading the Daily Mirror to see how "Jane" was making out, we were joined by Sergeant Al Hubert. I had known Al from my first days with the Guards back on St. Helen's Island in Montreal. Al had just come back to the Regiment after serving with the Eighth Army in the desert. We got to talking about fighting in tanks. Al's hands were still mottled where he had got burned escaping from a tank that had brewed up. He gave me a good piece of advice which saved me from much grief later on. Al said - "When you go into action put on everything you've got no matter how hot it is, and be sure to wear your asbestos gauntlets." I remembered his advice and followed it to the letter when we went into action.

The Army was strict about shaving. We were inspected every morning and it was a crime not to have shaved. When we first joined up, some of us could get away with shaving only every second day, especially if we were fair-haired as I was. One day I remember I tried to get away without shaving. The sergeant didn't put me on a charge, he just said - "Stand a little closer to the razor next time, Osborne." After a while, many of us grew a moustache. It gave us a military look, or so we thought. The traditional Guard's moustache was a handlebar which you could wax at the corners. You were not permitted to grow a beard, that was a prerogative of the Navy - especially the submarine captains. Just before we sailed for Normandy our tank crew agreed that we would let our moustaches grow as large as possible, and then when we got to Paris we'd wax them. We must have been a fierce looking lot - enough to put the fright into any German. I think Gordie Hatch had the best one. We never thought about the complications it might cause if we were burned on the face.

"Then a soldier,
Full of strange oaths, and bearded like the pard ..."
- William Shakespeare (1564-1616) - As You Like It, Act II, Scene 7 (1599)

APOCALYPSE NOW

One Sunday afternoon in late January, Doug and I were strolling along the street in Brighton. As it was about four o'clock, I was dying for a cuppa. I spied a sign which read "B. I. CANTEEN". "There's a spot Doug." And before you could say "Heil Hitler", we were across the street and up the stairs. I marched right up to the counter and ordered - "Two cups of tea and two rock cakes, please." The lady behind the counter served them up and when I went to pay she wouldn't accept anything. It was then that we realized that this was some kind of religious group, and remembering a similar experience in Camp Borden, I began to wish I didn't have such an addiction for four o'clock tea. We swallowed our tea and sat down docilely to listen to a sermon. The evangelist, or whatever he was, had an open Bible in his hand and pointed to a large map of Europe on the wall. He "proved", by an exposition of the Book of Revelation, that the Second Front would take place soon, and in Denmark. Imagine our amazement. We went back to Crowborough and burst into the hut exclaiming - "Hey fellas, wait till you hear this. The Second Front is going to take place in Denmark." When they stopped whatever they were doing and looked silently at us, Doug added, "The Bible says so." Imagine our surprise when we woke up on the sixth of June and heard over our tank radios that

IF YOU
ARE IN A BUILDING
WHEN THE
AIR-RAID SIREN SOUNDS

DON'T RUSH INTO THE STREET!
STAY WHERE YOU ARE

The Floor Warden will tell you what to do
—OBEY HIS ORDERS PROMPTLY

THE ENEMY'S PURPOSE
IS TO CAUSE PANIC

Panic spreads like a Bush fire,
and can be as disastrous!

You can baulk the enemy
by KEEPING COOL and
following instructions

the Allied armies were landing on the beaches of Normandy. I never did learn many words from the little Danish pocket dictionary that I had picked up in the booksellers, but it sure cast doubts on the Bible as a textbook for military prophecy! By the way, in case you are wondering, "B. I." stands for "British Israelism." [British Israelism asserts theologically related claims of a genetic link to the early Israelites] "Something rotten in the state of Denmark," but they do make good tea.

CROWBOROUGH 1943-1944

For eight months we lived in "Bomb Alley", a narrow corridor which marked the shortest route between the Channel ports and London. Many a night we would go outside the hut when there was a heavy raid on to watch the spectacle. We always knew when a raid was coming because we were located near some giant pylons which marked the wireless station that broadcast to Europe. These pylons had red lights on their tops. When a raid was forecast by our radar, the lights went out. We learned to distinguish between the howl of the Merlin engines of the R.A.F. and R.C.A.F. and the sort of lumpy snarl of the German aircraft engines. From our camp at Crowborough we could see the fires over London reflected on low cloud. Now and then there would be a large red glow and the fires would flare up and then die down. More bombs exploding or was it a gas storage tank going up? The search-lights combed the sky. Sometimes one would catch an enemy raider in its weaving tentacles like a moth caught in the beam of a flashlight. When this happened, the other searchlights would quickly converge on the unhappy aircraft, holding it in its criss-cross pattern of lights. Then the anti-aircraft guns would go to work. All the while, the German pilot would be twisting and diving trying to shake off this illumined spider's web of light. You could see him jinxing and turning to escape the long fingering tentacles. If he was lucky, or skilful enough, to shake the searchlights and the barrage then the night fighter boys would be lurking around in the darkness ready to pounce on him. London was an inferno of twinkling lights from the barrage, spouting salvos of heavy and light Ack/Ack. Suddenly the long weaving beams of light would snap off and the distant thunder of the guns would die down until the next wave of bombers arrived to stoke up the fires begun by the first lot. Often a lone bomber, which had escaped the London defence, would fly over our camp hightailing it like a scalded cat for home and safety. However, before the crew sat down to their bacon and eggs, they still had to reckon with our coastal defences and still more night fighters patrolling up and down the Channel. These boys knew the enemy raider was coming and the W.A.A.F.s would be vectoring them on to the Jerry. So if his dreams were of some fräulein like "Lili Marlene", he still had a long way to go to safety.

"Underneath the lantern
By the barrack gate
Darling I remember the way
You used to wait
'Twas there that you whispered tenderly
That you loved me
You'd always be
My Lili of the lamplight
My own Lili Marlene."
- Hans Leip (1893-1983) - Poem: The Song of a Young Soldier on Watch (1937). Set to music by Norbert Schultze in 1938. Recorded by Lale Andersen in German in 1939 and re-recorded in English in 1942. Lyrics translated by Norman Baillie-Stewart.

KNOCK-OUT

The Canadian Army Boxing Championships were held in January of 1944. I had managed to make it to the Divisional finals because my opponent in the Brigade finals could not make the weight. I got a big thrill

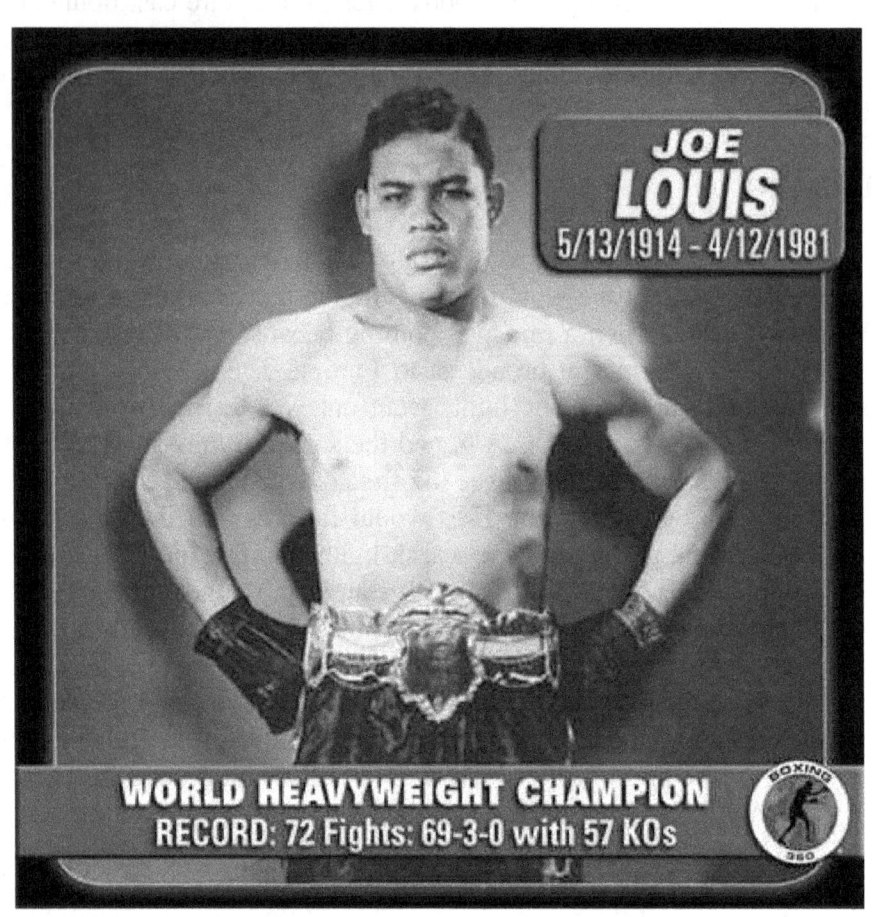

because Tommy Farr [British and Empire Heavyweight Champion, 1937] was the chief referee. He had come up from his pub in Brighton that he ran after retiring from the ring. I was surprised at his build. I was taller than he and I was boxing as a lightweight! He had very broad shoulders. After all, he had been a Welsh miner in Tonypandy, hence the nickname "the Tonypandy Terror". I asked him who was the hardest puncher he had ever faced. I expected him to say Joe Louis [World Heavyweight Champion, 1937 - 1949], whom he had challenged for the world title, but he surprised me by saying Max Baer [one-time World Heavyweight Champion, 1934]. Farr said - "Baer hit me in the second round and I really don't remember much until the sixth." Well, I went into the ring that night against this boy who had been the champion of Canada. In the first round I don't think he threw a single punch. He just kept moving around and studying my style. In the meantime I was scoring with my left jab and was way ahead on points at the bell. Nick "Nicky" Nickilo was in my corner and Nicky was a first-class fighter for whom I had a great deal of respect. "Go out there now, Ossie," Nick whispered into my ear, "and give him the old one-two." So when the bell sounded I sprang off my stool, met my opponent in the centre of the ring, hit him with a straight left and crossed my right. The next thing I remember I was sitting on my stool in my corner and Nicky was saying - "It's all over, Ossie." Apparently this boy was a clever counter-puncher and he was just waiting for me to throw my right. The moment I did, he let me have the shot that knocked me down and out. It was the first time that I had ever been knocked down and counted out in the ring.

That night there was an air raid. An enemy bomber, with a full bomb load, crashed near the drill hall where the boxing was being staged. There was a bout in progress at the time. The lights went out momentarily. The arena floor seemed to heave up and subside. Everybody instinctively dove under a bench and some under the ring, including the referee and the judges. When the lights came on, here were these two guys pounding away at each other in the ring. It brought down the house and relieved the tension. There is a sequel to this story.

The morning after the boxing tournament, I was awakened before Reveille by the orderly sergeant. "Osborne," he said, "take two men and a driver. Take weapons and ammo. Go down to the cookhouse now and get your breakfast. Go to this map reference. Stay there until you are relieved by the R.A.F. Regiment. A bomber has crashed and you are to guard it until the R.A.F. arrives." You can imagine the three men were not too happy at being awakened before dawn and told about this assignment. I got in front of the 8 cwt [Canadian-made 1/2 ton truck] with the driver, the other two got in the back. We started off in the fog and darkness. Nobody was saying a word. Each of us was nursing his own grievance about this lousy war. I was nursing a sore jaw. Our job was to guard the German bomber that had crashed the night before and narrowly missed the drill hail where the boxing was going on. We rumbled on in the fog and I kept studying the map to bring us to the crash site. Suddenly out of the mist there loomed the figure of a Norwegian airman. I noted that he was wearing a Norwegian badge on his cap. I had seen this same badge on the caps of Norwegians stationed on Toronto Island (Little Norway) way back in the winter of 1940-1941. I ordered the driver to halt and signalled the airman to hop in the back. We started off again and I studied my map. We must be getting near to the map coordinate now. There came an urgent pounding on the canvass at the back of the cab. I stopped the truck, got out and went round to the back to see what was up. Imagine my shock when one of the men said - "Hey, Corporal, we've got a Jerry in here!" He had got quietly in the back with my boys when I had signalled him to do so and my lads, in their sullen mood, had paid little attention to this hitchhiking stranger until one of them fixed his gaze on the newcomer's belt buckle. It bore a swastika! At this point he snapped out of his sulky reverie and began pounding on the back of the cab. As soon as the German airman realized he was recognized he handed them his luger, fully loaded, and other things among which was a Nazi silk flag. He could speak good English as he had been a student at Oxford for a short time before the war. He informed us that he was the only member of his aircrew that had survived the crash of the previous night. The only injury he had received was a superficial cut on his shin which he had bandaged with a piece of the silk torn from his parachute. It was funny, when I

first saw him looming up out of the fog, I had noticed that bit of white cloth around his leg and it had puzzled me. He kept repeating -"Hitler kaputz! Hitler kaputz!" We gave him a cigarette and some chocolate. For him the war was over and he had survived it and seemed grateful. We turned him over to the local constabulary at the next village. He made it very clear that he would have preferred to remain with us. When you stop and think of it, he could have shot us all and taken over our truck. In the foul mood we had all been in, and with the element of surprise on his side, it probably wouldn't have been too difficult. Fortunately for us he was a defeated enemy. What a contrast to the arrogant, swashbuckling airmen I had seen on my first contact with the enemy back in 1940! "Hitler Kaputz!" he kept repeating. I hope our Intelligence boys got a lot of useful information out of him. As far as I know, this was the last big bomber raid on London before the arrival of the V-1's. Statistics published after the War showed that this was the heaviest raid on England by the Luftwaffe since the winter of 1940-1941. 200 aircraft in 2 waves attacked London - Focke-Wulf FW190's and Messerschmitt Me410's followed by Junkers Ju88's and Dornier Do217's. The night was January 21, 1944. Oh, yes, the Norwegian insignia on his cap? I asked him about that and he explained that it was a badge worn by Luftwaffe crews who had been stationed in Norway.

MONTY INSPECTS US - FEBRUARY 29th, 1944

In the spring of 1944, Monty visited us. We had heard all about him of course. How he had routed Rommel in the desert and now he was going to lead us to victory over Rommel again - this time in Europe. We were lined up ready for inspection and he drove onto the field in a jeep. He was wearing his famous black beret. The jeep stopped in the middle of the field and he called out - "Gather round me, chaps." We broke ranks and ran. Oh how I ran! I was always a good runner and I decided to beat them all to Monty's jeep. Which I did! He stood up in the jeep to talk to us. He told us we would be called upon to capture and hold a strategic Hill which was being fiercely defended by a nasty lot of little men who would resent our presence and do everything they could to throw us off the Hill. He oozed confidence and spoke of the upcoming battle like the captain of a cricket eleven would speak to his team before an important match. "We'll hit the enemy for six," he said, "and see him off!" I liked Monty. I felt that in him we had a General who could lead us to victory over that old "Desert Fox". I also felt that he was no "brass-hatted Colonel Blimp" fighting our war with the strategy and mentality of 1914-18. Our tails were up and we were ready to go.

In a letter dated March 3rd, 1944, to my mother I wrote:

"I guess I told you about seeing General Montgomery. He stood us at ease and walked slowly among us as he said 'so we could get a good look at him and so he could see what manner of men we were'. He was wearing his old battle dress and black beret. He then called us around him and he stood on his jeep and talked to us. What he did say is not for letters of course, but he did say he had a bet on when the war would end and that he had no doubt we would 'see the enemy off' (A typical English expression meaning to beat the enemy). Anyway, we all feel confident in Monty. We could not have a better leader."

Not all the casualties in wartime are among the Armed Forces. What about the thousands of young girls who became pregnant and whose soldier, sailor, or airman was shipped overseas on the next draft, never to be seen by her again? Girls who became intimate with men in uniform often knew little about them. The romantic aura of a uniform turned their heads and many ended up with a baby, the real name of whose father they didn't know. This is the side of war that is not publicized. But these girls and their children were no less the casualties of the war. There was a barrack room song that went like this:

"Around the park she pushed a baby carriage
She pushed it in the springtime and in the month of May
And if you asked her why the hell she pushed it

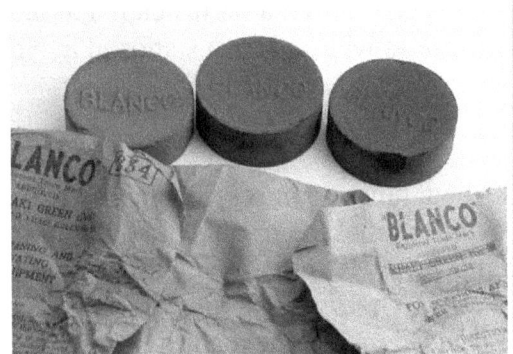
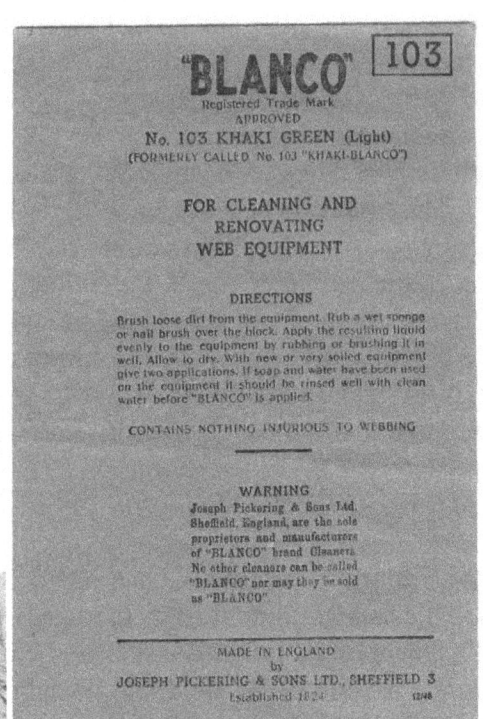

She pushed it for a guardsman who was far, far, away."
- The original copyright was the 1917 version by George A. Norton, titled 'Round Her Neck She Wears a Yeller Ribbon. The long version of this Cadence was adapted and used by many branches of military and many different countries. This was also the inspiration for the song "Tie a Yellow Ribbon Round the Ole Oak Tree" performed by Tony Orlando and Dawn in the 1970's. In Canada, the yellow ribbon represented commitment, belief and hope in the Canadian soldiers and is still represented today.

Rape was also a frequent charge, but a very difficult one to prove. One day at Crowborough Camp, early in 1944, we were all paraded by the C.O. while a girl and her mother walked slowly through the ranks so she could pick out the soldier that she said had raped her. Apparently all she knew about him was that he was wearing a red shoulder flash. As we were lined up waiting, I turned to the N.C.O. standing beside me, a more respectable man was not to be found in the whole Canadian Army, and said facetiously, "It would be just like her to point her finger at you!" Believe it or not, that's exactly what she did! When she came to him, she turned to the C.O. and said - "That's the man!" Of course it wasn't. Corporal Blank had an iron clad alibi. He had been Duty Corporal the night in question and hadn't been outside the camp. Mais, c'est la guerre!

A ROYAL VISITOR - MARCH 9th, 1944

On the evening of the 8th of March we were ordered to get our web equipment Blanco'ed [Blanco was a compound used to clean and colour webbing], our brass shined, and our boots polished. We were also told that Lights Out would be at 2000 hours, because Reveille was to be sounded at 0300 hours. We embussed in the dark and after a couple of hours we climbed out cold and stiff and marched to a rendezvous where we were joined by other units of the 4th Division. By about 0900 hours, we formed part of a line of troops which must have been twelve to fifteen miles [19-24 km] long. What was up? Rumours were flying - Somebody said that we were to be inspected by Prime Minister Mackenzie King - that must have been a liberal! - Somebody else said they overheard the Adjutant say it was General Crerar [General Officer Commanding First Canadian Army in North-West Europe]. The Orderly Room Corporal was reported as hearing the Colonel say it was General Eisenhower. So the rumours flew up and down the line. In the meantime we were freezing and stamping our feet to restore circulation. My hands were blue with the cold because we weren't allowed to wear gloves - only the officers could wear gloves! Then away down along the line to our left we could hear orders ringing out - then we, too, were ordered from the "Stand Easy" to the "Stand at Ease" - then the ringing order - "Canadian Grenadier Guards - Guards - 'Shun'!" Our boots came down like a rifle crack. Guardsman Fitzgerald on my left whispered out of the corner of his mouth - "Somebody's coming." "Steady in the ranks", bellowed the Sergeant-Major. "Who is it?" I whispered. There was a pause - then Fitz whispered back - "It's the King!" Sure enough, the King, our King, George the Sixth, was walking slowly, an aide carrying his sheepskin lined greatcoat. He was inspecting his troops before the invasion of Europe. I thought what if he stops and speaks to me? My heart was pounding in my chest. He was looking my way - he was coming over - he stopped in front of Fitzgerald. The retinue behind his Majesty stopped and the King addressed himself to Fitz. "I see you are wearing a pilot's wings - and yet you are a private in the Tank Corps - how is that?" Fitz explained that he had been a pilot in the Air Force but had remustered to the Army. The King looked a bit puzzled and moved on to continue his inspection. If Fitzgerald had told him the full story it would have gone like this. In his flying course in Canada he had graduated tops in his class. Along with three others, he had been kept at home as an instructor. This wasn't too bad at first. Then the news began coming back from the rest of the class who had gone overseas. Some had been decorated with the D.F.C. Others had been killed. The four instructors got together in the mess one night, and thoroughly "browned off", they decided to do something about it. There was a Wing parade on Sunday so they drew lots to see which two would be the first to carry out their plan to draw attention to their plight. Fitzgerald's name was not drawn so he and another instructor were to wait until the next Wing

Honorary Captain (H/Capt) John Anderson
[Later awarded the Military Cross]

parade. The two whose names had been drawn took off early, on some pretence, and when the whole Wing was neatly drawn up on the tarmac they came screaming in just off the deck and buzzed the lot. Needless to say when the Wing C.O. picked himself up and dusted off his uniform he wanted to see the two Pilot Officers in his office, pronto. When they appeared he demanded an explanation for their conduct. They explained that they had asked many times to be posted overseas and no one paid any attention. All their friends, who weren't as good pilots as they had been, were flying Spitfires and shooting down Focke-Wulf's and Heinkel's and getting "gongs" while they were just sitting around here in Canada and getting browned off. The Wing C.O. listened to their complaint. "Very well, gentlemen, if it's an overseas posting you want, then you shall get it." The next day they were posted overseas. Seeing the success of their two pals, Fitz and the other instructor prepared for their act the next Sunday. Again, when the whole Wing was drawn up in its Sunday best, the two instructors repeated the performance and beat-up the Officer's quarters for good measure. This time the Wing C.O. was not amused! They were stripped of their rank and thrown out of the Air Force. They were given the choice of going to either the Navy or the Army to serve in the ranks. Fitz, because he knew about air-gunnery, thought the Armoured Corps would be best. That's how he joined us and became one of our best tank gunners. It also explains how he was sporting a neat pair of Wings over his "Spam Medal".

WE MEET OUR NEW PADRE

This week we have been bivouacked near the old town of Lewes. Our tanks are parked right on the edge of the escarpment. It has not stopped raining since we arrived. Today, when we were queued up for our dinner ration - tea in one mess tin; everything else in the other - with the tea tasting strongly of disinfectant and the rain pouring into the lot, Doug turned to me and said - "It's gawdawful stuff, we wouldn't feed it to pigs back home." The chap behind me, a newcomer to the Regiment, observed "Is it really that bad?" "Just wait till you taste the goddamn stuff," I said. That night, with the rain pattering steadily on the tarp that we had slung on the leeward side of our tank, we were huddled into our sleeping rolls. Actually, we had learned to make ourselves quite cosy. George had the Primus Stove [camp stove] going and the smell of coffee was quite exotic. I had put an extension on the wireless and we had a headset hooked up under the tarp bringing us some dreamy music from the B.B.C. Outside it may be the foulest night on record, but inside our bivouac we were snug and warm. The newcomer, enticed no doubt by the aroma of the coffee, poked his head through the flap in the tarp and enquired - "May I join you?" "Sure, come on in," we chorused, "there's always room for one more." George handed him a steaming mug of our brew. After a while the new lad pulled out a mouth organ and we had quite a sing-song before he ducked out into the rain and darkness. "Some of these new guys aren't so bad," Gordie said, "I wonder where he comes from?" "One of those new reinforcements just down from C.A.C.R.U." [Canadian Armoured Corps Reinforcement Unit], I offered, "anyway he's a darn good harmonica player."

Imagine our surprise the next day when the stranger we had met first in the dinner line, and later when he had entertained us with his harmonica playing, turned up at our Church parade wearing a clerical collar. Boy, were our faces red! We had been one of the first tank crews to make the acquaintance of our new Chaplain - Captain John Anderson.

THEY ALSO SERVE WHO ONLY STAND AND WAIT

"Waiting, waiting, waiting, always bloody-well waiting, soon there will come a day when we'll bloody-well wait no more"

These words of an old army song that we often irreverently sang, to the familiar church tune of "Holy, holy, holy", summed up our feelings during the first days of June as we waited for the Invasion. During this

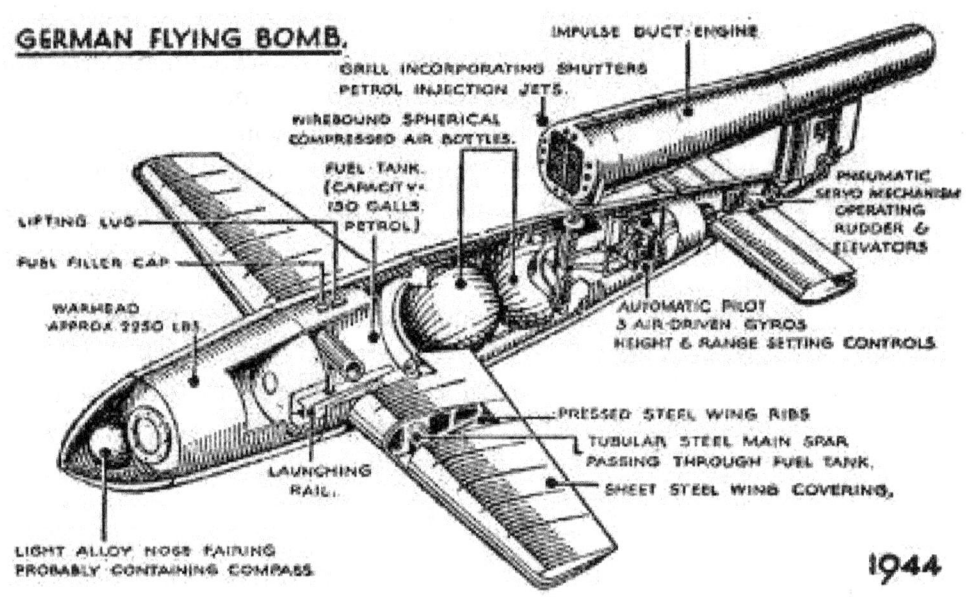

period we were still stationed at Crowborough. On June 13th, Hitler launched his secret weapon the V-1 [German: Vergeltungswaffe 1] flying bomb [cruise missile]. We called them Buzz Bombs or Doodlebugs. Our camp was in the middle of Buzz Bomb alley - mid-way between London and the Channel. At the coast there was a screen of anti-aircraft batteries which engaged these targets as they approached over the Channel. If they got past the Ack/Ack, as they frequently did, then the fighter boys took over. A new fighter aircraft - the British Hawker Tempest [an improved derivative of the Hawker Typhoon] - was proving very successful in bringing them down. Some pilots were chalking up some very big scores. We saw all the action because we had front row centre seats in the Fighter Zone. Beyond us were the barrage balloons and London. The V-1's had a distinctive throbbing noise that you couldn't mistake for an aircraft [they were the first aerial vehicle powered by a pulsejet engine]. They came hustling along, not very high up, as they scooted over our camp. The fighter pilot would line up behind the Buzz Bomb and, when he had closed the range to about 300 yards, we'd see his guns twinkling. Then there would be a terrific explosion. These little flying birds carried a ton [1870lbs - 850kg] of High Explosives. For a second or two, the pursuing aircraft would be engulfed in the smoke and flying debris, then emerge unscathed, do a steep bank and a victory roll and race back to pick up another customer to add to its score. It wasn't too bad during the day because you had time to take cover, but at night it was nerve-wracking. You'd lie there in your bed and listen as the throbbing sound of the Buzz Bomb grew rapidly louder and louder - then the motor would cut out and the devilish thing would begin its deadly dive toward the earth. You prayed that it wouldn't hit the camp. Doug and I decided that it would be safer to sleep out-of-doors. If the hut was hit you wouldn't stand a chance, but we figured that if we were lying outside at least we could see the darn thing coming and roll into a slit trench where nothing but a direct hit could kill us. It was beautiful June weather so we camped beside our slit trench. At night, the flame from the rear of the Doodlebug made the thing an easy target for our Tempest pilots. One day, I saw a pilot getting into position for the "kill" and then the motor of the Buzz Bomb cut out and it started its glide toward the centre of the town of Crowborough. It was a Saturday afternoon and the diabolical thing would have wiped out hundreds of people who were crowded into bus stations, cinemas, shops and pubs. The pilot sensed the gravity of the situation and acted quickly. He skilfully manoeuvred his plane alongside the descending bomb, tucked his wingtip under its short wing and rocked it. He did this a couple of times until he had deflected the course of its downward glide. The bomb exploded harmlessly on the outskirts of the town. The pilot's skilful and daring action undoubtedly saved many lives. He could no doubt see the crowds in the centre of the town and knew he had a chance to save them. I hope his courageous act was duly recognized.

Another time, one of the Buzz Bombs exploded just beyond our camp. Doug and I walked down the hill into the ravine to examine the damage. It had landed in a marshy area. The bomb had burrowed itself into the ground and hit a nest of adders and it blew these reptiles right out of the ground and draped them over the branches of the leaf blasted trees. It was a weird sight - all these dead adders hanging from the branches. It reminded me of a painting by Salvador Dali [1904-1989 Spanish surrealist painter].

I don't suppose anyone kept score of how many of these Buzz Bombs passed over our camp, but it must have been over a thousand. They gave me the jitters. I was prepared to lay down my life for my country and the cause I believed to be right, but I prayed that it would be in a fair fight and not to be obliterated by anything as impersonal as a Doodlebug. On the 18th of June, during a Sunday morning church service, a flying bomb scored a direct hit on the Guard's Chapel in Wellington Barracks, London. It killed 58 civilians and 63 members of the Armed Forces. One of those killed was Captain Johnny Gall, an officer from our Regiment.

During this very trying period our Chaplain, Captain John Anderson, announced that he would be conducting a service of Holy Communion every morning in one of the rooms in the N.A.A.F.I. While others sought to drown their anxiety over the bombs by "rolling out the barrel" in the wet canteen nearby, a

| Private | Private First Class | Specialist | Corporal |

| Sergeant | Staff Sergeant | Sergeant First Class | First Sergeant |

| Master Sergeant | Sergeant Major | Command Sergeant Major |

few of us found a source of strength in the Padre's daily Eucharists. Here, with death plummeting out of the sky, we experienced *Peace in War*.

CROWBOROUGH - PROMOTION

Every generation has one happening that to miss out on is to miss the one thing your generation lived and died for. I suppose it was like that in the 11th century if you didn't take part in the Battle of Hastings, or not to have been with Henry the Fifth at Agincourt, or not to have sailed with Drake and missed the rout of the Spanish Armada, or not to have stood with the Old Guard under Wellington at Waterloo, or not to have fought at Vimy Ridge. In our generation it was the Invasion of Normandy. Those who missed out on it must always feel a little cheated. The ones I really feel sorry for are those who volunteered for enlistment, then spent the duration of the war in Canada - those who never even got to a theatre of operations. I know some like that who joined up with the First Contingent in 1939 and were stuck in some camp as instructors all during the war. The Invasion was the great adventure of our generation and to have missed out on it must have been disappointing.

"And gentlemen in England now a-bed
 Shall think themselves accursed they were not here,
 And hold their manhoods cheap whiles any speaks
 That fought with us upon Saint Crispin's day."
- William Shakespeare (1564-1616) - Henry V, Act IV, Scene 3 (1599)

There was a song that we used to sing which went like this:

" ... You'll get no promotion this side of the ocean,
So cheer up my lads bless 'em all"
- Fred Godfrey (1880-1953) - "Bless 'Em All" (1917)

I had joined the N.P.A.M. [Non-Permanent Active Militia] before the war at the age of 17. Prior to that I had been in the High School Cadet Corps. In the N.P.A.M. I had the opportunity to enrol in an Officer's Training Course. Being very young and very keen and used to studying, I ate up the lectures on Map Reading, Military Law, Gun Laying, Signalling, etc. When the time for the exams came I knew that I could write them as well as anyone in the class. I also discovered that the results, which would determine who would be promoted, were a farce. It had all been decided before ever pen was put to paper or the exams came down from Military District H.Q. One candidate, who was older than me by about five years, and who was not too bright, kept looking over at my paper to see what the answers should be. When the results were finally posted, he was awarded a commission and I was promoted from Gunner to Lance-Bombardier! In spite of this experience, I was still naive enough to think that an able man could rise through the ranks to an officer's commission, like cream rises to the top of milk. This was my ambition. My reasoning went like this - If I am a good soldier, if indeed I am intelligent and have leadership qualities, then this will be recognized, and I'll get my chance at O.C.T.U. [Officer Cadet Training Unit]. I really did not believe that you had to have "pull" to get ahead in the Army. Soon after we arrived in Aldershot, England, some outside examiners arrived and we were all given a series of I.Q. tests. These tests were to be used for promotional purposes. I enjoyed writing the tests. One test dealt with the use of words, another involved identifying different types of tools and instruments, still another was a test on maths and so on. I felt I had done quite well on the tests. As I was crossing the parade ground after lunch one day at Willams Barracks, one of the men who had been conducting the tests stopped me and enquired: "Your name is 'Osborne' isn't it?" I acknowledged that it was. "Well," he said, "I'm not supposed to tell you this but you and two other corporals got the highest marks in the Regiment on the tests we have been conducting." "Who were the

other two?" I asked. "Corporals Ryan and Irvine," he replied. "Your score was 165. We're recommending you for O.C.T.U. I just thought I'd tell you so you would know. But remember - don't say I told you." I thanked him and walked on air to the Squadron Office. O.C.T.U. - Hooray! At last I'd get my chance at Sandhurst too! After finishing my business at the Squadron Office, I hurried back to the barracks to tell Bill Ryan and Walter Irvine. That was in December, 1942.

Toward the end of May 1944, just before D-Day, when our tanks were all waterproofed and ready to go, I received word that I was to report to the Squadron Office, the O.C. wanted to see me. Ryan and Irvine received the same summons. What could it be? We dutifully reported at 1330 hours. What was up? Were we going to be selected for an advance party? Would we miss D-Day? Thoughts like this raced through my mind. Corporal Ryan was called in first. It was my turn next. Irvine and I sat on the bench outside the office waiting and wondering what was being said to Ryan. Then the door opened and Bill came out. Just before I was paraded in I had time to ask: "What's it all about, Bill?" "That commission," he answered over his shoulder. Then I went in. I gave a smart salute. The O.C. was sitting at his desk with a confidential file in front of him. "Stand easy, Osborne," he said somewhat apologetically. "You have been recommended for Officer training but I feel sure you don't want to miss the upcoming party. You are our Squadron Wireless N.C.O.," he continued, "and we couldn't get anyone to take your place at this late hour." I could feel my blood pressure rising. I was getting angry. Struggling to control my voice I asked: "Sir, when was this recommendation made?" The O.C. cleared his throat as he shuffled the papers in front of him. Studying the papers in the file on his desk he said, "In December 1942." "Just what I thought," I replied acidly, "when I joined this man's army I had one ambition in mind - to win my commission. I had determined to get it not by favouritism or patronage. Why, sir, was I not informed about this before now?" I knew damn well why I hadn't been informed before, and why Ryan and Irvine hadn't been told too, because they didn't want to lose us from the outfit. Now the O.C. was getting embarrassed. His face reddened and he began to hum and haw and offer the usual platitudes and lame excuses. I had him on the hot seat and I decided to make him sweat. "Sir, I have earned the right to O.C.T.U. and I want it!" I, of course, had no intention of leaving the Regiment at this late hour, but I wanted to make him squirm a bit. He was obviously taken aback by my reply and began to expostulate with me. He said - "Corporal Ryan has just been in here and he turned it down preferring to remain with the Regiment." "That's his business," I snapped, "I have earned the chance to go to O.C.T.U. and I choose to go." He sensed that he was losing the debate, so he tried another tactic. "Come, come, now Osborne," he said in his sweetest tone, "You are a key man in your area of expertise in the Squadron. We just cannot lose you from the team at this time." I had a good mind to tell him that was his problem, not mine, but I could see the game had gone far enough and I didn't want to be insubordinate. "Look here, Osborne," he said, "you'll make a much better officer if you see a little action first." On that point I could not help but agree wholeheartedly. "I promise you," he said, "if you go into action with us, when the first opportunity comes up, I will see that you get your chance to return to England and Sandhurst." "All right, sir," I agreed, but I knew full well that by the time that happened, he or I, or both of us would probably be pushing up poppies. When I saluted and went out, Irvine went in and I met Bill outside the door. He asked me what had transpired and I told him what the O.C. had promised. "You'd better ask for that in writing," he said and we both laughed. When I went over to the canteen that evening the lads were singing - "There'll be no promotion this side of the ocean so cheer up my lads bless 'em all." Only they weren't saying "bless".

JUNE 26th, 1944

Today is my twenty-fourth birthday. It is just four years since I enlisted in the Guards. Yesterday Doug and I celebrated my birthday. We invited two A.T.S. girls to a picnic under the trees near the Tank Park at Crowborough. It was a lovely sunny afternoon. A parcel from my mother arrived the night before. It contained chocolate empire cookies [jam filled shortbread], orange juice and maple sugar. The girl that I

Women's Land Army

KEEP CLEAR UNEXPLODED BOMB

was paired off with was Dorothy, and neither she nor her friend had ever tasted maple sugar. We walked the girls to the bus stop where they caught the bus for their billets in Tonbridge. I wonder where I'll be for my twenty-fifth birthday.

"I have a rendezvous with Death
On some scarred slope of battered hill"
 - Alan Seeger (1888-1916) - I Have a Rendezvous With Death

DOODLEBUG

We are confined to 24-hour passes now and limited to how far we can travel from Crowborough. There is really no place you can go, so I decided to do some walking tours. The countryside is lovely in June with the blossoms out - truly it is the Garden of England. I packed a lunch and set off with my haversack and a map. The sun was in my face as I walked and after a few miles I was getting pretty hot. I came to a small village called Frant. There was an old pub with its door open. I am not a drinking man but I just had to quench my thirst. I went inside and there were three or four old men sipping their beer. They nodded in my direction. I went straight up to the bar and ordered a pint of cider. I downed it in one gulp and ordered another. The old gentlemen eyed me keenly. I drank the second one down but not quite as fast as the first. I put the glass tankard on the bar, picked up my haversack and marched out into the sunlight. The pub was situated on the village green and I crossed the road and sat down on a grassy bank. I suddenly felt awfully sleepy. I slipped my haversack under my head and lay back. I must have passed out because when I woke the sun was high and I was sweating profusely under its glare. The pub door was closed but the four old men were sitting on a trestle on the green, smoking their pipes. They smiled at me as I roused myself and nodded as if to say, "Aye, lad, thee'll not drink our cider as thee does your Canadian beer." I walked along the road going south toward Wadhurst. It was a super day and the sky was cloudless. Away in the distance I heard the familiar sound of a Buzz Bomb. I squinted toward the south. Sure enough there it is was, getting bigger every second and coming straight for me, going like a bat out of hell. Then all of a sudden its motor cut out. "My Gawd, it's coming down right where I am," I said to nobody, because there was no one about. They say a drowning man sees his entire life passing before him. I don't know about that, but I do know what thoughts passed through my mind. "I'll be blown to bits and no one will ever know what happened to me." I hadn't told a soul where was going when I left camp - would they find enough of me to make an identification? Maybe my dog-tags would survive the blast. The road had about a four foot high bank on each side. I flung myself flat on the side of the road and waited for death. I heard the damn thing pass over head and then there was a tremendous explosion. I climbed shakily to my feet and peered over the bank. There it was, what was left of it, lying like a fallen bird out in the field. I walked over to where it lay and looked at the German printing on its broken parts. Just think, a few minutes before it had been fired by the enemy. Now it lay, its destructive explosive spent, a tangled mass of grey metal. Boy, that was a close one! I gave it a kick and walked back to the road. If I had been carrying my pistol I would have shot it!

I walked on to Wadhurst where I hoped I might meet a Land Army girl that I knew who worked on a farm there. I located the farm all right and was informed that the girls hadn't come in from their work in the fields. I cooled my heels by walking up and down the lane in front of the farm house. I must have walked up and down for more than an hour. Then I sat on the stone wall and drew in deep breaths of the smell of blossoms from the fruit trees. Passersby looked at me curiously. I'm sure they knew why I was waiting.

"O what can ail thee, Knight at arms,
Alone and palely loitering?"
- John Keats (1795-1821) - La Belle Dame sans Mercy (1819)

Finally, Lily appeared and I asked her if she would go to the movies with me in Tunbridge Wells. Alas, she said that she was not allowed out tonight. I caught a bus to Tunbridge and consoled myself by thinking of my Land Army girl and her provocative uniform - beautiful green turtleneck sweater tucked into brown breeches.

At Tunbridge, I strolled through the gate of the famous Public School. I could hear the "plick-plock" of a cricket match and wandered over to the green and sat down under a giant tree and watched the game. In the midst of war and on the eve of what was sure to be the gawdawfulest battle in British history - something that would make Waterloo look like a mere skirmish - these lads were playing the gentleman's game - *Pax in Bello*. I thought of Tom Brown's Schooldays and Vitaï Lampada and recalled that somebody had said that the Battle of Waterloo was won on the playing fields of Eton. Would some future historian look back on the Invasion of Europe and say that it was won on the ball diamonds of America or the hockey rinks of Canada? My reverie was interrupted by one of the Masters who came strolling over to where I was sitting. He removed his pipe from his mouth and began chatting with me. I shared my thought with him and he seemed surprised to find a corporal in the Canadian Army indulging in such philosophy. His wonderment grew when I began quoting Newbolt's lines:

"There's a breathless hush in the Close to-night -
Ten to make and the match to win -
A bumping pitch and a blinding light,
An hour to play and the last man in."
- Sir Henry John Newbolt (1862-1938) - Vitaï Lampada [The Torch of Light] (1892)

We shook hands and I passed out of the school gate into the High Street and caught the bus to Tunbridge Wells.

TUNBRIDGE WELLS

As it was getting near supper time, I decided I'd better go on to Tunbridge Wells and look for a billet for the night. A Serviceman's Club recommended that I use a civilian billet and gave me the address of a woman who wished to rent a room to a serviceman. I called at the house and she seemed pleased to receive me, and the ten shillings I paid her in advance. That price also included my breakfast next morning. I left my small haversack with my shaving things and went out to see the sights of Tunbridge Wells. I arrived back at my digs just as it was getting dark. My landlady's son had arrived back from the desert war. This was one of the great secrets of the War that these Desert Rats were brought back to Britain, given leave, and readied for the Invasion. Soon two of his mates dropped in and I could feel the atmosphere definitely turning unpleasant. These lads had been to the pub, had a few beers, and discovered that in their absence from England the Canadians had taken over their pub and their girls. I could sense trouble ahead and decided that discretion was the better part of valour. I went out into the kitchen and found my landlady quite upset. I told her not to worry, that I understood, and said that I would just slip away quietly and, since it was a nice warm night, I would find some place to sleep. She apologized for the unfriendly attitude of her son and his pals and wanted me to take my ten shillings back. I refused, she was a widow, and I knew she could use it. She made me promise to at least come back for breakfast and I said that I would. As I was talking with her I heard her sons two cronies slip out the front door. How I wished I had Doug with me! I figured that they were waiting to ambush me. I went upstairs, got my haversack, said goodnight to the landlady, and went out the front door. As I strode toward the gate I figured that these two guys were waiting for me beyond the hedge, and that as soon as I opened the gate and stepped on to the sidewalk, they would jump me. I released the latch on the gate and kicked it open, but I did not step through. Just as I had anticipated, one of the Limeys lunged at me - but I wasn't there. As a result he overreached himself and struck out at thin air. I

21 ARMY GROUP

PERSONAL MESSAGE FROM THE C-in-C

To be read out to all Troops

1. The time has come to deal the enemy a terrific blow in Western Europe.

   The blow will be struck by the combined sea, land, and air forces of the Allies—together constituting one great Allied team, under the supreme command of General Eisenhower.

2. On the eve of this great adventure I send my best wishes to every soldier in the Allied team.

   To us is given the honour of striking a blow for freedom which will live in history; and in the better days that lie ahead men will speak with pride of our doings. We have a great and a righteous cause.

   Let us pray that "The Lord Mighty in Battle" will go forth with our armies, and that His special providence will aid us in the struggle.

3. I want every soldier to know that I have complete confidence in the successful outcome of the operations that we are now about to begin.

   With stout hearts, and with enthusiasm for the contest, let us go forward to victory.

4. And, as we enter the battle, let us recall the words of a famous soldier spoken many years ago:—

   "He either fears his fate too much,
   Or his deserts are small,
   Who dare not put it to the touch,
   To win or lose it all."

5. Good luck to each one of you. And good hunting on the mainland of Europe.

B. L. Montgomery
General
C.-in-C. 21 Army Group.

1944.

then stepped quickly out and nailed him with a solid left hook and he went down like he was pole-axed. His pal, who had been waiting on the other side, now swung a haymaker right, which I could see coming a mile away even in the darkness and ducked. I recoiled from my left hook and hit him with a straight right. With a yelp, he fell in a heap on top of his mate and I stepped smartly over both and strode off down the street in the darkness. I hate to think what would have happened to me if I had not sensed their plan and made one of my own. That type would not hesitate putting their army boots to your head if you were down. I was eternally thankful that I had learned to box. It was the first time that I had ever used my dukes outside of the ring. As my old boxing instructor back home in Magog used to say - "I don't want none of you lads fighting outside the ring, but always remember - it's better to be able to and not have to, than to have to and not be able to." How right you were Stanley Bain! That night I slept in an air raid shelter. There was a washroom in it and in the morning, after a shave, I went back to the widow's house. I made no mention of the incident with her son's two pals and she never mentioned it either, but I could tell by the pleased look on her face as she served me my breakfast that the two drunks had got more than they bargained for.

When I got back to Camp, I met Doug and told him about my short leave and how I had narrowly escaped getting beaten up. "That'll teach you not to go on leave alone," he jibed, "I always said you weren't safe to be out alone after dark!"

That was the last leave I was to have. The fight with the two Limeys was the preliminaries to the hard fighting that lay ahead. The bell was now clanging for the main bout.

"For who is he whose chin is but enriched
With one appearing hair that will not follow
These culled and choice-drawn cavaliers to France?"
- William Shakespeare (1564-1616) - Henry V, Act III, Prologue (1599)

OFF TO FRANCE

We started from Crowborough on our great adventure just as the sun was setting. It was 2100 hours on the 19th of July. We went down the road past the Half-Moon inn at Friar's Gate. Cheerio Half-Moon, I'd like to come back and visit you when all this is over. The locals were standing outside and giving us the thumbs up sign and raising their glasses. "Good luck, Canada!" they called out as GENEVIEVE and GERALDINE and GRETCHEN and GILDA and GRENADIER and GOOSE and GREYHOUND and GIRAFFE rolled past [All the tanks in the squadron had names that began with the letter G]. We travelled all night - through Tunbridge Wells, Sevenoaks, Chiselhurst, and on to Forest Gate, near Woodford Camp. As we traversed London we were bracketed by flying bombs. Londoners were just going to work. Many cheered us as we rumbled past. They knew where we were going and they knew that the sooner we got there the sooner the V-1's would cease. It must have been a heartening sight for them to see so many tanks rolling along to fight Hitler. We crossed London and came into the marshalling area. Here we were sorted into four craft loads with a nominal roll for each. Each one of us was tagged and each vehicle marked with a ship number. We were issued with Escape Kits, or as they were officially called "Special Ration Pack, Evaders, For The Use Of." They were small, compact kits with emergency rations, map, compass, pills to make water drinkable, pills to keep you awake, needle, thread, etc. I'd never seen so much stuff compressed into such a small package - even porridge and chocolate! We were also issued with "invasion money" - specially printed franc notes. The weather was perfect. I went to the tent assigned to me. There was straw on the ground in the tents but when I examined it, it was literally crawling with cockroaches. I slept outside the tent that night. The next day we boarded our ship at Tilbury Docks. A flying bomb destroyed one of our trucks on the way to the docks and killed the driver. On board ship we had boat drill and inspection at battle stations. I was anxious to get going before we became victims of a Doodlebug. At last we cast off and moved to an

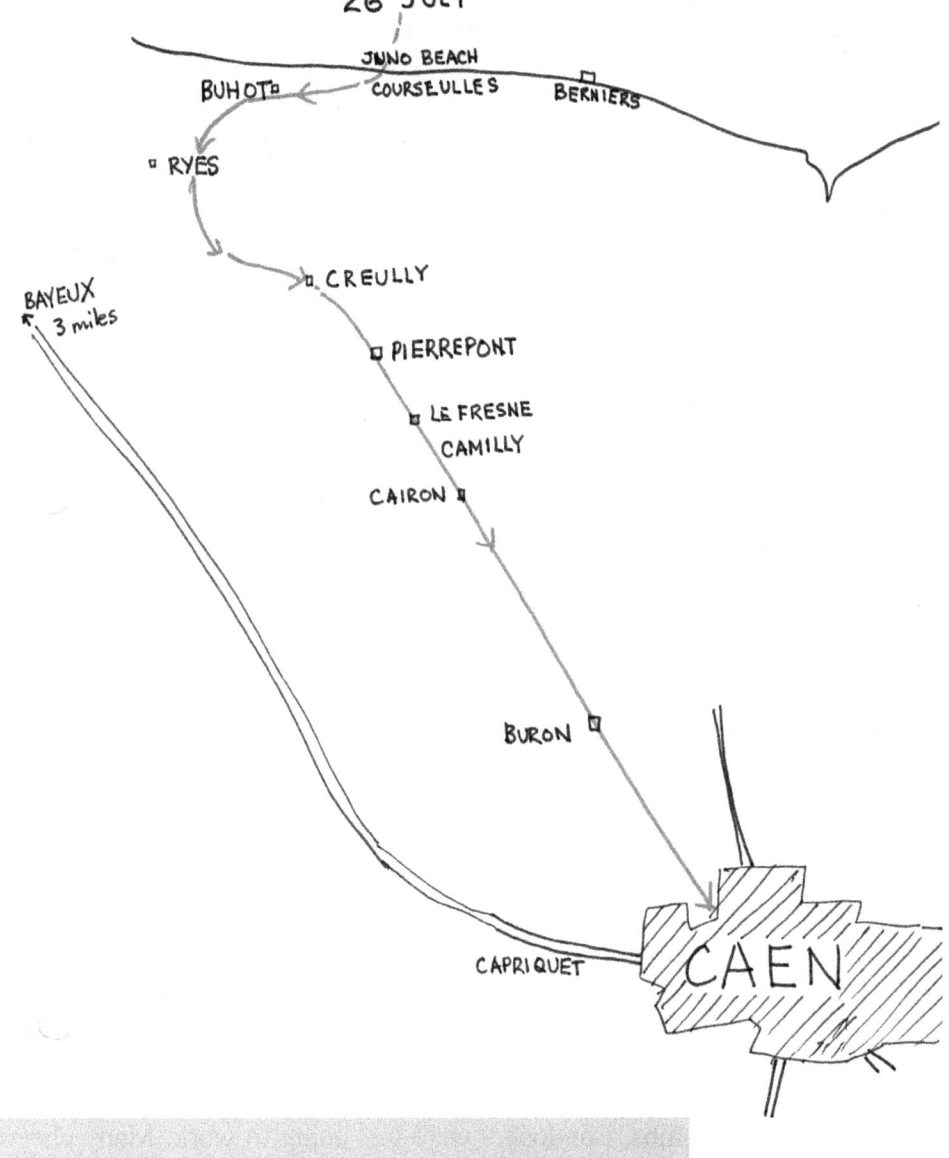

anchorage off Southend. It was the 21st of July and a beautiful evening. As I looked back up the Thames I was reminded of a painting by Turner. The sky was all streaked with gold and red and it was reflected in the river. We sailed out with the Advance Party - out into the Thames Estuary - on a calm sea and headed for Dover. I leaned over the rail and watched London fade into the sunset.

GOING TO NORMANDY - ENEMY COAST AHEAD

It was a déjà vu experience going to Normandy. Nine hundred years before, the Osbornes had come over with William the Conqueror. Now it was the Battle of Hastings in reverse. General Montgomery's ancestors had come over with William too. The Normans - who were really Vikings - were now returning to Normandy. As we approached the Straits of Dover, the ship cut its speed and we all held our breath wondering if the coastal guns would shoot at us. We could see the searchlights fingering the sky on both coasts as we crept silently through the narrow channel.

"The sea is calm to-night.
The tide is full, the moon lies fair
Upon the straits; - on the French coast the light
Gleams and is gone;"
- Matthew Arnold (1822-1888) - Dover Beach (1867)

We are through and we can breathe again. Now the coastal guns open up - the counter-battery work begins - but we are safely past. Daylight brings the promise of a fine day as Spitfires roar low over us heading for France. During the slow passage up the Channel we engage in many activities. Somebody got hold of our gunner, Gordie Hatch, and shaved off half of his beautiful moustache. He took it in good part and begged them to finish the job. There were boxing matches. I got involved in a Spelling Bee. There were only two of us left but I went out on "phlegm." As the Normandy coast loomed up out of the midday sun I wondered what my distant ancestors' thoughts had been when they first set eyes on the white coast of England. Were they wondering what Harold's Saxons would be like as I was now wondering about the Germans waiting for us? My reveries were cut short rudely by a broadside from H.M.S. Warspite [Battleship] as she sent a salvo screaming landward into a Nazi panzer lair. As we got ready to climb down the scrambling nets into the L.C.T.'s [Landing Craft Tank] that would take us and our tank ashore, a Royal Navy lieutenant, calmly smoking his pipe as he leaned his elbow on the rail and gazed shoreward, said to me: "I say, Canada, I'm jolly glad it's you that's going in there and not me." Cheerful bloke, wot? "Thank God we've got a Navy and there'll always be an England!" As Doug used to say, imitating a British accent, "By gad, we'll fight to the last bloody Canadian!" Hand over hand we climbed down the scramble-nets into the bobbing L.C.T. The engines of the craft revved up - we were away!

DOWN RAMPS

We could see the beach ahead. Then the command - "Standby to Beach!" "Down Ramps!" GIRAFFE's engines roared into life. We hit Juno Beach at Courselles-sur-mer and ran up some steel matting to firm ground. While Jack and the others blew off the water-proofing and worked to put her in fighting trim, I decided to brew up a cup of tea. We had been issued with a little metal gadget - actually two collapsible parts that you fitted together crosswise and inserted a little paraffin disc or capsule. This was supposed to make instant boiling water. I think I used up a box of matches and never did get the thing ignited. I learned a lesson, never depend on a new thing like this without trying it out beforehand. As we moved up the beach I saw the grave of a boy from Sherbrooke that I used to race against on bikes. He had been a dispatch rider and was killed on D-Day. It made you think. We drove on for about five miles and found a laager [a place where armoured vehicles are parked] in an orchard just outside the village of Buhot. It was now getting

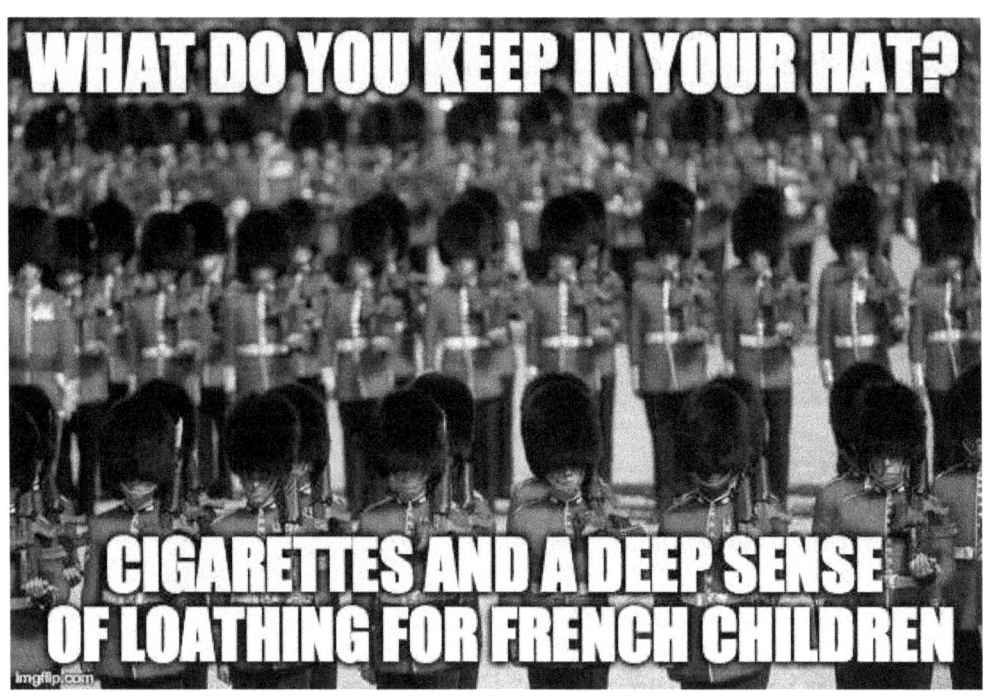

dark. Just as we got settled in, Jerry bombed us with some propaganda leaflets. They were really aimed at British troops. One I picked up read - "Tommy, where do you think your girl is tonight?" The picture showed an American G.I. in bed with an English girl. Good propaganda, cleverly designed to create division in the Allied team. Another had the caption "You Americans are sooo different!" It showed a nearly naked English girl in her bedroom being fondled by a fully dressed American sergeant. But Dr. Goebbels [Paul Joseph Goebbels, Reich Minister of Propaganda] had misunderstood the British character. Tommy would be mad, but he would just fight that much harder so that he could get home the sooner. As usual, German propaganda failed to achieve its purpose. Besides, their bomb aiming was lousy!

The next day I witnessed a beautiful dogfight over the beachhead. A Spitfire and a Me109 were having a duel. They looped, they dived, they spun out, they zoomed upwards, they rolled, neither pilot being able to manoeuvre his opponent into that position for the kill. Both were skilled pilots pitting their brains and ability in this exhibition of acrobatic skill. Suddenly a second Spit arrived, coming to the assistance of his friend. The Jerry pilot was having none of this, he turned tail and streaked for home hotly pursued by the two Spits. The Spitfire may have been a match for the German plane in a dog-fight but in straight pursuit it was no match for the speedy German who pulled away easily and in moments was out of sight. The two Spits turned back lazily and headed out over the Channel looking for more action. I thought of Bill Bellingham and wondered if he was in one of those Spits and if he were thinking of me down on the ground.

When we drove through the battered villages, the townsfolk would line the curb waving the tricolour. "The Tommies are coming!" they shouted. "No! No!" we would call back from the turret of our tank, "Les Canadiens!" Their faces would light up, tears would come to their eyes and they shouted above the roar of our engines and clatter of our battle tracks on the pavé - "Les Canadiens! Les Canadiens! Viva le Canada!" I was never so proud to be a Canadian. Not a Tommy. Not a Yank. But a Canadian!

JULY 28th, 1944

I am sitting in the turret of the tank and a priest comes alongside and begins to speak to me in French. To my amazement I can understand what he is saying. He is with the underground and he wants to use my wireless. I am reluctant to change the channel on my set. He is persuasive. He must listen in to a certain frequency. I tell him he can listen in, but he must not transmit. I don't want to give away our position to the Jerry intelligence. I get him up on the turret of the tank and he tunes in to some pre-arranged channel. After a few moments of listening he gets quite excited. He jumps down from the turret, leaving the headsets dangling, and starts dancing around and gesticulating wildly. I get the message - "Les Americains avait fait un coup a St. Lo et les boches sont courant!" ("The Americans have broken out at St. Lo and the Jerries are on the run!"). It is the moment the underground have been waiting for. They are to rise up now and help us throw the Germans out.

A young boy came alongside the tank. He asked for "Cigarettes - chocolate - pour papa." We had both stashed away inside the turret, but I wasn't going to give him any. I took a good look at him. He must have been about 9 or 10 years old. "Quelle age avez-vous?" I asked. "Treize ans.", he replied. He didn't look 13 to me. His legs were skinny and he looked undernourished. Damned if I'm going to give you any cigarettes, chum, even if you do say they are for 'Papa'. My mother had sent me a box of cod-liver oil capsules. That's what this kid needed. I reached inside the turret and fished them out. She had bought them at the Rexall Pharmacy in Magog, Quebec, and the instructions on the package were in English and French. Good. "Ici, mon petit." I tossed the package to him. "Take these to your mother; she'll know what to do with them. "He looked disappointed. "Prenez à votre mère," I told him. He walked away. I just hoped he wouldn't throw the

CANADIANS PATROL ONE OF CAEN'S LESS-DEVASTATED STREETS

package away round the corner of the next hedgerow or, worse still, try eating them. "Prenez à votre mère!" I shouted after him.

As we moved into the city of Caen I was struck by the terrible devastation. First it had been the target for our bombing. Now it was the target for the enemy. I had seen bombed cities before - London, Bristol, Exeter, and Plymouth - but I had never seen anything like this. There didn't seem to be a single house that hadn't been hit. Amidst the ruins stood the imposing twin towers of William the Conqueror's Abbaye aux Hommes. I wondered where the famous Bayeux Tapestry was. I hoped it had been removed to a place of safety. Engineers working with bulldozers cleared the rubble for us to move ahead. I saw what must have been a university library. The corner wall had fallen into the street and precious books - some medieval manuscripts - were lying in the street amid the dust and plaster. Oh the terrible destruction of war! Finally, we came to the bridge that our engineers had built over the River Orne into the Caen suburb of Faubourg-de-Vaucelles. They had put up a sign "London Bridge". The Jerries knocked it down every night and our men rebuilt it every day.

VERRIERES RIDGE - JULY 29th, 1944

We took up battle positions today. As we moved up, the regiment we were relieving moved down the road past us in the opposite direction. They were tanks of the 5th Battalion, Royal Tank Regiment - the famous "Desert Rats". At one point we halted and so did they. I shouted across from the turret to the commander of the British tank. "What's it like up at the front?" I asked. Between the salvos of shells that were going over our heads from some Long Tom five-fives [155mm caliber field gun] dug in on the other side of the road, he answered my question. "Well, Canada, I was in North Africa - that was good hunting. I was in Sicily and Italy - that was hard fighting. But up there - that's nothing but bleeding suicide!" It wasn't long before I discovered what he meant. We went through an underpass in the railway embankment and as we fanned out into the wheat field I counted over 48 burned out tanks. By the stench, some still had their dead in them. Apparently Jerry had let them all come through the underpass without firing a shot and then when they were all nicely bunched up just beyond the tunnel exit, he opened up - knocking out the last tank just as it emerged from the tunnel - effectively sealing off the escape route. Then he proceeded to knock out the others, one after the other, like targets on a shooting range. It must have been bloody suicide. Now I knew what the Desert Rat meant. Verrières Ridge lay in front of us and the Jerries were holding it.

"We go to gain a little patch of ground
That hath in it no profit but the name."
- William Shakespeare (1564-1616) - Hamlet, Act IV, Scene 4 (c. 1599)

SOLIERS, IFS, FRANCE

Contrary to Hollywood movies, the Front can be awesomely quiet. It was often like that the week we spent at Soliers before the big breakout on the 8th of August. We had moved into this field under the cover of darkness and used the numerous hay stacks to camouflage our tanks. I'm sure that Jerry knew exactly where every one of our tanks were. Every time we got a meal ready, he would mortar and shell us - so he must have been watching us. At night he dropped flares and bombs. One night I got the wits scared out of me. It was a beautiful night, soft pale moonlight. "How sweet the moonlight sleeps upon this bank!" [William Shakespeare (1564-1616) - The Merchant of Venice, Act V, Scene 1 (c. 1596)]. About 0300 I was on watch in the turret. Jerry began a bit of mortaring. I could hear the Nebelwerfers - the six-barrelled mortars winding up [15 cm Nebelwerfer 41]. We called them Moaning Minnies [also sometimes called Screaming Mimis]. One shell landed about 100 feet [30m] in front of our tank and a white cloud began drifting slowly toward us. "Gas!" I said to myself. When we came ashore at Bernières-sur-Mer (Juno Beach), which had

been liberated by The Queen's Own Rifles of Canada on the 6th of June, 1944, we had ditched our respirators as excess baggage. Now we were for it! Should I wake the crew sleeping peacefully under the tank? Should I break the wireless silence and inform H.Q.? My imagination was working overtime. It does that at three o'clock in the morning! I could see the headlines tomorrow morning in the Canadian newspapers GERMANS USE GAS IN NORMANDY - CAEN ANOTHER YPRES FOR CANADIANS. I didn't do a thing. The white cloud drifted harmlessly past the tank. Nobody else reported it. I never did. I suppose it was a smoke bomb that a German gunner had fired by mistake, but it sure scared me for a few moments. A mortar shell landed within inches of the left front track of GIRAFFE but it didn't explode. If it had, it probably would have wiped out our crew. It just lay there - a dud - and we lived with it for the next few days.

During the day it was desperately hot in that hay field. Just ahead of us to the right was a small railway station with the name SOLIERS painted on it. One afternoon, as I scanned the ridge ahead with my binoculars, I saw a Jerry climb out of his slit trench on the forward slope of the high ground. He placed a portable gramophone on the parapet and put a record on it, lighted a cigarette and sat there smoking and enjoying the music. It was so still that I thought I could actually hear the music. I could have nailed him where he was with my machine gun but it hardly occurred to me to do so. Here was a musical interlude in the midst of war - *Pax in Bello* - and we were both enjoying it. When the record ended he removed it carefully from the turntable, closed up the lid of the gramophone, and disappeared like a gopher into his hole in the ground.

Today we had a bottle of beer with the rations. It was Allsopp's English Ale. I had never tasted beer but I felt that I must drink it. The Jerries had poisoned all the wells so we could not use them and the sun was broiling hot. We perspired a lot and were badly in need of water. I didn't want to get dehydrated. I opened the bottle and took a swig. It was warm and awful tasting stuff but it was wet and in that heat was welcome. Some of the lads got into the local cider brandy made from apples. It was called Calvados and was pretty potent stuff.

The flies were something I had never seen before. Great huge things, like bumblebees. Apparently they came from feeding off dead men and animals - and there were a lot of these flies buzzing around. When they got into the turret, they flew around like a bluebottle and we had a deuce of a job trying to hit them. It struck me as rather ludicrous. Here we were sitting in a tank which was an arsenal, looking at the enemy and our main concern was to kill a fly!

Because we had had no rain, the dust was terrible. It got into everything. And of course you couldn't move a vehicle without creating a dust storm, which immediately brought down shelling. This was particularly hard on our B-Echelon who had difficulty bringing up rations to us. They moved at night but even then the dust gave them away. Signs reminded us - "DUST MEANS DEATH!"

We ate better here than anywhere else in the war. George, our co-driver and bow-gunner, became the self-appointed cook. He could take the army rations of spam and tinned potatoes and dish them up like a gourmet dinner. But woe betides anyone who interfered with him while he was cooking. For months we had been saving delicacies from our parcels from home and George dug into these hoardings to give us some real treats. Right under Jerry's nose too! And just as we would sit down under the tank to eat, Jerry would start shelling us. We swore that he could smell the coffee brewing.

THE MOST EXCLUSIVE CLUB IN THE WORLD

Probably the most terrible thing about war is that you learn to hate. The time comes when the enemy becomes a bunch of bastards that you hate with all your heart. Yet, if you could sit down with him as an individual and talk shop with him no doubt you could have a pleasant evening together. You could compare tanks and their performance and, as one tank man to another, share the life of a crewman. I recall reading a book by a British air ace in which he found himself in an English hospital bed alongside a German flier who had also been shot down. They had a good conversation comparing notes on the joys of flying. At the end of the evening the German pilot gave the British pilot his Iron Cross saying that he hoped it would bring him good luck.

"Had he and I but met
 By some old ancient inn,
 We should have set us down to wet
 Right many a nipperkin!"
- Thomas Hardy (1840-1928) - The Man He Killed (1902)

At the 1980 Reunion of the Regiment, Brigadier-General "Ned" Amy, O.B.E. [Order of the British Empire], D.S.O. [Distinguished Service Order], M.C. [Military Cross], C.D. [Canadian Forces Decoration], quoted this statement from a famous British general:

"I have always regarded the forward area of the battlefield as the most exclusive club in the world, inhabited by the cream of the nation's manhood - the men who actually do the fighting. Comparatively few in number, they have little hatred for the enemy - rather respect."

I think we could feel that way toward the average German soldier. But toward the S.S. [Waffen-SS, Protective Squadron] it was different. As far as we were concerned they were a bunch of bastards.

Water was terribly precious. We rationed it out carefully. One cup to a man. You had to use that for washing your face, shaving, brushing your teeth. Not much left over for anything else.

A funny thing happened during this period. In the night, we were ordered to move out from our position under the haystack in the field and probe in the region of Bourgebus and La Hogue to test the enemy's defences. A country road ran southwest toward Falaise and just at daybreak we halted on the road wondering what was in front of us. It was quite foggy and we just sat there listening - not a sound. George decided this was a good time to answer nature's call, so he collected the shovel from the back of the tank, got a roll of paper, and began walking down the road into the mist. He had just got the hole dug and operations underway when a light plane, flying very low, appeared out of the mist and began strafing us. George was caught with his pants down. He was trying to run back to the shelter of the tank with his pants shackling him about the knees and waving the shovel wildly. Rat-a-tat-a-tat-tat went the machine gun on the little plane and the spurts of dust from its bullets kicked up the road. George made it safely back to GIRAFFE, roundly cursing the German pilot. It was like a scenario from a World War I movie. I got the Ack/Ack .50-calibre Browning ready and prayed that the pilot would come round again. If he did, somebody else was going to get caught with his flaps down. But I still chuckle when I think of George, waddling like a duck, pants around his ankles, and the winking flashes from the Jerry plane. The next day the same thing happened to me - Jack Kane and Gordie Hatch had the laugh that time.

We returned to the wheat field having discovered that the enemy defences were pretty good. It was here - under the range of the German guns - that a famous order came through. "22nd Canadian Armoured

le jardin des Canadiens

En juin 1944, une vingtaine de soldats canadiens furent exécutés pour la plupart d'entre eux dans ce jardin d'agrément, créé vers la fin du XIXᵉ siècle derrière la grande aile de la cour de ferme. La sépulture de ces soldats se trouve aujourd'hui dans le cimetière militaire canadien de Bény-sur-Mer. Un monument, édifié avec des pierres tombées de l'église abbatiale, rappelle aujourd'hui l'événement.

Regiment (Grenadier Guards) will shine no more brass until further notice." That was a classic message. It should have been framed and placed in the Regimental War Museum. Actually, most of us had already taken matters into our own hands concerning "dress". Sneakers, we found, were far better for scampering around on the steel hull of a Sherman. Crew Commanders discovered that a piece of silk rag or a scarf helped to ease the chaffing around the neck when constantly swivelling the head looking for the enemy.

ECCE HOMO [Behold the Man; John 19:5]

Today we heard that one of our tanks had been brewed up and the R.S.M. went to get the dead crew members out to bury them. Our R.S.M. is a tough soldier - a true Guard's R.S.M. complete with handlebar moustache. When he got into the turret, the sight that met his eyes made him sick. He jumped down from the tank retching. Our Padre grabbed a shovel, mounted the tank, and scraped out what remained of the two members of the turret crew. There's one thing about our Padre, he's a real man and the more we see of him in action, the more we are coming to respect him and what he represents.

WINDY

An N.C.O. from the Recce crawled through the wheat to our tank. He wanted to make sure we were in radio contact with him. I admired these Recce boys. They were equipped with light M3 Stuart tanks that we called "Honeys". Their main armament was a 37-mm M5 gun which was useless against a German tank [mainly due to its limited range capabilities]. Their task was to seek out the enemy and tell us where they were so we could take them on. This often meant that they had to draw the enemy fire. When this chap spoke to me, his teeth were chattering as though he was freezing cold. The heat today was almost unbearable! I guessed that he was pretty "windy." I hadn't had any experience with this kind of thing and wondered if I should speak to him about it. I knew him to be a brave man and I didn't want to insult him. The most courageous man in battle is the chap who is scared skinny but who carries on in spite of his terror. I began to wonder what he knew, that I didn't, that was making him shake so.

A number of our tanks are getting strafed by low-flying light aircraft just at dawn. I saw Sammy Johnson fixing his .50-calibre Browning on its Ack/Ack mounting. "What are you doing, Sammy?" I asked. "Jesus, Ossie," he replied, "those sons-a-bitches are using live ammo!"

AUGUST 2nd, 1944

News received today that General Kurt Meyer's S.S. had murdered 19 Canadians.

[Murders at the Ardenne Abbey
During the Normandy Campaign, then SS-Standartenführer Kurt Meyer, commander of the 25th Panzer Grenadier Regiment, used the Ardenne Abbey for his regimental headquarters, as the turret allowed for a clear view of the battlefield. The abbey is the location where in June 1944, 20 Canadian soldiers were illegally executed by members of the 12th SS Panzer Division.

During the evening of 7 June, 11 Canadian prisoners of war, soldiers from the North Nova Scotia Highlanders and the 27th Armoured Regiment (The Sherbrooke Fusilier Regiment), were shot in the back of the head. This was a flagrant violation of the Geneva Conventions (of which Germany was a signatory) and therefore these actions constituted a war crime. The following day, 8 June, seven more POWs from the North Nova Scotia Highlanders were also executed. On 17 June, two more Canadian soldiers were also believed to have been killed at or around the abbey.

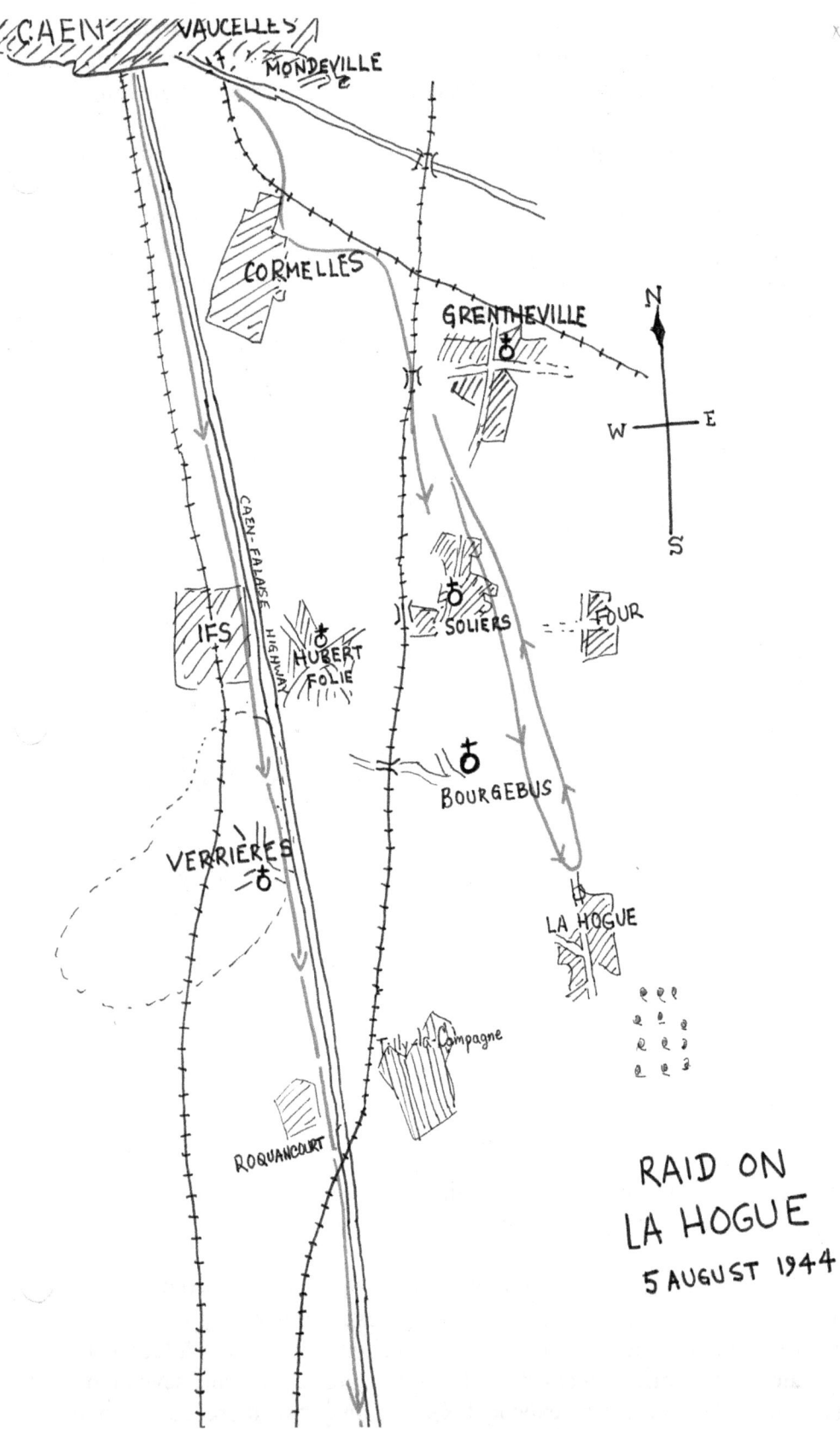

RAID ON
LA HOGUE
5 AUGUST 1944

Following a year of investigations from August 1944 to August 1945, the Canadian War Crimes Commission (CWCC), led by Lieutenant-Colonel Bruce Macdonald, strove to discover the details of the murders and who bore the responsibility.

Meyer was found guilty of "Inciting and advising soldiers under his command to refuse quarter to Allied troops." Sentenced to death on 28 December 1945, his sentence was commuted to life imprisonment on 14 January 1946. After serving nearly nine years in prison, Meyer was released on 7 September 1954.

Currently, in the garden of the Abbaye rests a memorial to the soldiers, unveiled on 6 June 1984. The inscription, followed by the names of those killed, reads: "IN MEMORIAM. ON THE NIGHT OF 7-8 JUNE 1944, EIGHTEEN CANADIAN SOLDIERS WERE MURDERED IN THIS GARDEN WHILE BEING HELD HERE AS PRISONERS OF WAR. TWO MORE PRISONERS DIED HERE, OR NEARBY, ON 17 JUNE 1944. LEST WE FORGET."
- Source: Wikipedia]

AUGUST 4th, 1944

Just as we were about to eat our supper we came under some heavy shelling. Jerry always manages to disturb our meal times. Tonight, Gordie Hatch and I were in the turret when Jerry started bombing us. It got so bad that we closed down the turret hatches. There was one loud "crump" and then another. The enemy knew where we were and was raining down bombs upon us. Gordie said - "Ossie, if we come out of this alive, it's a date for dinner at The New Sherbrooke Hotel." "You're on, Gordie," I said and we reached across the turret and shook hands on it.

"Would I were in an alehouse in London! I would give all my fame for a pot of ale and safety."
- William Shakespeare (1564-1616) - Henry V, Act III, Scene 2 (1599)

AUGUST 5th, 1944

It is desperately hot again today and not a cloud in the sky. I came off my duty watch in the turret and slipped down into the shallow trench we had dug under the tank. George was getting the lunch ready and I knew better than to talk to our "chef" when he was cooking. I lay up near the front of the tank where it was cooler. I thought I heard a noise out in front. I listened carefully and I was sure I could hear someone creeping up on us through the wheat field. I warned George and I cocked my pistol and waited. If this was a Jerry expecting to slap a "sticky bomb" on GIRAFFE, he was in for a surprise. I could hear the man creeping closer and closer. Just then a blond head appeared in front of my pistol. "For Gawds sake don't shoot, Ossie!" It was Lieutenant The Lord Shaughnessy who had been up front on a Recce.

Doug McKnight had taken part in the raid on La Hogue, in which our Regiment, along with the infantry from the Lake Sups, had tested out the enemy's defences. After the raid Doug came over to see me. I was glad to see him because this was our first real action and Doug had beaten me to it. He walked toward our tank carrying a German machine gun over his shoulder - a souvenir of the raid. I needed some fresh camouflage for GIRAFFE and Doug said he knew a good spot to get some, so I set off with him, swinging my machete. As we walked along in the moonlight near a hedge row, I suddenly froze. Not ten yards away was a German heavy machine gun, with the two gunners sitting right behind it, and it was pointed straight at us. In that moment I knew that I was a dead soldier. I was staring right down the barrel. For a split second I wondered if I was already dead! Then I heard Doug say - "They're dead!" I breathed again. We went over to the gun but were careful not to touch it in case it was booby-trapped. There was not a mark on them as far as we could see. Their eyes were open and they were in the act of firing. One man was feeding

22nd Canadian Armoured Regiment Memorial

Inscription: THIS M4 SHERMAN TANK BEARS THE OPERATIONAL DESIGNATIONS OF THE 22nd CANADIAN ARMOURED REGIMENT (CANADIAN GRENADIER GUARDS) AND IS DEDICATED TO THE MEMORY OF ITS SOLDIERS WHO FOUGHT IN NORTHWEST EUROPE FROM 1944 TO 1945 WITH COURAGE, HONOUR AND SELFLESS DEDICATION. THEIR VALOUR AND SACRIFICE CONTRIBUTED TO THE LIBERATION OF OCCUPIED EUROPE AND THE UNCONDITIONAL SURRENDER OF ENEMY FORCES.

WE WILL REMEMBER THEM

FALAISE	THE SCHELDT	VEEN
FALAISE ROAD	THE LOWER MAAS	TWENTE CANAL
THE LIASON	THE RHINELAND	BAD ZWISCHENAHN
CHAMBOIS	THE HOCHWALD	NORTHWEST EUROPE 1944-45

the ammo belt into the gun, the other had his finger on the trigger. We concluded that a mortar bomb must have landed very close and they were killed by the blast. Either that or a bomb blast from an aircraft. It was a frightening experience. "Cowards die many times before their death." [William Shakespeare (1564-1616) - Julius Caesar, Act II, Scene 2 (1599)]. We cut the camouflage and Doug helped me carry it back to GIRAFFE. We said, "Goodbye" and "Good luck". I watched him stride away with the Jerry machine gun over his shoulder. He reached the corner of a hedgerow and in the shadow it was difficult to see him. He stopped and turned toward me and saluted. I saluted back. It was a soldier's farewell. Then he was gone.

AUGUST 6th, 1944

We were withdrawn from the front today and went to a rest area near Vaucelles to get ready for the big offensive. Even here in the environs of Caen we are still within range of the German's biggest guns and, of course, his bombers at night.

AUGUST 7th, 1944

This morning we were taken to a Mobile Bath Unit. We took off all our clothes, waited in line, and then went through a shower and delousing machine. It was just like an assembly line. As you emerged you picked up a clean set of underwear. While we were waiting there stark naked, we suddenly realized that not twenty yards away crowding the fence were about sixty French girls all admiring our beautiful physiques! More kept arriving by bicycle. They must have been coming from some factory that was on its lunch break. This was a kind of Follies Bergeres in reverse. "Never mind," someone observed, "It'll be OUR pleasure when we get to Paris." "Guardsmen are used to being in bear skins!" chimed in another. The funny thing about it was I experienced no erotic feeling whatsoever and the other men seemed to feel the same. War novels may combine sex and battle but I don't think it happens in actual fact. As far as we were concerned, those French girls peering over the fence might have been just so many French cows - we felt no excitement at all. Viva la difference!

This afternoon we spent tidying up. I washed some socks and wrote some letters - the first chance I have had since arriving in Normandy. Tonight I saw a pitiful sight - civilians - old people - children - some with two-wheeled hand carts or pushing wheel-barrows loaded with their belongings - leaving the city. Where were they going? Someone said they were going to sleep in the Fleury Caves. Caves that had been made when quarrying stone to make the great English cathedrals hundreds of years ago. I feel sorry for these people. First they had got our bombing which had almost reduced their city to rubble, now they are getting the German bombing as the enemy hits back at us.

It is sweltering hot tonight. The mosquitoes remind me of a summer night back home. They wriggle under our battle dress and nibble our ankles, wrists and face. We're all ready for the big offensive now. It looks like this will be one of the biggest battles of the war. The Jerries are stubbornly holding the high ground around Falaise. Field Marshal Rommel has thrown a ring of steel around that ancient town. OPERATION TOTALIZE is a carefully planned offensive designed to break the enemies grip on Falaise and to destroy his panzers in Normandy. We put spare tracks on the front of our tank today to reinforce the armour plate. The tank has been gassed up and the ammo carefully stowed in the racks. Just to be sure, we have scrounged some extra rounds and they are lying on the floor of the turret. We'll fire them first. It is now late in the evening but still daylight as the sun sinks in a great fiery red ball through the dust haze that hovers over the hedgerows. There is a peaceful hush over the villages and countryside of Normandy - that ominous silence we are coming to know so well - which is the prelude to battle.

Yea, though I walk through the valley of the shadow of death, I will fear no evil: for thou *art* with me; thy rod and thy staff they comfort me. Thou preparest a table before me in the presence of mine enemies.

Psalm 23 (KJV)

"It is a beauteous evening, calm and free,
The holy time is quiet as a Nun
Breathless with adoration; the broad sun
Is sinking down in its tranquility;"
- William Wordsworth (1770-1850) - It is a beauteous evening, calm and free (1802)

We are all thinking the same thing. Will I be alive to see the sunset tomorrow? I was making a last minute check of the gear stowed on the back of the tank when our chaplain came along. "Tell your crew I'll be back very soon with the Holy Communion," he said, and continued down along the line of Sherman tanks drawn up on the left side of the road. "O.K. Padre," I replied. The padre - John Anderson - is a young fellow and fairly new to our Regiment. We haven't really got to know him yet. I go forward to alert the crew. There is Jack. Should I tell him? He is a devout Irish Catholic, but I know that no Roman Catholic padre will be along tonight. There are R.C. padres, but they are attached to French Canadian or Irish Canadian regiments. Ours in an Anglican regiment. I decide to tell Jack anyway. There is nothing to lose and, at a time like this, on the eve of our greatest battle, Jack might appreciate it. "Thanks, Ossie," he replied, "I would like to join you."

Working along with Jack in the hull of the tank is George, our co-driver and forward gunner. Now, George is Jewish and I know that Jews don't come to a Christian communion service. Should I invite George? I decide against it. I don't want to offend him. I climb up into the turret where Gordie, our gunner, is making a final check on the armament. He is a good Anglican. "The Padre will be along any minute with the Holy Communion, Gordie." I said. "Thanks, Bob." he replied as he made a final adjustment to the Browning machine gun and wiped it affectionately with a rag. I knew Gordie would be there, the Eucharist meant a lot to him.

Here we are the four of us, all friends who have trained together in Canada and England. Now we are about to engage in the toughest assignment of our lives against Adolf Hitler's supermen. Some of us will get killed. Should I not at least invite George? There will be no rabbi along tonight to bring him the comfort of his faith.

As I ponder this question and climb out of the turret I can see the Padre hurrying towards us with his communion kit. As I jump down to meet him, George sticks his head out of the co-driver's hatch. Without a further thought I said, "Here's the Chaplain with the communion, George, you're welcome to join us if you wish." Had I said something wrong? Perhaps I should have checked it out with Captain Anderson first. But there was no time. Already the clock was ticking away the minutes before zero hour. Oh well, the Padre would probably never know anyway and George might not accept the invitation. George didn't move or reply. He just stayed there, half in and half out of the forward turret hatch. I can see him now just sort of stuck there with a strange look on his face. I can't describe it - almost as if he was smiling; only he wasn't.
We followed the Padre across the ditch by the roadside and through a gate into a garden. I remember that because there were cabbages and one was right under my knee as I knelt down. Can you picture us there in that French garden as the long summer twilight turned to dusk - the Padre in his battle dress and the three of us in our dirty tank suits? Captain Anderson began a prayer - something about "The Lord mighty in battle". My eyes were closed but I could hear someone approach and kneel down at the other end of the line beside Jack. "Through Jesus Christ our Lord," said the Padre, bringing the short prayer to a close.

Then he read the Twenty-third Psalm. I could hear someone quietly repeating the words along with him, but it was now too dark to see who it was. "Yea, though I walk through the valley of the shadow of death," intoned the Padre. That's just where we were going. Down into the deep dark valley, and the German Eighty-Eights [German 88 mm anti-aircraft and anti-tank artillery gun] will be cracking at us from every

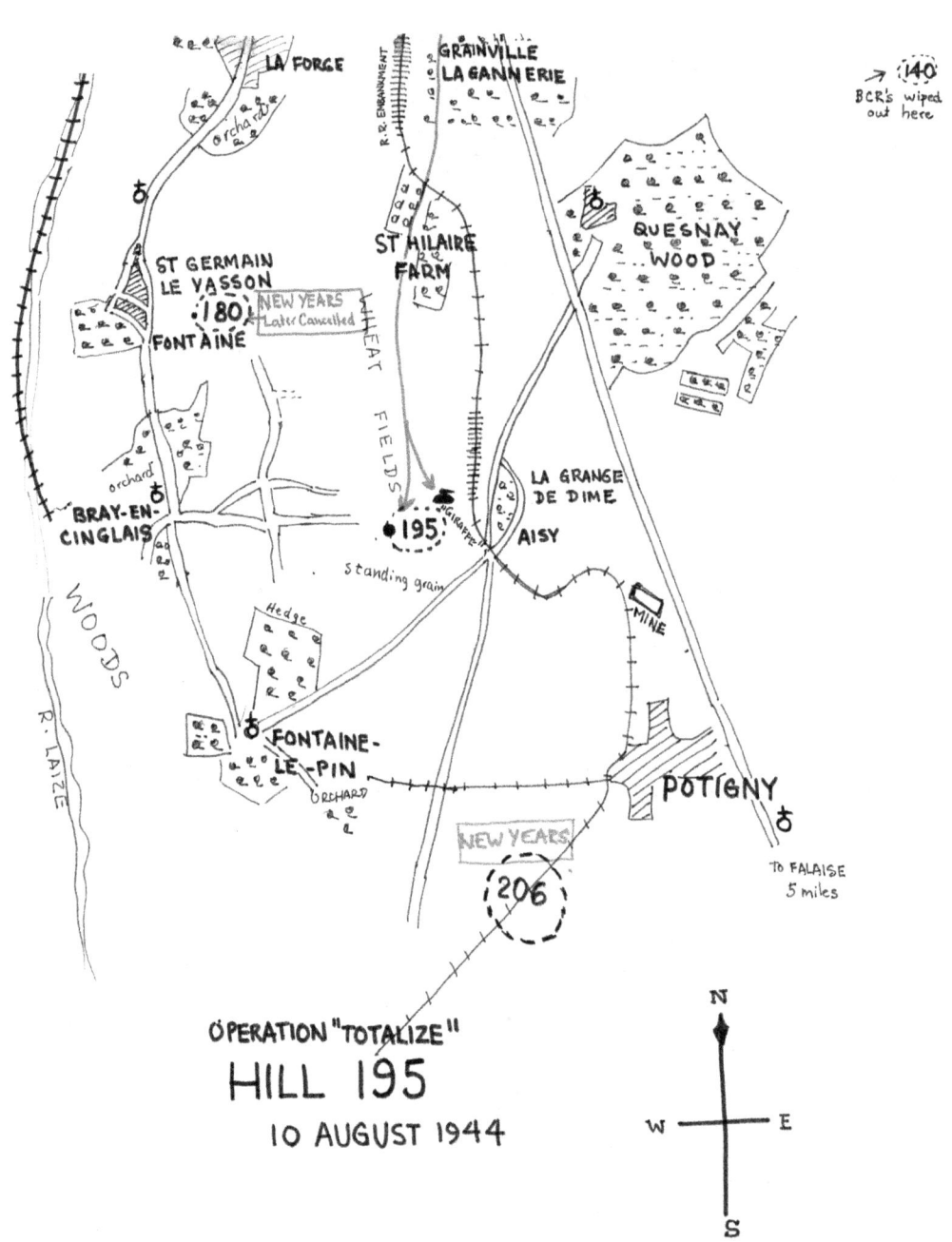

side. "I will fear no evil." But the writer of that Psalm hadn't seen what an Eighty-Eight could do to a Sherman tank. "Thou preparest a table before me in the presence of mine enemies." The Jerries were dug in waiting for us. Soon we will be in their gun sights. "Surely goodness and mercy shall follow me all the days of my life: and I will dwell in the house of the Lord forever." We held out our oily and grimy hands to receive the wafer. Then we received the wine from the common chalice. "The blood of Our Lord Jesus Christ", said the Padre. The wine burned its way down our dusty throats and seemed to light a fire in my stomach. The Padre dismissed us with the blessing. I don't suppose that the whole service lasted more than four or five minutes - if that long. There was no ornate altar, no stained glass windows, no organ music, no robed choir, no kneeling benches, no priest in vestments - not even a table - yet everything was there - faith and hope and fellowship.

"Soldier's luck, lads, and God bless you," said Padre John Anderson, and then he disappeared in the darkness to minister to the next tank crew along the road. George got up from his knees and walked back to GIRAFFE with us.

OPERATION TOTALIZE

After the sun had set, there was an eerie silence over the Normandy countryside. This was the hour before the big attack. OPERATION TOTALIZE was designed to destroy the enemy in Normandy and open the way for Victory. Lieutenant-General Guy Granville Simonds C.C. [Order of Canada], C.B. [Order of the Bath], C.B.E. [Order of the British Empire], D.S.O. [Distinguished Service Order], C.D. [Canadian Forces Decoration], our Corps Commander, had laid his plans carefully. First, the fleet of Halifax and Lancaster Bombers, from the 2nd Tactical Air Force, would pulverize the enemy's flanks. To make sure no bombs fell on our front, the artillery were to mark the flanks with green and red shell burst - green for the left side and red for the right. Our Division, the 4th Armoured, and three British divisions would then push off on either side of the Caen-Falaise highway - Canadians on the west side and the British on the east. The Polish 1st Armoured Division would also strike out to the east of the highway. The Infantry were to go into the attack along with the Armour in open tanks which had had their 25-pounder guns removed. "Unfrocked Priests", we called these vehicles. It was difficult to attack at night so General Simonds, with typical Canadian ingenuity and initiative, had hit upon an idea for artificial moonlight - searchlights bounced off clouds. Some said he got the idea from the lights on baseball fields at home. We waited. It was awfully still and terribly exciting. The adrenalin was flowing. I kept glancing at my watch. Some fellows stood around their tanks smoking. Then, over the Regimental net, came the command - "Mount!" There was a scramble as crews dropped their cigarettes and climbed into their tanks. Then came the order - "Start Up!" Hundreds of tank engines coughed and roared into life. I wondered if the enemy had any idea what was about to happen. I almost felt sorry for him! My watch was ticking off he minutes - 2257 - 2258 - 2259 and as I looked up, there in the night sky coming out of the north, were the bombers - a thousand of them in a great air armada. What a sight! What precision timing! They were over us and we could see the stuff going down, and above it all we could hear the crash of our artillery. To our front we could see the flashes of the bombs and hear the thunderous explosions. Now and then there would be a big explosion - they must have hit an ammunition dump - something purple flared up. The earth was pulsating and shaking like an earthquake with the tremendous detonations and the pounding of the big guns. I had to scream at the top of my voice to make myself heard, and even then I could only see the other person's lips moving and guess at the words. Now an even bigger roar as the massed artillery of the Canadian guns shattered the air. Somebody who had been at the Battle of El Alamein said that this was a far bigger barrage. I recalled the film we had seen in Brighton - "Desert Victory". What a fantastic barrage this was - the whole front flickering with the incessant flashes of the guns. Every two minutes the barrage lifted and crept forward. It was difficult to hear on the I/C over the diapason of the guns. Now we were rolling. I looked for enemy prisoners and knocked out Eighty-Eights. I saw none. Perhaps nothing could survive such a holocaust. We followed the

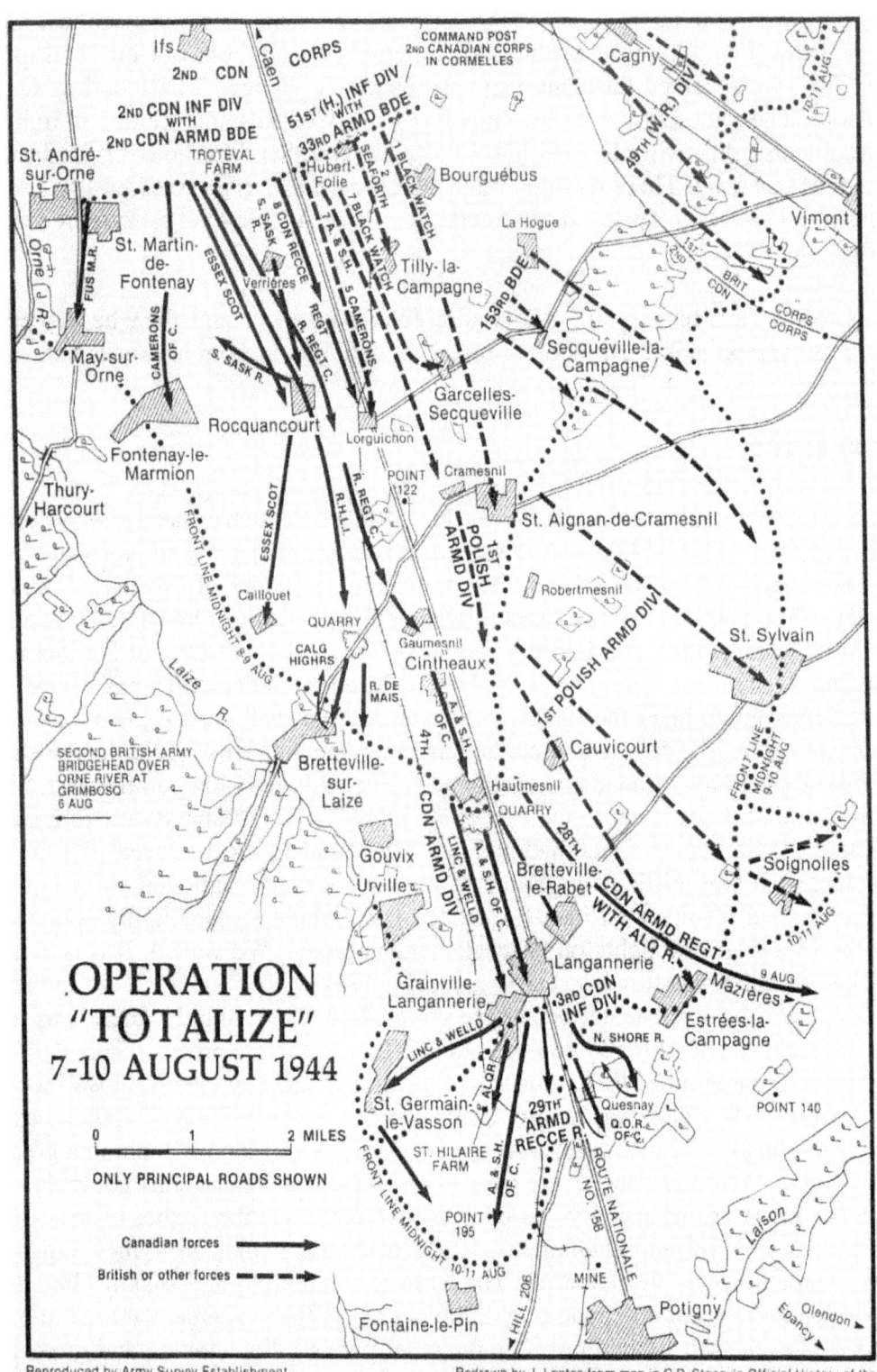

tank in front, and he was following the one in front of him, and somewhere way out in the lead was a Pathfinder tank which was being directed on course by a radio beam. I wondered how Don Ross, our Troop Commander, could see anything up there in the turret - the dust that was being stirred up was stifling. I noticed Very Lights [flares] going up on the left. I saw tracers from a tank machine gun. We rolled steadily on. A shadowy figure staggered by - I guess it was a Jerry who figured he was safer to walk straight into us than to run back and get caught in that creeping barrage. A tank on its side, no sign of the crew. They must have fallen into a bomb crater. A big explosion on the left - I guess a supply dump was hit. We clattered steadily on - the Ack/Ack from the 40mm Bofors guns giving us the line of advance - pointing the way like red billiard balls struck by a giant cue into the darkness. I thought of the bomber boys. They would be back in England now - eating their bacon and eggs. "A good prang," they would be saying. We rolled steadily on through the ring of steel we couldn't break through before. It was a piece of cake now. I glanced at my watch - 0230 - a waning moon and some bright stars. Sometime later, dawn was breaking and we were through the enemy's defence line and pushing ahead on the high ground south toward Falaise. Jack must be tired. He has driven all night. We came to a halt, time for a five minute break. We climbed out stiff and cold and looked back. It was a fantastic sight - tanks and unfrocked priests everywhere. Some clusters of prisoners coming up out of the wheat fields. We motion them on - keep walking - your war is over - you lucky bastard! Some were S.S. and they were bastards - never trust them - even as prisoners they would surrender with a grenade in each hand. Our orders were to hit them first, hit them hard, and keep on hitting them. They hate our guts and we don't give them any quarter.

I wondered what the news reports back home would be saying - August 8th, on the anniversary of the great Canadian break-out in the last war, Ludendorf's "Black Day" and the "beginning of the last hundred days" at Amiens. Was this history repeating itself? I made a rapid calculation - 100 days - The war would be over by Christmas!

The attack seems to have gone well. We have broken through Jerry's defence line. Now it's "On to Falaise!" Don is reading to us over the intercom. He's got a small pocket copy of Shakespeare:
"And these few precepts in thy memory
Look thou character. Give thy thoughts no tongue,
Nor any unproportioned thought his act.
Be thou familiar but by no means vulgar."

"Hey, Ossie, pass down the coffee tin", Jack calls up from the driver's seat. He needs a pee. Some crews used a spent shell casings but we preferred the Maxwell House Coffee tin! "Good to the last drop!"

"Those friends thou hast, and their adoption tried,
Grapple them unto thy soul with hoops of steel,"

Shakespeare can be so relevant. I guess that's the secret of his greatness. Like the Bible - it always seems to be speaking right to you. If we come through this, we'll never, never, forget the comradeship we've had together in this crew.

"But do not dull thy palm with entertainment
Of each new-hatched, unfledged comrade. Beware
Of entrance to a quarrel, but being in,
Bear 't that th' opposed may beware of thee."

By George, that's good. I hope the Jerries feel that way now...

LIEUTENANT-GENERAL G. G. SIMONDS, C.B., C.B.E., D.S.O.,
G.O.C. 2ND CANADIAN CORPS
(From a watercolour portrait by Major C. F. Comfort)

THIS WEEK'S COVER is a portrait of Major General Guy Granville Simonds, C. B. E., D. S. O., who, when he led the First Division of Canadians into action in the Middle East with Britain's famous Eighth Army, was the second youngest general ever to take a Canadian division into action. Appointed a major general at thirty-nine, General Simonds was forty when he reached Sicily, and his record was bettered only by General Sir Arthur Currie, who took our First Division into battle in France in the Great War at the age of thirty-nine.

Tall and slender, with an imposing mustache, an English accent, and a touch of austerity in his make-up, General Simonds is a permanent force officer with eighteen years of Army service.

Born at Ixworth, England, General Simonds came to Canada as a youngster.

His wife and two daughters live in Winnipeg. Educated in the classical military tradition—at R. M. C., the Staff College at Camberly, and Sandhurst and Woolwich—he went overseas as a major in 1939. He was attached to Montgomery's tanks and infantry as an observer for General McNaughton when Rommel was driven out of Africa. A few months later, in Sicily, Montgomery presented him with the Distinguished Service Order for his leadership of the Canadians in the fighting in central Sicily.

A quick thinker with a gift for lucid expression, General Simonds is regarded as one of the Army's men of brains, a young man who is just getting started but whose record indicates that he will be one of Canada's top fighting men.

"Give every man thy ear but few thy voice."

By the sound of the chatter on the Command net they're not heeding Polonius' advice - but we are. We haven't broken our wireless silence yet.

"Take each man's censure but reserve thy judgment.
Costly thy habit as thy purse can buy,
But not expressed in fancy—rich, not gaudy,
For the apparel oft proclaims the man,"

So it does. Look at those prisoners shuffling by in their German uniforms.

"And they in France of the best rank and station
Are of a most select and generous chief in that.
Neither a borrower nor a lender be,
For loan oft loses both itself and friend,"

That reminds me, did Jack ever pay me that fiver he borrowed? Yes, I remember he did - just before we left Crowborough.

"And borrowing dulls the edge of husbandry.
This above all: to thine own self be true,
And it must follow, as the night the day,
Thou canst not then be false to any man."
- William Shakespeare (1564-1616) - Hamlet, Act I, Scene 3 (c. 1599)

"Orders coming over the Command net, Don." I switched him over while he pocketed the little copy of Shakespeare. On the I/C now, Don was speaking. "Driver halt! I've got to go to an O-Group. You take over Ossie." Don took off his headsets and climbed out of the turret. I left my niche in the turret and climbed up on the top to have a look around. Everybody else got out for a stretch and smoke. We have broken through all right and debouched on to a wide plain. Tanks are fanned out everywhere but no enemy shooting at us. I look toward the northeast and see bombs dropping from a great fleet of aircraft - a great pall of smoke. What the hell? Bombing about three or four miles BEHIND us? I check the map - somewhere in the vicinity of Vaucelles. They are U.S. Heavy Bombers, and all kinds of stuff is going down. I call Gordie and Jack up to have a look. Damn funny, this bombing. "Polish up that white star on the top of the turret, Ossie," says Jack, "I don't want any of those Yankee boys plastering us." "Aw shut up, Jack," says Gordie good-naturedly, and then imitating a Brooklyn accent, "You'll get a poiple heart." Every time Jack jammed his finger, or bruised himself with a spanner, we kidded him about getting a Purple Heart. If Jack, originally from Brooklyn, New York, had been in the American army instead, he would no doubt have half a dozen medals by now. With us, he's lucky to be sporting a "spam medal."

A tiny artillery O-Pip plane, a Taylorcraft Auster, is trying to attract the attention of the bombers and call off their bombing of our troops. He flies up, wildly doing all kinds of aerobatics and firing off Very Lights to draw them off. "Well, fellas", I said, "if they're bombing the enemy positions, then we're half way to Berlin!" Don arrives back. There has been a terrible mistake. Bombs have fallen among our echelons - a lot of support vehicles have been knocked out. What will this do to our early gains? We mount up and move forward. Captain Cassils has run into a sticky situation. A Tiger firing out of the window of a farm house. We listen to Charlie Cassils' message to his Sergeant. "You pin him down from here and I'll make an end run to the right and put the boots to him." I could just imagine some prosaic German Intelligence Officer trying to decipher that! "Put the boots to him? Put the boots to him? Wass iss de matter wit dese

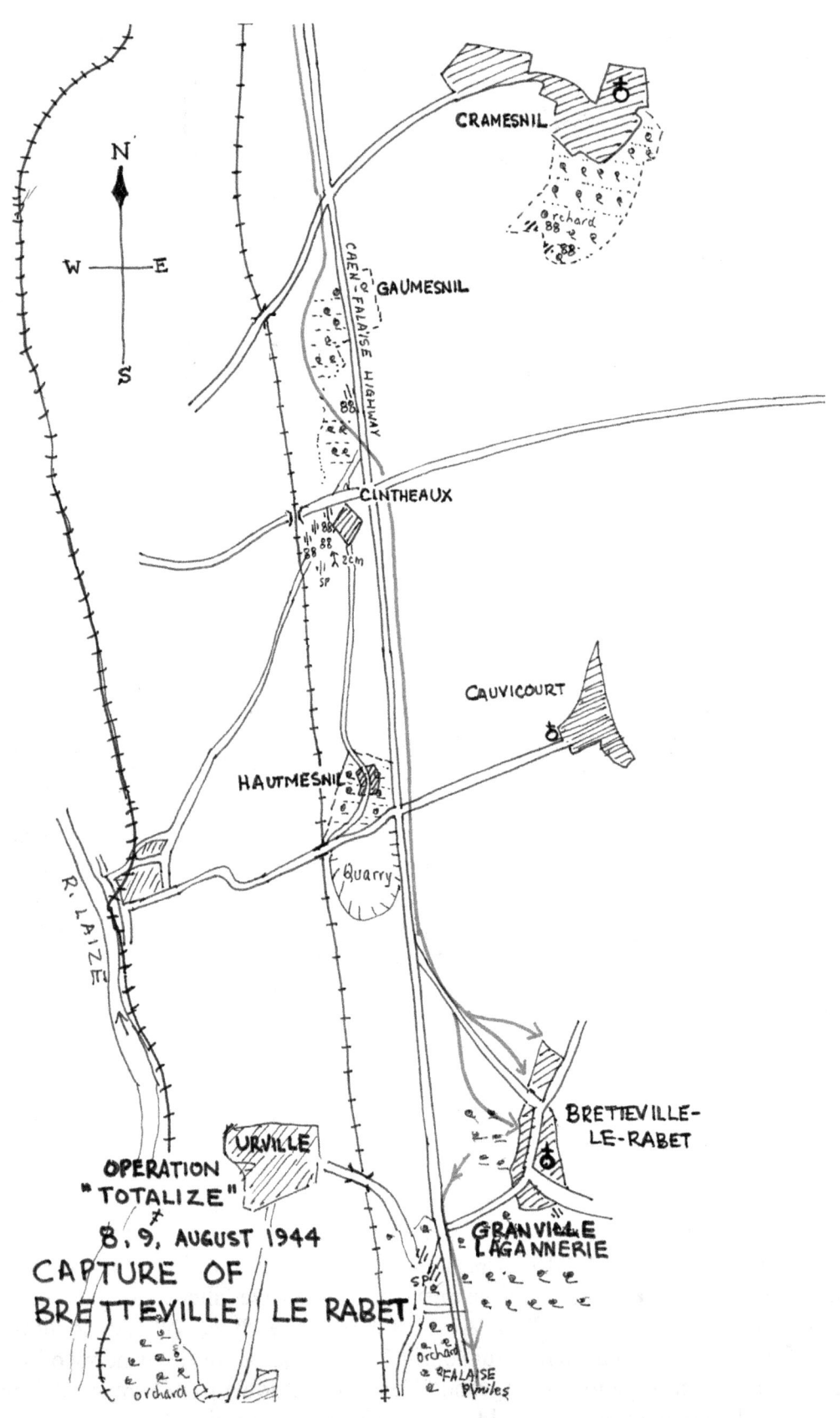

Kanadians?" I look at my watch. It is 1600 hours. By the messages coming over the wireless I can tell there is a lot of action in No. 1 and No. 3 Squadrons, but so far it's all quiet on the No. 2 front. Typhoons rocketing off to the left. When I am in the turret, most of what I can see is to the left (east) as we advance south. That must be the British or the Poles getting some air support. I recognize Major Smith's voice on the radio - I think his tank has been hit - yes, it's been knocked out - but he's cool - we don't want to lose "Snuffy" - he won his M.C. [Military Cross] in Italy and we need his experience. There have been some casualties. I hope Doug is O.K. Heavy fighting is reported around Gaumesnil Wood. I can see Don studying his map. He hands it down to me. Where's Gaumesnil Wood anyway? Here it is just north of us. A lot of chatter on the net. Things are livening up! "We've been blooded" as the British say.

Don is called away again for another O-Group. We wait. Some Engineer types ask me to move my tank back. There is an U.X.B. [UneXploded Bomb] and they are going to detonate it. We must be a thousand yards from it for safety. I watch them through the binoculars as they attach a detonating device - two metal bands - around the bomb. Then they drive away in their jeep - stop - get down into a slit trench and "whamo!" - she blew! The shock wave hit me right across the forehead like a giant slap. I think the bomb must have been one of ours - a two thousand pounder. I move the tank back to the original position so Don can find us.

"Arms on armour clashing bray'd
Horrible discord, and the madding wheels
Of brazen chariots raged; dire was the noise
Of conflict;"
- John Milton (1608–1674) - Paradise Lost (1667)

The harbour area is just north of Gaumesnil. We have settled down for the night in a haystack. The Jerries had made a little room in it and a hollow shaft with a ladder and lookout at the top. It was a strange feeling to realize that only last night the enemy slept here.

Sometime well after midnight, we were awakened and told that we are going to make a pre-dawn attack on Bretteville. We name it The Rabbit. There were a number of Norman towns with this name - Brettevilie-sur-Laize was only three miles from Bretteville-le-Rabet - hence the nickname, The Rabbit. Don has come back from another O-Group and says that our intelligence has discovered that about nine hundred fresh German troops have just arrived on our front in the area of The Rabbit. They have forced-marched, so the Intelligence/Operations say, all the way from Denmark. I was reminded of the B. I. Canteen! They are members of the 89th Infantry Division. They are tired and our job is to attack them before they get a chance to rest and dig in. It is a beautiful summer night with a waning moon, a night when young men like us should be making love, not war. The order came through to "Mount" and "Start Up" and we pushed off into the night. Our Rendo is at a place named Hautmesnil and here we regrouped and renetted our wireless sets. At 0330 hours we led off - that's No. 2 Squadron - with a company of the Lake Sups. Four or five of them were perched on the back of our tank. We are passing uncleared territory and now we swing left and overlook the village. Just before dawn we begin shooting - tracers and High Explosive rounds exploding in the village. By now the enemy was alerted and began answering our fire. No. 1 Squadron opens the attack circling around the perimeter of The Rabbit with all guns blazing. Don gives us the fire order and we lob a few shells into the village. There is a lull as prisoners begin to come out and up the hill toward us. The forward companies of the Lake Sups go in to winkle them out. Don is called away to an O-Group.

Wc still have our four or five men on the back. I am standing in the turret surveying the scene when a sniper zings a shot off the turret. Then another sang past. The next shot was very close to my head and I heard it ricochet off the turret ring. The infantry pile off the back and take cover on the ground behind the

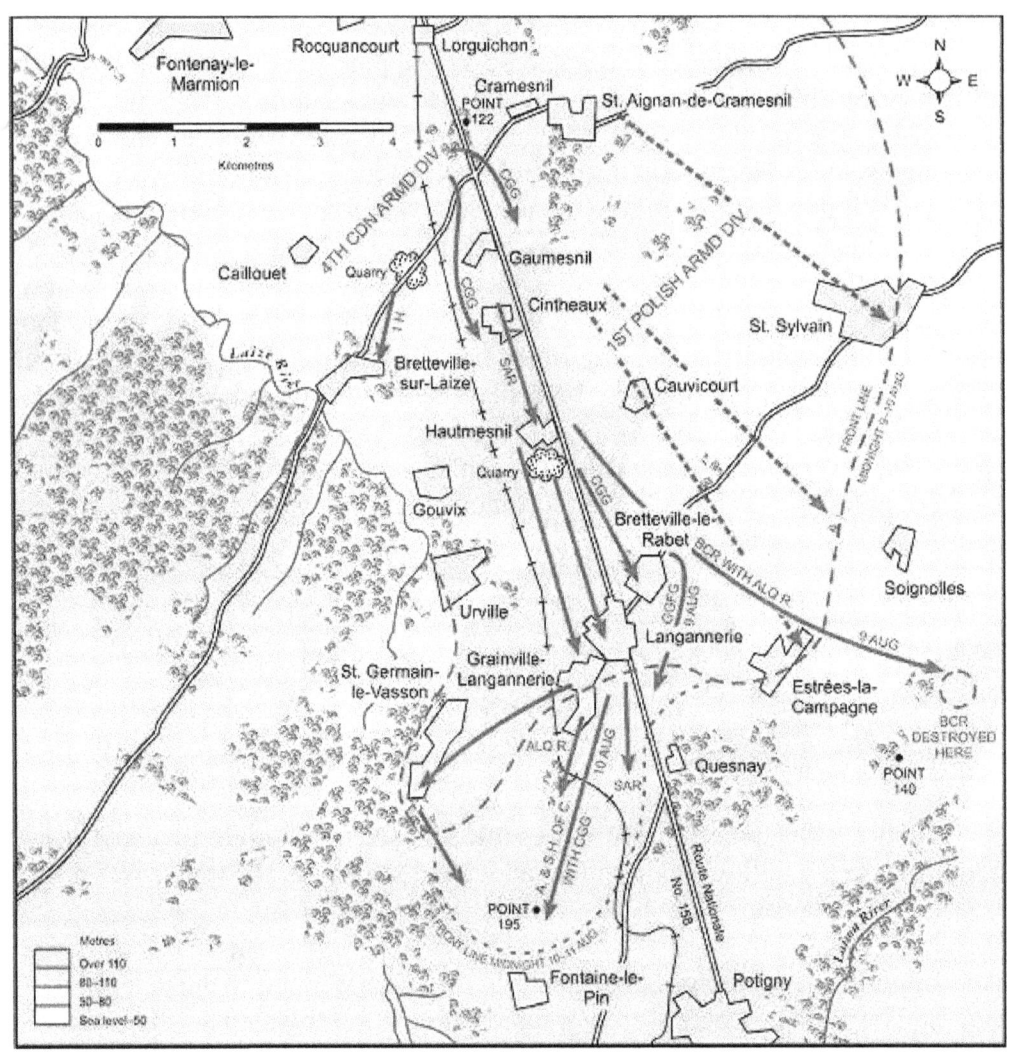

tank. I raise my turret flaps to provide some protection and pull my head in like a turtle. I know the next shot will be right through my noggin. I suspect the sniper is firing from the church tower. I speak on the I/C to Gordie Hatch, "Gunner traverse left - steady - ON - Church tower - one round A.P. [Armour Piercing] - Fire!" The gun cracked and GIRAFFE lurched as the breach clanged open and the recoil ran out. The spent casing fell into the canvass bag. Another shot from the sniper. This was getting too close for comfort. I spoke to the gunner again: "Gordie, give him a couple more, into the belfry of the church." Again GIRAFFE's gun blasted. I couldn't see any result of our shooting. The sniper fired again, an inch from my ear! "Gordie, those A.P. shots must be going clean through, let's try an H.E. [High Explosive] round." I dropped down into the turret and set the fuse on a five second delay. When I was clear of the breach I said: "Fire when ready and be damn quick about it!" I crouched in the turret. The gun boomed - there was a long pause. I watched the belfry for a hit. Then the doors of the church blew open - followed by plaster dust and smoke. There was no more trouble from the sniper. By now the Lake Sups were clearing the village. Prisoners were streaming up the road toward us with their hands on their heads. This was my first really close-up look at our enemy since arriving in France. There were some blond S.S. You could tell they were S.S. because they were sporting the two crooked lightning streak insignia. The superman conquerors we had seen on the Pathé News [cinema newsreels]. One of them was combing his beautiful locks. I recalled that the Greeks saw nothing unmanly in the Spartan three hundred combing their long hair before the battle of Thermopylae. Funny things you think of during a battle! These prisoners were arrogant and proud. One was badly wounded in the abdomen but he refused to let our medical men assist him and hobbled along supported by two comrades - holding in his guts like link sausages with his hands. There was raw courage here. You had to admire them. They were tough, these S.S. of the Hitler Youth Division. More prisoners filed past the tank. These were older men and boys. These were the troops that had walked all the way from Denmark or Norway. They were glad to be out of it - you could tell that by the looks on their faces. The Lake Sups must have taken sixty prisoners already and still they kept flushing them out and shepherding them up the road toward our tanks. The battle was over. We had lost a tank, or two, but generally speaking it was an easy victory. Don was back now. The plan was for the B.C.R. [British Columbia Regiment] to pass through us and press on to capture Hill 195. I jumped down from GIRAFFE and got a tin of Carnation Milk, punched a hole in it and drank it down to celebrate the capture of The Rabbit.

AUGUST 9th, 1944

The B.C.R.'s leap-frog through us and we follow them up the Falaise Road. The sides of the road are strewn with knocked out vehicles - some of them lying on their sides and burning furiously. There was a pall of smoke through which the sun gleamed like a silver disc. The 51st Highland Division were moving up too and they were singing - "Mairsie dotes and dosey dotes and little tamsey divey". A bit further along, the forward companies were held up by heavy shelling and sniper fire. There was a rumour of a 62-ton Tiger lurking around too. Some of them were evidently skulking around in the numerous copses and behind the hedgerows. The enemy defences were stiffening. A truck was overturned and burning hotly. An infantry company that was held up by this obstacle were sitting by the road making tea! All I could think of was that song Noël Coward used to sing - "Everything stops for tea". With death just up the road ahead of them, these "Jocks" still found time for a "Nice cuppa". "Hello, Canada, were just having a brew up, won't you join us for a spot?" I glanced at my watch - it was exactly four o'clock. Why not? A jolly good cup of tea would go down well right now. How could we possibly lose this war with a spirit like that? I jumped down from the tank and joined these lads in their tea time.

The big push on to Falaise seemed to have been slowed down. Don said to me, "Come on, Ossie, let's walk up forward and see what's going on." We walked up the road with its smashed vehicles and signs of war. A dead German, cut right in half, was dangling over a fence, his twin lightening streak marking him as S.S. Others were lying face up with the flies crawling over them. The smell was becoming familiar - that sickly-

sweet stench of death. To the left there seemed to be a tank battle going on. We crawled through a hedgerow and lay on our bellies and, with the binoculars, we watched the annihilation of the B.C.R.'s. Later we heard that they had got off their centre-line, reported that they were on top of Hill 195, when they were actually on Hill 140. The fighting was still going on and tanks were brewing up as the Eighty-Eights and Tigers of the 12th S.S. and 21st Panzer turned the slopes of the hill into a shooting gallery. "What a massacre!" we said as we crept away from the hedge and crossed the road and made our way back to the Squadron.

On our advance along the Falaise road, we passed through the village of Hautmesnil. Gordie was spraying the hedge-rows and deserted houses with the machine gun. From my periscope on the left side of GIRAFFE, I saw a young woman suddenly dart out of a house clutching a baby in her arms. "Hold it, Gordie!" The co-ax [Most tanks have a coaxial machine gun mounted to be aimed and fired by use of the main gun control] stopped at once. Gordie was grateful that I had spotted her. He had a wife and baby back home and had a snapshot of his baby over his gun sight. We developed a habit of spraying hedges and houses with the machine gun to flush out any Jerries who might be hiding there and who would shoot us in the back as soon as we had passed by.

"'And I hit everything within reach,' cried Tweedledum, 'whether I can see it or not!'"
- Lewis Carroll (Charles Lutwidge Dodgson: 1832-1898) - Through The Looking-Glass (1871)

It is getting dark and a slight rain is falling. We seem to be coming under some mortar fire too. The Squadron Leader is having engine trouble. Don, our commander, sends me over to the Squadron Leader's tank while he takes over ours. "What's wrong, 'Shorty'?" I asked the driver. John Halladay had the back of GREYHOUND open and was tinkering with the engine. What a time for a breakdown. I climbed into the turret and put on the head-phones. Art Smythe looked up from his gun sights. "Oh, it's you, Ossie, hadn't we better report we're out of action and need the L.A.D.?" [Light Aid Detachment]. "Let's wait a minute or two Artie, maybe Shorty can get it going again." It was very dark now but I could see Shorty disappear into the murk with a pair of wire-cutters in his gloved hand. In a few moments he was back and tinkering with the engine. Then I hear that oh, so sweet sound of GREYHOUND's engines roar into life. Shorty is back in the driver's seat. "What was wrong, Shorty?" I asked over the I/C "Oh nothin' that a piece of fence wire couldn't fix," he answered. Halladay was one of those prairie boys - brought up on tractors - very practical - ideal tank men. I thanked God for men like him, "Let's go, Shorty", I said, "see if we can catch up to the rest of the Squadron."

OUR POLISH ALLIES

When the great armoured phalanx struck out from Caen toward Falaise, the 1st Polish Armoured Division was on our left flank just to the east of the axis of our advance along the tree lined Caen-Falaise highway. The Poles weren't too worried about keeping to their centre-line, they had old scores to settle with the Germans. I suddenly remembered that the war had started over Hitler's invasion of Poland. These Polish tank crews were fanatical in their eagerness to come to grips with the enemy. Each crew member had one aim and that was to kill a German. Sergeant Les Wells told me this story. Three Jerries surrendered to him but he could not cope with them and command a tank as well, so, seeing a Polish soldier he went over to him and explained that these three prisoners had surrendered and he asked the Pole to escort them to the rear. "Yah, yah, Kanada, I understand." Sometime later that same day Sergeant Wells met the Polish trooper and he recognized him at once. "Ha, Kanada," he said, "you want see those Germans you gave me?" Wells said he feared the worst as the Pole led him around behind a hay stack. The three Germans were lying dead - shot through the head. "But you ... you ... you can't do that!" spluttered the sergeant. "These men surrendered to me ... I thought you understood ... this is contrary to the Geneva Convention."

Troops of Les Fusiliers Mont-Royal supported by 'Sherman' tank of the Sherbrooke Fusiliers hunt, Falaise, France, 17 August, 1944. (Donald I. Grant)

Canadian tanks move into position for attack toward Falaise, between Hubert-Folie and Tilly-la-Campagne, August 8th, 1944.

"Geneva Convention," he repeated slowly, "Geneva Convention." Then with scorn in his voice he asked, "Kanada - were you in Poland? Were you in Warsaw?" These Poles were the wildest bunch of tank men I had ever seen. As far as they were concerned the only good German was a dead one. They even outclassed the Jewish lads in their desire to kill, kill, kill. Who could blame them? They had been waiting five years for this and they had old scores to settle with the Nazis. "Take that you bastard. That's for my little sister raped in the village. And that's for my old grandmother shot down in cold blood in the farm kitchen." Geneva Convention? Baloney! or should I say - Polish sausage!

AUGUST 9th, 1944 - FALAISE ROAD

We are in harbour tonight in a wood not far from Bretteville-le-Rabet. Don has just come back from another O-Group and called a SITREP of his own to "put us in the picture". We, Halpenny Force, are going to spearhead the attack. We start out tonight and follow the east side of the railway until we reach the railway embankment south-west of Grainville-Langanerie. This is our first objective and it has been given the code name CHRISTMAS. If we don't run into trouble we should make it to CHRISTMAS before midnight. For the first time in this operation we are to be the leading squadron. "As long as we keep that railway on our right we can't stray from our centre-line", I was telling myself. The ambushed B.C.R.'s were still haunting me. As Don explained the battle plan for Halpenny Force, I thought how close it paralleled that of GRIZZLY in East Anglia. Our task was to smash through, capture a hill and hold it. There was even a mine - a real one this time - at Potigny. If we could only do as well now as we had done then, this would be a piece of cake. I wonder where the British 9th Armour are tonight. My reverie is broken by Don gathering up his stuff and climbing out of GIRAFFE. Don explains that there is to be a switch in commanders. Major Peter Williamson climbs in to take over from Don - "ours not to reason why" - and we move off into the night. We reach our objective and report CHRISTMAS just before midnight. The original plan is to push on now to Point 180, just south-east of St. Germain-le-Vasson, and code-worded NEW YEARS. But now that has been changed and we are to push on to Point 206, which has also been given the code name NEW YEARS. Orders have just come through to "Stand by at 10 minutes to proceed to Point 206." "Waiting, waiting, waiting, always bloody well waiting...." (sung to the tune of Nicaea (1861) - John Bacchus Dykes). I feel the call of nature and get out and take the shovel from the back of the tank. I dug a hole on the side of the railway embankment. I hope I don't step on a mine. It's quiet but I can hear sporadic machine gun and rifle fire up ahead. Our own infantry - the Algonquins and the Argylls - are up there somewhere. I hope we don't get to shooting at each other in the dark. I climb back into GIRAFFE and listen in on the net. Somebody has reported a Tiger skulking around the orchard at St. Hilaire Farm. Then the report is denied.

"Tiger, Tiger, burning bright
In the forests of the night"
- William Blake (1757–1827) - The Tyger [Tiger] (1794)

AUGUST 10th, 1944

We all knew this was going to be one hell of a day. The most nerve wracking encounter that a tank man has to face is a frontal assault on a prepared position. The crayon dispositions of the various formations on the map gave the impression of an orderly attack, but in reality the situation ahead of us was in a state of confusion. Nobody really knew if the Argylls were in possession of Hill 195. They had apparently gone through Cintheaux and Hautmesnil and then leapfrogged right through the corridor to Hill 195, without a big battle for Grainville and Langannerie, or so it seemed. Word was that the South Albertas were supporting the Argylls. And where were the Algonquins? Somewhere up in front of us with the Argylls presumably. The state of flux up ahead continued all night as we sat waiting on the 10 minute notice to

move. At last came the dawn and at 0752 came the order to move off and we began rolling through orchards with the little hard green apples falling off the trees into the turret and making the floor like a roller-skating rink. We were going along in a line like a bunch of sheep. I just hoped Jerry wasn't luring us into the kind of trap he had sprung on the B.C.R.'s. Then I thought of all the formations up ahead and I couldn't believe we could have the same thing happen to us.

We bypassed Quesnay Wood on our left as the early ground mist was just beginning to lift on what promised to be a beautiful hot summer day. With the Wood behind us, we swung to the right up the slope to St. Hilaire Farm and passed it into the corridor which led to Hill 195. Everything seemed to be going well but you had the feeling that at any moment a Tiger or an Eighty-Eight would hit you. It was a very tense and dangerous feeling. We now began to run through the wheat field to seize our immediate objective at the top of Hill 195. We reached the crest and began to descend the forward slope. There we stalled. What were we waiting for? Nobody seemed to know what to do next. Suddenly we were in trouble. We began to get shot at from the screen of anti-tank guns and Tigers lurking in the heavily wooded area west of Fontaine-le-Pin. The objective, Point 206, was now within our grasp and the minehead buildings at Potigny were clearly visible. The sun was getting high and it was terribly hot in GIRAFFE. Around 1100 hours Lieutenant-Colonel Halpenny called an O-Group to lay out his plan of attack. Major Williamson left the tank and I jumped up on the commander's seat. I had no idea what we were supposed to do next. Fortunately he had left his binoculars for me. I then ordered George to come up in the turret and take my place as loader. It is a good thing that I did for in the next moment all hell broke loose. Tanks in front of ours were hit and burning - their crews bailing out. Some of our forward tanks started to back up. It became apparent that we had got ourselves in a box very much like that in which the B.C.R.'s had found themselves yesterday and in which they were almost totally destroyed. We couldn't back out as the escape route was also coming under murderous fire. General Kurt Meyer's [nicknamed "Panzermeyer"] fanatical 12th S.S. Hitlerjugend [Hitler Youth] Division were going to have a field day supported by Eighty-Eights and Tiger tanks. It was later disclosed that the enemy had found a map on an officer captured at Hill 140, with the battle plan marked on it. They knew our objective was NEW YEARS - Hill 206 - and he prepared his defence against us. An ambulance with a huge red cross painted on it was lying on its side and burning furiously. Those bloody bastards! The red crosses on that ambulance were nearly 5 feet [1.5m] high.

"I was not angry since I came to France until this instant."
- William Shakespeare (1564-1616) - Henry V, Act IV, Scene 7 (1599)

We are now in a desperate situation. We can't advance and we can't retire. We can't even see the bloody enemy. We are being shot-up with Eighty-Eights on every side. I heard somebody say "Retire" over the radio. Retire? Where to? We began to back up from the forward slope to the crest of the hill. For a moment I thought our own artillery was shelling us by mistake. But it was not so - it was those damned Tigers and Panthers in Quesnay Wood. In less than ten minutes, eight of our Shermans were brewing up - Freddie Hill's among them. Our only hope so far as I could see must come from the North as No. 2 Division or No. 3 Division broke through to rescue us. If only we could silence those guns in Quesnay Wood. Could we break out? Do a "Charge of the Light Brigade"? Not a chance - they had the hill covered - both backward and forward slopes, "Sunray" [code name for the Regimental Commander] was urging us to maintain the momentum. The order was to "Press on!" At last we began to get some help from our Tactical Air support. The artillery began to lay down red smoke and the Tyffies came down and rocketed the marked targets. If we could just silence the fire from Quesnay Wood, we could turn all our fire power in the direction of the enemy at Fontaine-le-Pin.

At the foot of the hill the C.C.S. [Casualty Clearing Station] had been set up and the regimental medical officers were overwhelmed with the casualties coming in. The infantry stretcher bearers were bringing in

tank crewmen as well as their own lads. Tank men horribly burned - with legs shot off and others in need of amputation. I felt for the morphine syrette in my left breast pocket. Yes, it was there. The evacuation route for the ambulances and jeeps was like a shooting gallery.

The battle-experienced officers now began to show their worth and some of the inexperienced ones too. Captain Curt Greenleaf was calmly walking about in a pair of high boots he had probably taken off a German officer and was regrouping No. 2 Squadron to fight back. He was awarded a well-deserved M.C. [Military Cross] for his leadership. Squadron Leaders Major Ned Amy of No. 1 Squadron and Major "Snuffy" Smith of No. 3 Squadron, both decorated for their gallantry in Italy, were a great steadying influence when near panic was gripping the Regiment. They went from tank to tank encouraging the crews and regrouping the remnants to fight back. My stomach was in a knot but outwardly I was cool and clear headed. Some Argylls were cowering in a gun pit where they had an anti-tank gun. The poor lads were shaking with fear. I guess they were afraid we might not see them and run over them with our tanks and of course the Jerries were pounding them with mortars and small arms fire as well as Eighty-Eights. The poor blighters had been there all night too. I leaned out of the turret and yelled at them - "Get that damned gun into action!" It worked! They responded to my command - snapped out of their terror and began firing toward Fontaine-le-Pin. Just then, what looked to me like one of our Bren-carriers, came speeding diagonally across our front. I thought it must be some of the Argyll boys pulling out fast, though I wondered how they had got so far out in front. It occurred to me that they might have been out there all night on a Recce or had been captured and were escaping back to our lines. The vehicle had a little white flag fluttering from its aerial. While I was puzzling about this - it took about two seconds - should I shoot or hold my fire? - it would be awful to kill our own lads. I remembered the Mosquito shot down by mistake at Hove. Sergeant "Sandy" Forsyth, on my right, thought it was enemy and fired on it. The vehicle blew up with a tremendous explosion. It was an enemy secret weapon - a "Beetle Tank". These little robots, officially named Goliath Tracked Mines [German name: Leichter Ladungsträger Goliath], were operated by remote control through a 2000 foot (600 metre) cable attached to their rear. They carried 130 or 220 lbs (60 or 100 kilograms) of High Explosives and were powered by an electric or gasoline motor. I don't think any of them did us any damage.

The heat inside GIRAFFE was getting unbearable. It was around 120 degrees [120 °F = 50 °C] outside the tank. In this blast furnace we had to think and fight for our lives. It was now high-noon and added to the scorching sun was the heat of the tank engine and the burning cordite. I had on my winter underwear - woolen long johns - my woolen battle dress and, over it all, my tank coveralls. The sweat was just pouring into my boots. It was trickling into my eyes and made them smart. If you touched the outside of the tank it blistered your hand. The landscape was shimmering in the sun making it hard for Gordie, the gunner, to get a good shot. I took off my web belt and holster and laid it on top of the wireless. I glanced over at George. He didn't look too happy. More Typhoons arrived and - swoosh - they fired their rockets into the enemy tanks not more than 1500 yards (1371 metres) in front of us. Such close tactical support was tremendous. These were the boys who had careened around in our tank at Crowborough. I wondered if Hal and Jim were up there and if they were thinking of us. Their shooting was deadly accurate. It had to be when they were working in such close support. More red smoke on the ridge in front of us - it looked like candy floss. Tanks began to get hit and brew up. I saw Sergeant Johnny Andrew's tank get hit and watched him and his crew bale out. Then he went back, climbed on the blazing tank and pulled out his wounded gunner - Moe Lutsky (Sergeant Andrews was awarded the Military Medal for this brave act). Somebody on the blower informing me that they were playing a machine gun off GIRAFFE's hull. We were on the extreme left end of the fighting line and very vulnerable. I acknowledged the message. What the hell could I do? I could see the sparks flying off the left side, but the Jerry machine gunner didn't worry me much, it was the Tigers out in front that I was worried about. If I directed my co-ax on to the machine gunner, I could no doubt silence him, but in the meantime we would get nailed by the Tiger. I couldn't use the bow gun because George,

The Tiger tank captured intact by 22 Battalion at La Romola stands alongside one of 4 Armoured Brigade's comparatively small Sherman tanks

THE MONTREAL DAILY STAR, MONDAY, JANUARY 28, 1946

Present O.C.

LT. COL. C. A. GREENLEAF, M.C., who commands the overseas battalion of the Canadian Grenadier Guards, which he is leading home to Montreal. Colonel Greenleaf is one of the few original members of the unit remaining with the battalion that was mobilized in 1940.

who operated it, was up in the turret in my place. I kept searching for the Tiger. More tanks brewing up. Again somebody on the radio urging us to hold on and fight back. I acknowledged the message and said we would hold the flank. Then to my chagrin I discovered I was on the I/C. Damn! I remembered how I had once chuckled when Lieutenant Freddie Hill had made the same faux pas. The crew must have thought I was a bloody fool. Gordie Hatch's voice over the I/C - "I can see him Ossie! See him? There - to the left of that hedgerow!" I raised my binoculars slowly. "Yes - O.K. I see him too." A big lumbering 62-ton monster all camouflaged with pieces of hedge. He was moving - his gun swinging on us. I gave Gordie the fire-order - "Gunner! Traverse left - steady - ON. Thirteen hundred - enemy hornet - FIRE!" In that same instant I could hear a noise like an express train approaching - then a sickening rending crash as the Tiger's shell smashed into us. There was a blow on my left ankle like somebody had hit me with a baseball bat - I fell off the seat on which I was standing, on to the turret floor.

AFTER THE FIRE, A STILL SMALL VOICE

There was a loud hissing - the fire extinguishers? - I could sense Gordie pushing his way up and out - and George heaving up with all his strength - then the fire - I knew I couldn't last long - 4 or 5 seconds - the flames were licking my face - up my nostrils - it felt like ice water being poured through my veins. Death wasn't far away now - another second and it would be all over for me - then I seemed to be twisting and turning and writhing dizzily - a horrible feeling of vertigo - like in a boxing match when your opponent has nailed you with a left hook and you are going down and out. The whole tank seemed to be writhing in its death throes. Then freedom - clean air - above the tank looking down - was this death? No pain - I seemed to be floating in mid-air about 20 feet [6m] above the tank - I could see the battlefield below - then - thud - I was back in my body and I was lying crumpled up in the wheat field. (Corporal Warren "Johnny" Buck was moving his tank up behind ours and years later, at a Regimental Reunion, he said I exploded out of the turret like a cork out of a bottle of Calvados!). I was on fire - my clothes were almost gone - my hair was alight - I thought my front teeth were smashed out - I ripped off what was left of my smouldering battle dress tunic - I groped in the pocket for the morphine syrette - broke off the glass tip and jabbed it into my arm - I thought - "They'll find what's left of my tunic - just the yoke with the "GRENADIER GUARDS" red shoulder flashes, and they'll report me dead. I tried to crawl away from the burning tank - which was going up now like fireworks on the First of July. I remember thinking of all that ammo - those grenades - phosphorus bombs - Browning ammo - and those 4000 cigarettes! What an inferno. My face was really hurting now and I pressed it down into the wheat where the dew felt cooling. Then I looked down at my feet. My boots were full of blood and the laces had burst. Was my foot off? I couldn't tell. I tried to crawl away from the tank. A burst of machine gun fire whistled over my head. "Keep down, you bloody fool!" I told myself. Some bullets went through the calf of my leg. A searing pain at the back of my neck and I realized that it was the metal band of the headsets glowing red hot branding my neck. I ripped them off. I looked down at my hands - Thank God I had kept my asbestos loader's gauntlets on - what had once been white fabric was now charred threads but my hands were untouched by the flames. I could hear the growl and whine of tank engines, and the squeak and clank of tank tracks. A new terror seized me. Our boys were regrouping - they were going to move down from the crest of the hill again. They'll run over me - now I knew how the infantry felt - they'll never see me lying in this wheat - I struggled to raise myself up in hopes that they might see me - a tank stopped close by - I heard someone say "Look at that poor devil!" I must have looked like the devil with my burnt, blackened face and my clothes were smouldering rags. The Crew Commander, Lieutenant George Stanbury, jumped down from his tank and knelt down beside me and gave me a shot of morphine - "That'll help you," he said comfortingly. I knew I shouldn't have 2 shots of morphine so close together but I was too far gone now to care. I just lay in the wheat and waited for death. Somewhere I could hear George Holden crying out - "O my God help me!" Poor George - I couldn't see him anywhere. I tried to answer him but my lips were so swollen I could only mumble. My eyes began to scab over too. This was the end. I felt like I was going down a long dark tunnel. So this was what death was

These pictures of GIRAFFE were taken by Lt.-Col. George Hale, D.S.O. in May of 1945 when in company with Lt.-Col. C.A. Greenleaf, M.C. he visited the battleground at Hill 195. Notice how the turret is turned upside down as it landed on 10 August, 1944. Also see how I tried to get some cover from the tree and brush which would have been thicker in August.

Major G. R. Hale
D.S.O.

like - not too bad - I thought "I wish I could live just so I could tell people not to be afraid of death" - it was so easy - no more pain - I was floating away - then, just at the point where I should have left this world, I felt myself returning. The pain came surging back - I gave up trying to live - I let go - it seemed like I heard a voice saying: "Oh no you don't. I gave you your life and I'll take it away." "O.K." I answered, "Whoever you are - God? If you're so great - you take over."

I don't know how long I lay in the wheat field after that. The pain was terrible. To keep my mind off it I began reciting Shakespeare:

"Methinks I am a prophet new inspired
And thus expiring do fortell of him:
His rash fierce blaze of riot cannot last,
For violent fires soon burn out themselves;
Small showers last long, but sudden storms are short;
He tires betimes that spurs too fast betimes;
With eager feeding food doth choke the feeder:
Light vanity, insatiate cormorant,
Consuming means, soon preys upon itself.
This royal throne of kings, this seat of Mars...."
- William Shakespeare (1564-1616) - Richard II, Act II, Scene 1 (1595)

I could hear someone crawling through the wheat toward me. "It's a Jerry," I thought, "he'll put a bullet through my head." I reached instinctively for my pistol only to recall that I had unbuckled my web belt and holster and left my pistol on top of the wireless set. "Oh, Hell! I can't even take one with me as I go!" I moaned. The wheat parted in front of my face and a friendly voice said, "You can't stay here Ossie - the stretcher bearers can't come up this far." It was Joe Arnold - a tank driver who had just lost his tank but had escaped unhurt. "I can't walk, Joe," I managed to blubber through swollen lips, "my leg is broken." Joe didn't say another word. He picked me up and put me across his broad shoulders and carried me right through the wheat. For some unexplained reason no shot was fired at us. A minute before, you couldn't have raised a hand in that wheat field. When Joe felt he had carried me to a place of safety, he put me down gently. I thought my foot would fall off. "You'll be O.K. here Ossie," he said reassuringly, "I'll send the stretcher bearers up for you." I remember the terrible pain and the thirst. I remember the medical orderly too. He was from the Argyll and Sutherland Highlanders. He worked fast. The poor guy was scared but he was doing his job bravely and efficiently. He cut away what was left of my trousers and put a shell dressing on my buttocks and a tourniquet on my leg. After a few minutes two stretcher bearers arrived, lifted me onto a stretcher and carried me down the hill to the casualty clearing area. I later heard that the medical orderly got the Military Medal for his brave work that day. He deserved it. It must have been hell giving first aid under conditions like that. Joe Arnold deserved a medal too. The stretcher bearers put the stretcher down beside some others. [Due to his injuries and morphine, my father believed it was Joe Arnold who carried him across the field when it was in fact Lieutenant Donald Armitage Ross, C.G.G. who performed this selfless and heroic act and never felt it necessary to correct my father about it. This came up during an informal reunion where my mother, Beverley Osborne, was present and had a private conversation with Lt Donald Ross.]

We seemed to be near the road where we could easily be loaded on to the jeep ambulances that were shuttling back and forth to the R.A.P. [Regimental Aid Post]. I remember clearly that Lieutenant-Colonel Halpenny was there. I was surprised to find him so close to the action. He said - "You've done a good job, boys" and generally spoke encouragingly to us. He seemed very much in command of the situation. I wondered if he really knew how bad it was at the top of the Hill. I guess he did. Anyway he cheered us up

The GIRAFFE holed by a Panzer at Hill 195 Normandy - Aug 10, 1944
The tank blew up and the turret landed back on the hull upside down!

Gdsm [Jack] Kane (Driver)
Gdsm [Gordie] Hatch (Gunner)
Gdsm [George] Holden (Co-Driver - acting as Loader & Wireless Operator)
Cpl [Robert] Osborne ([acting as] Crew Commander)

Gdsm Holden escaped but died of wounds.

and I shall never forget the lift he gave us by being there and speaking to us. A fellow on a stretcher next to me complained - "The damn bastards burnt my moustache off!" Moe Lutsky was lying next to me on the other side covered with a blanket. "Where did they get you Moe?" I burbled through my swollen lips. "They shot off both my feet, Ossie," he said. "That's tough, Moe." "I always had ingrown toenails, anyway," he chuckled. That was Jewish humour and raw courage at its best.

As we lay there at the bottom of the Hill waiting to be evacuated, I could see out of my swollen eyelids a tank driver that I knew. He was sitting bolt upright against a tree trunk and staring straight ahead. He didn't seem to be wounded as far as I could see and there were no signs of burns on his tank suit. I spoke to him but there was no answer. I called him by name. He gave no sign that he had heard me - just kept staring uncomprehendingly at the Hill. I turned to Jack Kane who was lying nearby. "What the hell's the matter with him?" I asked. Jack tried to shush me up. Then it dawned on me that the poor fellow was in a state of deep shock.

We were loaded onto jeeps - two stretchers to a jeep. As we drove out of the field and on to the Falaise road we came under some heavy shelling. The driver of our jeep turned it into the ditch and jumped off and lay down for cover. Some shrapnel hit the lad next to me and he bled to death.

I remember the jeep stopping and my stretcher being unloaded and carried up a long flight of steps. Was it a church they were using as a C.C.S.? Someone was speaking to me. "Remember me, Corporal?" I sure did. It was the fellow who took my chocolate ration and whom I had threatened to punch up if he didn't hand it back. Well, I was at his mercy now! He asked me how the Regiment were making out. I said that we were getting a hell of a beating but that we were fighting back. Then I passed out.

There are those who had said that we should have maintained the momentum. If we had pushed on through the night of 9th/10th of August, we might have captured Point 206 and reported NEW YEARS, but then we might have got into a SNAFU in the dark. Major-General George Kitching C.C. [Order of Canada], C.B. [Order of the Bath], C.B.E. [Order of the British Empire], D.S.O. [Distinguished Service Order], C.D. [Canadian Forces Decoration] was criticized for not pressing home the attack more vigorously. Hindsight is always 20/20 vision. I doubt that any troops could have done better than our brigade on the Hill. General Kurt Meyer's 12th S.S. Panzer Division and 89th Infantry Division were "old pros" and they had the advantage of waiting for us to come to them. They knew our plans because they had captured an officer carrying a flap showing the centre-lines and objectives of the Corps. So they set up their anti-tank screens, dug in and deployed their Panthers and Tigers. We ran into an ambush. If we made a mistake it was when we stalled after capturing the crest of the Hill. We should never have been caught in the open on the forward slope - the "killing ground". That day - August 10th, 1944 - the Regiment lost a third of its Shermans with 59 of their crews killed or wounded. Sergeant Walter Irvine, whose troop was L.O.B. (Left Out of Battle) that day, said it was an awful feeling to realize that so many of his friends were gone. The thing that stunned those who were left was that in half a day of fighting nearly half of No. 2 Squadron was killed or wounded. But the Grenadiers now had hold of Hill 195 and nobody was going to dislodge them.

"I praise you, Lord, because you have saved me and kept my enemies from gloating over me. I cried to you for help, O Lord my God, and you healed me. You kept me from the grave. I was on my way to the depths below, but you restored my life."
- Bible (GNB) - Psalm 30:1-3

"Death drew its ropes tight around me,
the horrors of the grave closed in on me ;
Then I called on the name of the Lord:

Near Bretteville-le-Rabet, 14 August 1944

'O Lord, save me!'
The Lord is gracious and righteous;
our God is full of compassion.
The Lord protects the simplehearted;
when I was in great need, he saved me.
Be at rest once more, O my soul,
for the Lord has been good to you.
For you, O Lord, have delivered my soul from death,
my eyes from tears, my feet from stumbling,
that I may walk before the Lord in the land of the living.
I believed; therefore I said, 'I am greatly afflicted.'
And in my dismay I said, 'All men are liars.' "
- Bible (NIV) - Psalm 116:4-11

AUGUST 10th-13th, 1944

My memories of the hospital at Bayeux are hazy and fleeting - like pictures flashed on a screen. A sequence of incidents interspersed with long periods of unconsciousness. One picture is of a night bombing raid on the hospital. The whole place was shaking under the concussions of the bombs and our own flak failing back through the canvass tents. Some of the nursing sisters were justifiably in quite a state of fright and I remember calling out: "There's nothing to worry about, everything will be all right!" I was so doped I hardly knew what I was saying anyway and after the fierce battle at Hill 195 I guess it really was nothing to worry about. Another image is of a Doctor and Nurse trying to give a blood transfusion to a badly wounded lad from the 12th S.S. Panzer - the Division we had been fighting at Hill 195. I expect that these boys had been fed a lot of propaganda and told that if they were wounded and captured by the Canadians that we would give them Jewish blood. At any rate he was putting up a terrific struggle to prevent them putting the transfusion needle in his arm. Finally, the Canadian doctor gave up in disgust - "All right then, die, damn you!" he shouted and walked away. And the wounded German died not long afterward.

In a letter written on August 15, 1977, Jack Kane wrote the following:
"I'll never forget, we were on opposite sides of the big hospital tent, and through the eye slits of my bandaged head I could see you lying on your belly, and your backside was just a big piece of charcoal."

I was not aware that any of GIRAFFE's crew were in the hospital with me. The last memory I have of the hospital at Bayeux is the sound of a tank engine, or at least what I thought was a tank engine. "Oh, my God," I thought, "the Jerries have broken through and they are so short of tank crews that they are putting me back in a tank." The next thing I remember is seeing someone leaning over me and he's wearing pilot's wings. Now I realized that the engine I had heard was that of an aircraft, not a tank. (An easy mistake to make because some of our tanks were equipped with a Wright Whirlwind aircraft engine. I recall an air alert being sounded in Brighton when our tanks were manoeuvring on the South Downs). The pilot leaned closer and asked - "How do you feel?" "Not too bad," I mumbled, "what is this, an aircraft?" "Yes," he said, "This is a Dak (Dakota or DC3) - we're going to fly you to England. It will be a little bumpy on takeoff but once we're airborne and over the Channel it will be smooth flying." By now the aircraft was filling up with stretcher cases and there were walking-wounded standing in the centre aisle. "How would you like an egg-flip?" the pilot asked. "Fine," I said. He came back with some kind of eggnog drink well laced with something else - rum? He put it to my lips and helped me drink it. The engines started revving up. The plane started to shake. I could feel the wheels jolting over the runway. As we gathered speed I thought the Dak would shake apart. The engines grew louder and steadier. The ground was slipping away. The shaking stopped. We were airborne. It was my first ride in an airplane.

A Memorable Victory
1946-01-18
The Montreal Daily Star

Caption: This photograph of the painting by Adam Sherrif [sic] Scott, of Montreal, Canadian war artist, will be of immemorial interest to all members of the Canadian Grenadier Guards. It depicts the action in which the tanks of the Guards smashed the German defences and captured Hill 195, an operation which was a stepping-stone to the ultimate isolation and destruction of the German forces in the Falaise pocket.

(See appendix for more on this painting by Adam Sherriff Scott)

The next thing I remember, I was lying on the stretcher on the tarmac. The sun was shining down on me and a W.A.A.F. was crouching beside me and asking - "How are you?" "I'm fine," I replied, "but where am I?" "You're in England - You're safe now - this is Swindon." I tried to place Swindon on the map of England. Then her lovely English voice again - "Is there anything I can do for you? Could I help you send a message to your next of kin?" "Yes - yes!" I said, "Send a message to my mother. Tell her I'm wounded but back in England." She began writing on one of those brown Field Service post cards. I still have that post card. It is stamped across one side - HAVE ARRIVED IN U.K. The rest of it looks like this:

I am ~~quite~~ well.
I have been admitted into hospital
{ ~~sick~~ wounded } and am going on well and hope to be discharged soon
~~I am being sent down to the base~~
~~I have received your { letter telegram parcel }~~
Letter follows at first opportunity.
I have received no letter from you
Signature only Robert E. Osborne
Date 13.8.44

The whole [pre-printed] card was filled out by the W.A.A.F. and signed by her. I did not even have the strength to sign my own name.

SWINDON - TAPLOW

The journey in the ambulance was a nightmare. Every bump in the road sent searing pain through my body. I don't know where they were supposed to be taking me. There was a famous hospital where burned air crew were taken. It was at East Grinstead. Whether they were heading for there I don't know. I only know that I lay in a sea of pain and was near death. The distance from Swindon to Taplow must have been around 65-70 miles (105-112 kms). There was a medical orderly in the ambulance with me. He hammered on the back of the cab and the driver came to a stop. He and the orderly got out and held a consultation beside the ambulance. I overheard the orderly say - "This chap is not going to make it - we've got to get him to the nearest hospital - fast - he won't last much longer." There was a further delay. I suppose they were studying a map. Then we rumbled off again. I drifted in and out of consciousness. We stopped. I was lifted carefully out. It was night. I could see just enough to know that I was being carried into a building. People were busy around me. I passed out. When I came to again I was aware of someone handling the casualty tag around my neck. A voice asked - "Can you hear me, Osborne?" "Yes," I mumbled. Again the voice - "You gave us quite a scare last night, but you're going to be all right now." "Thank you," I tried to form the words through lips that felt like inflated inner-tubes, "I appreciate all you're doing for me." I heard the voice speak to someone else - "Continue the penicillin and the blood transfusions. I don't want to move him too much for the next twenty-four hours. When he's stronger we'll have a closer look at him. There may be a fractured pelvis here too. Just keep him as comfortable as you can for the time being." The voice was that of Doctor Howard Hamlin and he was speaking to Nursing Sister Ostiguy. The place was No. 11 Canadian General Hospital on Lady Astor's estate at Taplow in Buckinghamshire.

"The last enemy to be destroyed is death."
- Bible (KJV) - I Corinthians 15:26

ELEVEN CANADIAN GENERAL HOSPITAL

TAPLOW, BUCKS   ENGLAND

—Nakash Photo
**Cpl. Robert Osborne
WOUNDED:**

WOUNDED IN FRANCE:
WOUNDED
Canadian Armoured Corps

OSBORNE, Robert Ernest, Cpl., D26348, Mrs. Bessie Osborne (Mother), Magog, Que.

Corporal Osborne was serving with the 22nd Armored Regiment (Canadian Grenadier Guards). He is the son of Mrs. B. S. Osborne, of Magog.

PAX IN BELLO

As I lay in the hospital bed between times of consciousness and unconsciousness with all the sounds of the ward floating toward me - for I was still unable to see because of the burn scabs over my eyes - I became suffused in a great sense of peace. It dawned upon my consciousness that for me the War was over and miraculously I had survived it. There was no longer any question of who would win. I felt that the battle of Falaise had been decisive. The Jerries were on the run and from the voice of the news broadcasters that I picked up intermittently, reporters like Matthew Halton, I knew that the enemy was getting a terrible pounding from our armour and aircraft. The broadcasters spoke of the "Cauldron" in the Falaise Gap. It had become a shooting gallery for our lads as the crack 21st Panzer and the powerful 12th S.S. that had given us such a hard time at Hill 195 were being pulverized. Those that were still alive tried to escape by night from the "Pocket". Those grey winding columns like some mortally wounded dragon in its death throes were being cut to pieces. But I no longer had to think of war. Before ever I was fit to fight again it would all be over. Just a few days ago I was surrounded by enemies bent on my destruction; now I was surrounded by friends bent on my recovery. I would breathe deeply and say to myself "breathe in health - breathe in life." Like those who echoed Émile Coué de la Châtaigneraie - "Every day in every way I was getting better and better." I *must* get well. I *will* get well. I had netted-in my last wireless set, fed the last belt of ammo into the Browning M.G., given my last fire order, spent my last day constantly facing death. From now on I was going to be embracing life. The time for hatred was over and the time for love was beginning. The only words that could express what I felt during these days of convalescence were those of the Bible - "The peace that passeth understanding" (Phil. 4:7). It is a wonderful, wonderful feeling. Only those who have experienced it can ever know what it is like because it defies all description. Every hour, every day of life from now on, was a bonus snatched from the jaws of death. Surely it is what Rupert Brooke meant when he wrote:

"We have gained a peace unshaken by pain for ever."
- Rupert Brooke (1887-1915) - Safety (1914)

TELL YOUR TROUBLES TO THE PADRE

14 Aug 44
No 3. C.A.C.R.U.
Cdn Army Overseas

My Dear Mrs Osborne,
This is just a note to let you know that your son is in hospital here in England and coming along nicely. As you probably know by now, that he was wounded in action and gave a very good account of himself.
I saw him today and he asked me to write you and let you know that he is on the road to recovery. His tank was hit and the shell broke his leg and he got a few cuts and bruises around his face. He also got some slight burns but from what I could see nothing appears to be very serious.
His spirits are good and he was pretty cheery considering that he had only arrived by air evacuation from France last night. The regiment was in a pretty busy spot for a time and gave a good account of itself.
You can address a letter directly to him at No. 11 Cdn General Hospital (R.C.A.M.C.) Cdn Army Overseas. You have a fine son and a man everyone is very proud of in the Regiment.
22 Cdn Armd Regt (C.G.G.)
Yours Sincerely
S.F. McAdam, Lieut.

No. 11 Canadian General Hospital.
19 August 1944

CANADIAN NATIONAL TELEGRAPHS

CASUALTY (REPORT DELIVERY)   OTTAWA

16 AUGUST 1944

TO:- MRS BESSIE OSBORNE
MAGOG P Q

10320 MINISTER OF NATIONAL DEFENCE SINCERELY REGRETS TO INFORM YOU D26348 CORPORAL ROBERT ERNEST OSBORNE HAS BEEN OFFICIALLY REPORTED WOUNDED IN ACTION TENTH AUGUST 1944 NATURE OF WOUNDS DESCRIBED AS PETROL BURNS FACE SHELL FRAGMENT WOUND BUTTOCK LEFT KNEE STOP WHEN ADDRESSING MAIL ADD WORDS IN HOSPITAL IN BOLD LETTERS AFTER NAME OF UNIT FOR QUICK DELIVERY STOP WHEN FURTHER INFORMATION BECOMES AVAILABLE IT WILL BE FORWARDED AS SOON AS RECEIVED

PREPAID   DIRECTOR OF RECORDS
                                OFFICER I/C RECORDS

MAGOG, P. Que.
August 20, 1944

MINISTER of NATIONAL DEFENCE
OTTAWA
Ontario
ATTENTION: 10320 Minister of National Defence
           Director of Records

Dear Sir:

With reference to your telegram of August 16th, 1944, concerning D26348 Cpl. Robert Ernest Osborne, it will be appreciated if you will forward to me as soon as possible, any information you may have regarding the whereabouts and extent of facial injuries of my son.

Yours very truly,

Bessie Osborne

(Mrs. B. S. C. Osborne)

Mrs B. S. Osborne,
Magog, P.Q., Canada

Dear Mrs. Osborne

I am writing this in the hope that by doing so, you may be spared needless fret and worry.

Your son Bob has just come into our Military Hospital here. He was recently wounded in Normandy, as no doubt you have been informed.

His wounds are painful; but not serious. He is coming along splendidly, and is a model patient. "The darling of the nurses." He has a few burns and some lacerations & shrapnel wounds which will take a time to heal, but you can he assured that there is no cause for you to be alarmed. Due to the position of his injuries, he finds it difficult to write, so I have taken it upon myself to write this letter for him. I knew you would want to hear from, or about him, as soon as possible.

I can give you no idea how long he will be here. Burns, as you know take some time to heal, and he will not be allowed to leave until he is completely recovered. He is being given the utmost in treatment and care, and by the way in which he is responding I should say it will not be too long before he is up and around again as fit as ever.

He is a great lad, cheerful all the time, and never a word of complaint at the tediousness of having to lie in an uncomfortable position. As I have said, the nurses "love him", and that fact alone is guarantee that every want is promptly looked after. "Our best patient", the nurses on his ward all say.

As a mother, I know you will not be satisfied until you have him by your side once again. Let us hope and pray that will be soon. Meanwhile, be thankful that he has come through his experience of battle in safety, and that when his hospitalization is over, he will come home to you safe and sound, the proud son of a proud mother.

Strangely enough, just as I finished the above paragraph, Bob's doctor dropped in for a smoke, and he tells me that they are tremendously pleased with him. The chief trouble, as I mentioned above, is the place where he was burned and hit by shrapnel, making it hard for him to be comfortable until they are healed - the rear buttocks. But the Doctor says he will be right as rain in a month or so.

So, dear Mrs. Osborne, you may be thankful that Bob is doing so well, and sleep peacefully in the assurance that it will not be long before his wounds are completely healed. Thankful, indeed, too, that he is alive, for he had an almost miraculous escape.

Until Bob is able to write, I shall keep in touch with you.

E.H. Costigan

H/Captain E.H, Costigan,

Chaplain (P), #11 Canadian General Hospital - Canadian Army Overseas

H. Q. C. R. U.
Cdn. Army Overseas.
22 Aug. '44.

Dear Mrs. Osborne,

I've just come back from a base hospital here in England where I saw your boy Bob, who as you probably know was wounded in Normandy. I have known Bob so long when I was chaplain with the Grenadiers & he certainly is a grand boy. I told him I would write to you today.

He has a broken leg and some few burns but he is doing very well & while I know you will be very sorry he is suffering at the moment you will have the very great consolation of knowing that soon he will be well & that you will have him with you safe & sound for many years to come. Some of his pals & mine have been killed but your fine brave boy has been spared to take care of you. He will be writing you himself soon.

With all good wishes,

Yours very sincerely,

F.J. Sinnamon. Major.

Canadian Red Cross Hospital, Taplow, Bucks.

August 22nd, 1944.

Mrs. B.S.C. Osborne,
Magog, Quebec.

Dear Mrs. Osborne,

Re: D.26348, Corporal Robert E. Osborne

Mr. Ralston has directed me to acknowledge receipt of your letter of August 20th, in which you ask for information regarding the present whereabouts of your son, the above named soldier, and the extent of the facial injuries which he received.

The Minister is keenly aware of your anxiety and every effort is being made by the officers of the Department to furnish the next of kin with the fullest possible information regarding battle casualties. You will be advised immediately by wire when this Headquarters receives further particulars.

In the meantime I have forwarded your letter to the responsible officers and can assure you that they will give prompt attention to any incoming message relating to Corporal Osborne.

Yours very truly,

(H. A. Dyde) Colonel,
Military Secretary.

Director of Records

Passed to you for necessary action and further reply direct, please.

Colonel,
Military Secretary.

No. 11 - TAPLOW

Dr. Hamlin came into the ward and said I would have to lie face down for a long time. I had been severely wounded in the buttocks and, when more healing had taken place, he was going to try some skin grafts. My left ankle (talus) was fractured and I had some gunshot wounds in my legs. I also had burns to my face and back of my neck. "Gee, Doc, how am I going to explain getting wounded there?" I asked - meaning my backside. "Well, Osborne, just tell the folks back home that you were wounded in Normandy," he replied. "Yeah," quipped the fellow in the next bed, "that's better than saying you were wounded at the front!"

Today, Dr. Hamlin came in and looked at my toes peeking out from the cast. "Let me see you wiggle them," he said. I tried as hard as I could but I couldn't move them at all. They were a dark purple. "You get those toes moving, son, or we're going to have to take that foot off!" This alarmed me and I tried and tried all afternoon to make my toes move. At last I lay back exhausted. I just couldn't seem to make my toes respond to the message my brain was sending them. I fell asleep and when I awoke I tried again. I thought I saw a slight twitch. Was I imagining it? I tried again and this time I was sure there was some movement. Nursing Sister Ostiguy came along and stopped in front of my bed. "How are you making out with those toes?" she asked. "Sister," I replied, "I may be imagining it but watch now and see if I am moving them a little." I tried again and this time I was sure. "You've got it," she said, "keep it going, the Doctor will be pleased to see what you've accomplished." "Not half as much as I am!" I replied.

While I lay face down on my bed I was conscious of a radio blaring. It got on my nerves but I did not want to complain because the other patients obviously enjoyed it. I heard for the first time the name of a crooner called Frank Sinatra. I also heard that the girls back home were swooning all over the place whenever they heard this voice. I tried to figure it out. How could they be so stupid as to swoon over this 97lb weakling. If they wanted a hero-figure, why didn't they choose someone like Clark Gable - a real man in my books. But this phoney guy Sinatra! I wasn't sure I wanted to go home. Maybe it would be better to remain in England and marry an A.T.S., W.A.A.F., W.R.N.S. or Land Army girl - somebody who knew what this war was all about than go back home to the unreality I was hearing over the radio. One song I did like was "I'll Be Seeing You." Another, which seemed appropriate to my situation, was:

"It's a lovely day tomorrow
Tomorrow is a lovely day
Come and feast your tear dimmed eyes
On tomorrow's clear blue skies ...
Tomorrow is a lovely day"
- Recorded by Frank Sinatra (1915-1998) - It's a lovely day tomorrow (1940)

A favourite was "Long Ago and Far Away".

When I first came into the hospital, I was so badly off that I hardly cared if I lived or died. The sister that dressed my wounds today was really cute. When she got through I said rather cheekily, "You know Sister, if I could get out of this bed and walk, I'd ask you for a date." Nursing Sister Fox replied, "You're getting better all right" and walked provocatively down the ward. They took me up to the O.R. today. The nurses were standing around the end of the table and the anaesthetist said - "Let me hear you count to ten." Long before I got to ten the Pentothal had done its work and I was off in cloud cuckoo-land. I woke up back in the ward to discover that I had a new cast on my leg. The orderly came to put a drying device over it. He told me that they had really planned to amputate my foot and I had been all prepped for them to do so. Just before he prepared to take it off, Dr. Hamlin walked over to window and stood there for some time

PTE. RICHARD EVERARD CONNOR, 21, was killed in action October 28, according to word received by his parents, Mr. and Mrs. Henry Connor, of Magog. Pte. Connor was born near Belfast, Ireland, May 24, 1923, and came to Canada with his parents in June, 1926. He attended Magog High School and was a former King Scout. Prior to enlistment he was employed by the British Overseas Airways Corp. at Dorval as an airplane engine mechanic. Pte. Connor joined up in May, 1943, and went overseas a year later. He served in France and Belgium as a regimental signaller with the Royal Hamilton Light Infantry for two months. Besides his parents he is survived by five brothers Robert and John of Magog, Lt. James Connor, R.C.A., Petawawa Edward, of Waterloo, and Norman of Vancouver, and one sister, Claire of Magog.

Major "Paddy" Sinnamon

deciding what to do. Then he turned quickly around and said, "I think we'll try to save it." What momentous decisions these surgeons had to make. Decisions that would affect a man's whole future.

FROM THE "MONTREAL STAR"

November 30th, 1944
MISSING - F/O W. H. L. BILLINGHAM, 21, eldest son of Mr. and Mrs. W. Bellingham of Magog, who has been reported missing following air operations overseas. He enlisted in the R.C.A.F. in March 1942 at the age of 19, qualified for his wings at Uplands a year later, and was posted overseas in June 1943. Flying Officer Bellingham is a former student of Magog High School.

KILLED - PRIVATE R. E. M. CONNOR, 21, son of Mr. and Mrs. Henry Connor of Magog has been killed on the Western Front. He was serving as a regimental signaller in the Royal Hamilton Light Infantry when fatally wounded.

FALAISE

> For the deeds of this proud September
> While we render to God the praise
> Let us pause, look back and remember
> The men who died at Falaise.
> ----------
> Their spirit has lived to guide us
> And forward our swift advance;
> On their phantom feet beside us
> They showed us the way through France.
> ----------
> They gave us her towns in order
> They went with us step by step
> From the Orne to the German border
> Through Paris, Rouen, Dieppe.
> ----------
> They helped our ranks to rally
> And follow the fleeing host
> Their courage swept us to Calais
> And gave us the Channel coast.
> ----------
> May shame be the lasting burden
> Of him who today forgets
> That these went with us to Verdun
> And opened the road to Metz.
> ----------
> In the moment of crowned endeavour,
> In the triumph of wonderful days
> Let us hold in our hearts, and forever
> The men who fell at Falaise.

- William Henry Ogilvie (1869-1963) - Falaise [unverified]

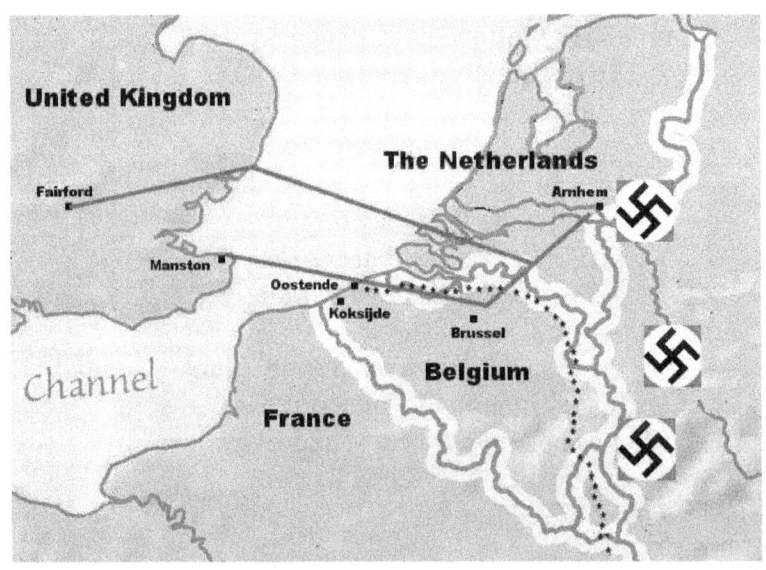

GOOD SHOW

"Good show!" they said as they sat at ease
In the Officers Mess shooting the breeze
and tippling drinks.
This was the praise they gave to the squadron
lost at Falaise

"Good show!" How could they be expected to know
Of the awful stench and the burning glow
of the brewed up tanks.
This was the memory of all the ranks
who fell fighting in that awful hell.

"Cheers!" they said as they raised glasses
to toast the memory of those that fell at 195
How could they know of the desperate plight
of those who didn't survive.
They could never know of the blood and fears of
those who were ambushed from the Wood.

"Good show!" they said as they stood at the bar
of the Brigade Mess and filled their jar.
This was the toast they gave to the ghosts of
men who would never come home again.

For them it will always be "Good show!" and "Cheers!"
let's have a few more beers!
How different to those who know.

- [Unknown reference]

TAPLOW - SEPTEMBER 17th, 1944 - A BRIDGE TOO FAR

It was a beautiful September day. The sun was shining and it was one of those rare English autumn days.

"Season of mists and mellow fruitfulness
Close bosom friend of the maturing sun ..."
- John Keats (1795-1821) - To Autumn (1819)

Somebody had the brilliant idea that our beds could be pushed outside. It was the first time I had breathed the fresh air since the tenth of August. It was a wonderful tonic for us. We lay in the warm sun and luxuriated in the smells and sounds and sights of Lady Astor's beautiful estate. It reminded me of those lazy, hazy, days we used to get at home at this time of the year, when the campers had left the cottages and there was nobody on the lake but the loons. I was just lying there revelling in these fantasies and letting the gentle sun penetrate me with its healing power. Then quite suddenly we heard the sound of aircraft and looking up we saw dozens and dozens of airplanes towing gliders. The aircraft were Dakotas [Douglas C-47 Dakotas] and the gliders were painted with white stripes around the fuselage. The sky was soon filled with them. Something really big was on. Maybe this was the operation that would bring final victory in Europe. Give the coup de grace to the reeling German armies. Still the planes and gliders kept going over

Cliveden ("valley among cliffs") is an Italianate mansion and estate at Taplow, Buckinghamshire, England. Once home to Lady Nancy Astor.

and the afternoon was filled with their noise. Later we learned that this was OPERATION MARKET GARDEN - the largest airborne operation ever mounted [in excess of 1500 transports and 1000 gliders on the first day and similar numbers the following day]. If it had come off, it would have shortened the duration of the war by months. Unfortunately, the unsuccessful attempt to gain the bridges over the Rhine was costly and probably delayed the Allied victory by months.

TAPLOW HOSPITAL

Just after lunch Dr. Hamlin came in followed by Nursing Sister Ostiguy. He sat down on the side of my bed and held my chin up so as to get a better look at the scabs on my face. "This is going to hurt, Osborne, but we've got to get those scabs off or your face will be badly scarred" "O.K. you're the doctor," I replied. Sister Ostiguy held a small tray and Captain Hamlin used a pair of tweezers to pick off the scabs. He was right, it did hurt like hell, especially around my chin and upper lip where the hair had grown right through the scabs. The area where my moustache had been was particularly painful. "We're almost done now," Hamlin said, as the sweat poured from me. When the last bit was removed he turned to the nursing sister and asked, "Do you have one of those things that women use to spray on perfume?" "You mean an atomizer?" "Yes." "I don't have one but one of the other girls has." "Can you get it for me?" "Right now, doctor?" "Yes, these burns on his left temple are third-degree and infected. I suspect septicaemia. I want to try spraying them with penicillin." Sister Ostiguy hurried off down the ward, her starched linen swishing as she went. She soon returned with the little atomizer and Dr. Hamlin went to work. While she shielded my eyes, he began spraying on the penicillin. "It's too near to your eyes, Osborne," he said as he squeezed the little rubber bulb on the atomizer, "I don't like infection in that area of the face." The method worked and the infection was arrested and cleared up, thanks to the invention of the new wonder drug "penicillin" and the practical ingenuity of Dr. Howard Hamlin.

This being Sunday we had a lot of visitors in the ward. A woman went past my bed took one look at me and immediately threw up.

TAPLOW - LADY ASTOR

Lady Astor visited the hospital often. When she came into our ward she made straight for my bed. I was her favourite. She told me that she had a nephew in General George S. Patton's United States Third Army tank force. I think that fact, plus the fact that I was burned up so badly, gave me a special place in her attentions. One afternoon she asked me if there was anything I would like her to bring me. I said, "Yes, my lady, there is. I'd love to have some grapes." The next time she arrived she brought me my grapes. She had had them flown in from the Mediterranean. Later, when I was on leave in London, I saw some in a shop and bought nine at the cost of a shilling a grape! Our hospital - No. 11 Canadian General - was located on Lady Astor's beautiful estate "Cliveden".

Today a chap was brought into the bed next to mine. "Hi, Mac, what happened to you?" "I don't know." "Whaddya mean - ya don't know?" This is the tale that unfolded. "I landed in England. The next day I was posted as a reinforcement to an outfit in France. It was night when I arrived at my unit. A sergeant told me I was to relieve a man dug in along a canal. He took me in the dark to the position. The enemy was on the opposite bank. That's all that I remember. The next thing I know I woke up in here. This is England?" "Yep, this is England," I reassured him, "you're in No. 11 Canadian General Hospital on Lady Astor's estate." Think of it, this guy's war lasted about two minutes or was it seconds? What a way to go! Because Mackenzie King wouldn't bring in conscription, lads were being sent over as reinforcements before they were ready.

Pte Mel Newman, RCAMC

IN MEMORY OF
REV. MEL NEWMAN

Obituary for Rev. Mel Newman   Published in The Ottawa Citizen from July 15 to July 18, 2015

Newman, Rev. Mel
WWII Veteran
June 15, 1922 – July 12, 2015
Peacefully, at the Perley & Rideau Veterans' Health Centre, while his son read to him from the Psalms. Beloved husband of June and dear father of Bruce. Predeceased by his son Brian. While serving in England, he came to realize that Jesus Christ is Lord and worthy of all praise. A United Church minister for over 50 years; Chaplain of the Kanata Legion and a Life Member of the Royal Canadian Legion. Friends are invited to visit at the Central Chapel of Hulse, Playfair & McGarry, 315 McLeod Street (at O'Connor) on Thursday, July 16 from 2-4 and 6-8 p.m. with a Legion Tribute at 7 p.m. Funeral Service in the Chinese United Church, 600 Bank Street on Saturday, July 18, 2015 at 11:00 a.m. In lieu of flowers, donations to the Jericho Road Ministries or the Good News in the Morning, would be appreciated.

"GUINNESS IS GOOD FOR YOU" - so the advertisement said. Today the doctor ordered Guinness' Stout for me. Since I am not a drinking man this was no big deal for me, but I was the envy of every other man in the ward. When nobody was watching, I would swap my stout with the sailor from the Haida [H.M.C.S. Haida (G63) Tribal Class Destroyer] in the next bed in exchange for his chocolate.

"Should but his Muse descending drop
A slice of bread and mutton-chop;
Or kindly, when his credit's out,
Surprise him with a pint of stout; "
- Jonathan Swift (1667-1745) - To Stella (1720)

HOSPITAL - TAPLOW

I got into conversation today with Ralph McVeigh, a wounded sergeant from the Black Watch [Royal Highland Regiment]. He was telling me about Le Régiment de la Chaudière who had gone in on D-Day. [Assigned to the 3rd Canadian Infantry Division and designated as a reserve battalion during the D-Day landings, June 1944. They came ashore at Bernières-sur-Mer, surprising the locals who hadn't expected to find francophone troops in the liberating forces. It was the only French-Canadian regiment to participate in Operation Overlord]. "Les Chauds" were dug in and a fierce attack was mounted against them. The Jerries came across an open field. The withering fire of the Chauds drove them back. The enemy regrouped and, supported by tanks this time, attacked again. Again the concentrated fire of the Chauds repulsed them. But the Jerries were not finished yet and a third time they came in, wave after wave. It was like the attacks during the First World War. The Chauds gave them everything they had but many were killed and wounded and the ammo was running out. This time the Germans broke through. Most Regiments would have retired, but not the Chauds. Those who were still alive, and could fire a weapon or toss a grenade, came up out of their slit trenches firing from the hip and throwing grenades, and even some with bayonets fixed, met the enemy hand to hand. Who said the French Canadians were not brave soldiers!

"Si tu veux être heureux, Vas entre Caen et Bayeux."
[If you would like to be happy, go between Caen and Bayeux]
- Norman Proverb

As I lay in my bed I had plenty of time to think. I wondered why it was that our side hadn't developed a flashless powder like the Jerries. When they fired at us there was just a little puff of smoke. When we fired at them the flash lighted up the whole countryside! Another thing that I wondered about was why we couldn't have special flameproof tank suits made of asbestos fibre. My hands had been saved by my asbestos gauntlets. Why couldn't my body have been protected the same way? It occurred to me that such a suit would be helpful to aircrew too. Perhaps somewhere behind a door marked "SECRET" the boffins were doing research on this. I hoped so.

We had an exceptionally good hospital orderly in our ward. His name was Mel Newman. He took a personal interest in my recovery. I remember when I didn't want to eat and he sat on the side of the bed and spoon-fed me. Today, the 17th of October, they brought me some crutches. I had been lying on my stomach ever since I had been wounded. I had anticipated the day when this change would come, so I had been doing some push ups in bed to strengthen my arms. Now was the time to get out of bed for the first time and try out my crutches, but I just felt I couldn't manage it. It was difficult because I had to get off the bed backwards - that is, facing the bed - and the bed, being on wheels, tended to move away from you. Newman encouraged me to try. He held the bed steady and placed the crutches on either side of me. I lay on my stomach and got crosswise on the bed then pushed myself backwards until my good right foot felt

the floor. Next I got the crutches under my arm pits. Now the big test - could I take the weight on my arms. Newman kept encouraging me and I had an audience in the other bed-ridden patients. I took a deep breath and pushed back off the bed and up on the sticks - there was a round of cheers and applause - I stood wobbling a bit - but I had made it. My head was a bit woozy because it was the first time I had been upright since the tenth of August. Now the next thing was to try to walk with the crutches. "You can do it," Newman encouraged me, "here, let me help you get started." He stood beside me and we picked out a limited goal for my first "solo". Over to Jim two beds down the ward. I started and it was easier than I had anticipated. Once you got the hang of it, it was fun and I was mobile again. I made it back to my bed, thoroughly elated, but quite exhausted. Now Newman said, "Keep practicing and as soon as you really get going on those sticks, we'll get a weekend pass and go up to London." That was just the incentive I needed. I could hardly wait to get going again. Soon I discovered how to get off the bed and on to the sticks without anyone helping me. I began to explore the ward and soon was able to go down as far as the Nurse's Office at the far end. "Well, now that you're so smart" the Nursing Sister said, "I think you should take a bath in the tub and when you've done that we'll wash your hair." It sounded like a good idea. Newman ran the bath. He left me and I managed to climb into the tub while keeping my left leg, which was in a cast up to the hip, resting on the side of the tub. It was wonderful to have a bath and just luxuriate in the warm sudsy water. When I came out the nurses washed my hair. "My gosh, he's a blond!" they exclaimed. The soot and dirt of the battlefield had made them think that my hair was dark.

In no time I was going great guns on my crutches. My explorations increased and I began to visit other wards. But pride comes before a fall and one day, as I came flying into the ward, I failed to notice some water that had been spilled on the shiny waxed linoleum floor. I put one crutch down on it and, of course, I went flying! But like those who crash in an airplane, I knew I must get up and go again or I'd lose my nerve.

Newman and I did go to London on leave. We went to the Matinee at the Stoll Theatre with two lovely girls to see "Lisbon Story". We sat in a box seat with a carpeted floor and soft cushioned chairs. What fun! During the Interval we had tea served to us. This was real living. The programme said, "The cost of teas in this theatre remains at the pre-war price of 1/-" When we emerged from the theatre, the London flower girls were selling violets and we bought our dates a bouquet.

"But buy a bunch of violets for the lady,
And tell her she's your own true love."
- Alfred Noyes (1880-1958) - The Barrel-Organ (1904), Line 105

Wherever we went people insisted that I go to the head of the queue and wouldn't let me pay on buses. My date said she wished she had me to go shopping with! Earlier that day we wanted to cross the road in the Strand just in the midst of the noon-hour traffic. The Bobby on duty could see that I was apprehensive about making it across. He held the rush hour traffic while I hopped across on my sticks. Nothing was too good for a man back from the front. I heard someone in the crowd say - "Ees one of them Red Devils just back from Arnhem!" My red Guards flashes made them think that. Who was I to disillusion them! I remembered all those gliders being towed by Daks. It was a noble sight. London never looked better to me as we enjoyed our lunch in Lyons Corner House. If you had served your King and Country, and had been lucky enough to get back alive, Londoners would open their hearts to you. The buzz-bombs had stopped now that the Channel coast was ours, but a more terrifying weapon, the V-2, was terrorizing the city. You couldn't hear them coming. The newspapers would just have a small notice - "AN INCIDENT TOOK PLACE IN CROYDON YESTERDAY". Behind that terse notice lay the complete obliteration of a block of flats, with its attendant death toll. What made this so bad psychologically was that everyone felt that the war couldn't go on much longer. We were winning. Who wants to be killed by a V-2 after surviving the

Merry Christmas
and
Happy New Year

1945

Sincerely,
Mel.

A GUINNESS A DAY

GUINNESS IS GOOD FOR YOU

Blitz and the Buzz Bombs? This was Hitler's last and most terrible vengeance weapon. No Typhoons could shoot down these V-2's, no anti-aircraft guns could engage them, no siren could wail to warn you to take cover. It was the ultimate in Hitler's secret arsenal. Londoners, who had survived so much, were getting pretty jittery. There was a story going around London at this time. A cockney woman was dug out alive from under the rubble after her home had been obliterated by a V-2. The W.V.S. [Women's Voluntary Service] member taking down information asked her, "Do you have a husband, Mrs. Smith?" "That I do," she replied. "And where is he?" asked the W.V.S. "Ees at the front, the bloody coward!"

News gradually trickled through about the other members of GIRAFFE's crew. Don, who had left us to take over as commander of GREYHOUND the night before Hill 195, had been wounded and lost a leg. I was sorry to learn that, but I was glad that he had survived because he was the finest type of officer. Gordie and Jack had been burned and invalided back to England. George had died of his wounds on August 10th. I also heard that my former Signal Platoon officer, Captain B. Ghewy, had been killed soon after the Hill 195 battle. I was grieved to hear that because he was a fine officer and a gentleman.

I had a number of visitors while I was a patient in No. 11. The first person to visit me was Colonel H. C. Griffith. I had just arrived from Normandy but somehow "Griff" found me. It showed his warm humanity and thoughtful concern for the lads of the Regiment. Some of the girl friends Doug and I knew also came to visit. Mary came one cold wet November day and so did Dorothy, the A.T.S. who helped me celebrate my twenty-fourth birthday. She brought me a leather-bound Collins Classic - Lorna Doone. She wrote on the fly-leaf "Best Wishes, Dorothy, Nov. 7th, 1944". Aunt Fanny and Uncle Charles Wigley were chauffeured up in their Wolseley. Unfortunately, I was in the Operating Theatre [Operating Room] that day so I did not see them. They brought my wrist watch with them. I woke up to find it on my bedside table.

HOMEWARD BOUND

Finally, the day came for me to leave Taplow and entrain for Liverpool. November 25th, 1944. The nurses, orderlies and some of the doctors lined up to see us off. We arrived at the port and were carried on board the Hospital Ship H.M.S. Letitia. We were not allowed to go up on the deck unless we were wearing our "blues" - blue trousers, blue jacket, white shirt and red tie. We didn't like the Hospital Blues because most civilians did not understand them and thought we were shell-shocked "loonies." Our ship travelled south through the Bay of Biscay and as far south as North Africa, then we turned westward following the route Columbus took. We sailed through the Azores. It was a beautiful night and the towns were lighted up, as was our ship - the big red crosses picked out by searchlights. This was to alert the German submarines that we were a hospital ship. That's why we could not go on deck without wearing our "blues". If a submarine captain spotted someone on deck wearing khaki, then he would be justified in thinking that we were carrying troops under cover of the Red Cross. There was a tiny deck at the back of our ward and I used to slip out of the bunk and climb the ladder and snuggle up out there sheltered from the wind. I liked to go up there just before I went to bed at night. Huddled there, out of the breeze, I watched the creamy foam from Letitia's churning propellers disturbing the plankton in the Sargasso Sea. In the daytime too, it was fun to watch the flying fish gaily leaping through the ship's wash and splashing down in the turquoise blue water. Then we turned north towards Bermuda. After that the weather turned cold, the sun disappeared and the sea took on the grey look of the North Atlantic. It was too cold now to climb up and out to my eagle's nest. We docked at Halifax on Friday, the first day of December.

HOME FOR CHRISTMAS

I was a stretcher case when I was put ashore from the Hospital Ship Letitia in Halifax. I could walk with crutches, and had done so for some time in England before leaving No. 11 General Hospital at Taplow, but

ENDS FIRST VOYAGE—Canada's newly-converted hospital liner Letitia—shown above—most modern vessel of its kind afloat—arrived at Halifax today, bringing hundreds of sick and wounded warriors from the European battle areas to spend a quiet Christmas in their homeland.

SS Letitia was an ocean liner, built initially for service with the Anchor-Donaldson Line. She continued to serve with its successor company Donaldson Atlantic Line, and was requisitioned for service at the start of the Second World War to serve as an armed merchant cruiser. She was withdrawn from this service in 1941 and became a troop ship. She was badly damaged in 1943 and on being repaired was made a hospital ship in Canada.

for the trip home I was officially a stretcher case. My trusty crutches, however, were carefully tucked under the blanket of my stretcher. I was carried on to the Hospital train and soon we were rolling through the night toward Montreal. How good the Canadian sounds were - the Crossing bells, with their Doppler effect - the long Canadian train whistle - so different from the saucy little "peep-peep" of the British railway engines.

One of the wounds on my buttocks had failed to heal properly although Dr. Hamlin had grafted skin on it. Just before I left No. 11 in England, they had taken me up for an X-Ray and Dr. Hamlin had explained to me that the plate showed a foreign body lodged in the left buttock. He said that it was causing the discharge and would have to be removed before the wound would heal properly, but he said he did not want to operate now, as I was booked to go home and this would mean postponing my return until after Christmas. However, he said - "These X-Ray plates will go with your records, Osborne, and as soon as you get home they'll take the shrapnel, or whatever it is, out." The nursing sister on the train said I would have to go straight to hospital as soon as we got to Montreal. I pleaded with her to let me go home first. Most of the other patients were getting a disembarkation leave that would allow them to be home for the holidays. I told her that my mother was a nurse who could change the dressings. "All you have to do," I said, "is to supply me with a good batch of surgical dressings." My mother was not a registered nurse - and I expect the matron knew it - but I had been in the Army long enough to know how to cut through the red tape. It being Christmas, and my story being a plausible one, the matron agreed to my plan. My mother and my sister and her husband met me at the old grimy Bonaventure Station in Montreal. It was a clear cold night. Three years ago the Regiment had said its "goodbyes" from here. One of the people who came down to meet the train was Major "Vic" Sadleir, my old Company Commander. It was good to see him and I tried to tell him we had upheld the honour of the Regiment in which he had served so nobly as a Sergeant in the First War and for some time as a Major in the Second. My brother-in-law, Dr. Leslie Shaw, drove us along St. Catherine Street so I could see the lights - the Christmas lights - after three years of blackout, boy, did they ever look good! I was humming that song:

"When the lights come on again all over the world, and the boys are home again ..."
- Written by Bennie Benjamin, Sol Marcus and Eddie Seiler - When the Lights Go On Again (All Over the World) (1943)

We got to the C.P.R. Windsor Station and I managed to hop over the snow drift at the edge of the sidewalk and hop-hop into the station. When I went through the gateway on to the station platform, I met Mr. Forrest, Johnny Forrest's father, who was collecting the tickets. He wanted to know about Johnny but of course I hadn't seen him since August. I hopped along the platform accompanied by my mother and managed to get up the steep steps into the train car. I was weak and almost overcome with the excitement of being home again. The long train ride from Halifax, during which I don't think I slept a wink, had taken its toll of my strength. When we entered the train car there were no vacant seats. It was a three hour journey home to Magog. Mother said, "I'll ask somebody to give you their seat." I was indignant. "You will not," I replied, "if these people can't see that I'm a returned veteran, wounded in battle, then to hell with them! I'll faint dead away on the floor first." I was angry and mother knew it. I hated to upset her but I couldn't help it. These people didn't really know that there was a war on. A woman with her teenage daughter was sitting beside where I was standing on my crutches. They must have overheard the conversation between Mother and me, but they never budged. Finally, as the train pulled slowly out of the station, my mother could stand it no longer. She touched the woman on the shoulder and said, "Excuse me, my son here has just returned from overseas. He has just come off the Hospital Train and he can't stand up much longer, could your daughter give him her seat please?" The woman, without even turning her head to look at us, replied, "My daughter and I have been in town all day going our Christmas shopping and we too are tired!" They made it clear that they had no intention of giving up their seat for me. I hoped I could control myself. I had an

St. Anne Hospital

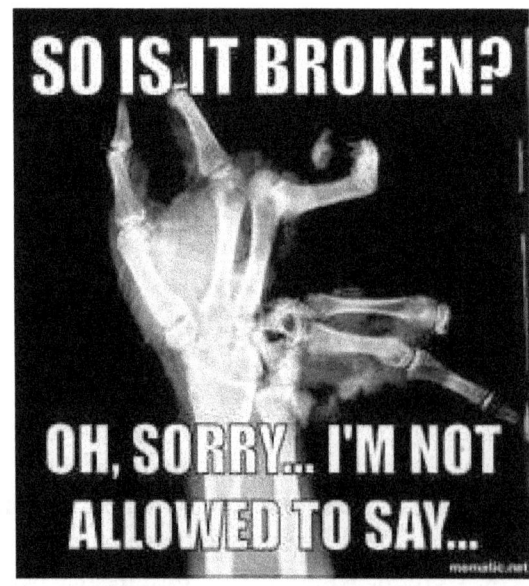

overpowering urge to lift my crutch and bash them over the head. Just at that moment the Conductor arrived to collect the tickets. "Westmount - Westmount next," he called. He looked at me and the full railway car. I noticed that he was wearing the ribbons of the First War on his uniform. "What's the matter, son, can't find a seat?" I saw him eyeing the gold wound stripe that I was wearing on my sleeve. "No, sir," I replied, trying to control my voice, "they're all taken." He leaned over the woman who had refused the seat and he just said one word - "Out!" She got up and left without a word and her daughter trailed after her. Mother and I sat down. This was Canada. This was home. They didn't even know there was a war on. I had been warned that it might be like this. A few buzz-bombs landing in Montreal would have done a power of good! As the train slowed for Westmount Station I thought to myself - "What a difference!" The policeman on traffic duty had stopped all the noon hour traffic in London to let ME cross the Strand! Think of that, he held up the London traffic for a full minute while I hobbled across the intersection on my crutches and the bystanders said, "There goes one of them red devils from Arnhem!" In Canada - my homeland - my own people wouldn't even get up to give me a place to sit.

A nice memory was the second night home. Just after supper I thought I could hear music and carollers. My mother went to the window and pulled the curtain aside. "Why it's the choir from the church!" she exclaimed. They had heard that I had arrived home and had come out on this cold night to welcome me. I hopped to the window and peered out. The choir was standing there under the street lamp in the softly falling snow. I could recognize some of the faces. Girls I had gone to school with. When they saw me at the window they began to sing - "God Rest You Merry, Gentlemen." It made me almost break down. I went to the door. My mother opened it and I stood there on my crutches. Then they struck up "It Came Upon a Midnight Clear". My thoughts flew across the Atlantic to Holland where my pals - Doug and Jack - and the others were still fighting desperately on the frozen polders along the Maas River. I wondered if it was snowing there tonight.

"O hush the noise, ye men of strife,
And hear the angels sing."
- Edmund Sears (1810-1876) - It Came Upon a Midnight Clear (1849)

"Come away from the open door, now," mother cautioned, "you'll catch your death of cold." I waved my crutch in salute to the carolers. They called out - "Merry Christmas" and "Welcome Home, Bob." I'll never forget that night with the snow falling and the church choir - after five long years of war it sure was great to be home again at Christmas.

HOMECOMING, 1945

My leave was up early in the New Year of 1945 and I returned to Montreal and was sent to Ste. Anne's Military Hospital. My mother had changed my dressings faithfully but the wound was discharging and getting more painful. I was put in a ward with a lot of other fellows. I looked around to see if I could recognize anybody from the Guards or anybody who had been on the hospital ship. I couldn't see a soul I knew and the atmosphere was so different to the hospital in England. There was no camaraderie among the patients. They all seemed to be staring at me as if I was some kind of a freak. What the hell, I thought, hadn't they ever seen a burned face before? In the afternoon "Grand Rounds" was announced and the chief surgeon, along with a whole retinue of sycophants, came trooping into the ward. We never had anything like this at Taplow. They went from bed to bed accompanied by the matron. They didn't stop at my bed and were actually passing by when I called out - "Aren't you going to look at me?" I wanted to tell the Colonel about the foreign body and its need for immediate attention. The whole parade stopped and the head surgeon looked at me like I had leprosy. "May I have a word with you, sir?" He just turned away and continued walking, followed by his parade. That made me really mad and I began calling him and the

Canadians should be told our boys were heroes too

Comment
Charles Lynch

If you grew up in Canada after the First World War, you probably joined in the ditty that went:

The Yankees think they won the war, Parley Voo!
The Yankees think they won the war, Parley Voo!
The Yankees think they won the war,
The (bleeping) (bleeping) (bleeps) of whores!
Hinky, Dinky, Parley Voo!

That song had its roots in the fact Canada was involved from 1914 on, while the Americans came in in 1917 and had less than a year of fighting, but claimed the victory for their own.

It was the same in the Second World War, insofar as American recognition that Canada had a hand in the hostilities.

At the time of the Dieppe raid, a few American Rangers were involved on the fringe of the assault, and Canadian troops bore the brunt of the operation. U.S. headlines read: "Yanks Hit Continent!"

Only long after, when it became clear that Dieppe was a disaster, did the U.S. media give Canada top billing.

Then came the Normandy operation, with Canada playing such an enormous part, only to have the U.S. and Britain share the credit, with scarcely a mention of Canada.

What the Americans tell their own people is one thing, but it's something else when they peddle their version of events in Canada, virtually eliminating our contribution to the victory in Normandy.

The current issue of *Time* magazine has a 17-page spread to mark the 40th anniversary of D-day, and the text is surrounded by advertisements solicited in Canada.

Yet the text depicts the Normandy operation as largely an American show, with some help from the British and "Commonwealth" forces.

In this Canadian edition of *Time*, the editors proclaim: "Never again, perhaps, would American power and morality so perfectly coincide. The Americans, from Eisenhower down, dominated the drama. The invasion, in a way, was a perfect expression of American capabilities: vast industrial energy and organizational know-how sent out into the world on an essentially knightly mission — the rescue of an entire continent in distress.

"So the experience of Normandy, bloody as it was, has a ring of moral freshness in the American imagination, a quality of collective heroic virtue for which the nation may be wistful."

Nobody can begrudge American writers these gropings, and no doubt the British are writing about their own D-day glories in similar fashion, as indeed we write about the Canadian accomplishments.

But what gripes me about the *Time* piece is that it is aimed at a Canadian audience, and thus represents a distortion, if not an insult.

Perhaps the fault is our own, for not seeing to it that successive generations of Canadians were reminded of what our own armed forces accomplished.

Perhaps we were not as good at propaganda and ballyhoo as the Americans and British, which is why the great heroes of Normandy and subsequent victories were all American and British, insofar as Canadians had any heroes at all.

One of the headlines in the *Time* piece says that "Every man was a hero." The quote was from U.S. General Omar Bradley, and he was talking about the casualties incurred by American troops on Omaha Beach.

The same could have been said of the Canadians on their beaches, and in the subsequent battles for Caen and along the Falaise Road, when the Canadians suffered casualties greater than the Americans did at Omaha.

After a litany of American accomplishments, and global reverberations, the *Time* piece ends with the statement that "All these things happened on June 6, 1944."

Time's massive Canadian readership deserves to know that a lot of other things happened on that day, involving young Canadians in their first battle, and fighting very well.

whole Medical Corps in Canada some uncomplimentary names. "Take that man's name and number," he said to the Matron, "and charge him with insubordination." "Thank you, Colonel," I said, "maybe I'll get some attention around here now." I was causing quite a stink which was exactly what I wanted. It turned out that what had happened was this. My bed was between two Zombies who had shot themselves in the feet so as not to be sent overseas. The head doctor thought I was there for S.I.W. [Self Inflicted Wounds] too. When he discovered his error he came marching right back into the ward and apologized to me. All the charges he was laying against me were dropped. I asked him how in blazes he thought I got the gunshot wounds, burns and fractures - falling out of a bunk in Longueil Barracks?

Not long after his visit, another surgeon came to my bed. "Roll over, Osborne, let's have a look at this wound that won't heal." He probed it and said, "Yes, I can feel the foreign body in there all right. We'll book you for the O.R. tomorrow and fish it out." "What I want to know," I said, "is how come you people didn't look at the X-Ray plates that accompanied my documents from England? It's all there in my papers and Dr. Hamlin sent instructions for you." "Your documents, X-Rays and all," replied the medical officer, "were probably lost in the fire at Longueil. The Zombies burned down the Admin building there last week." "Damn!" I replied, "are you telling me that everything that the medical people did for me overseas is lost?" "I'm afraid so, Osborne, we'll have to get you to give us your case history." "It's a good thing that I'm not suffering from amnesia," I said, "now I know why the Army does everything in triplicate!" I suppose that someday everything that was done at Bayeux and Taplow will arrive to be put into my file. At least I hope so. The next day, I went up for surgery. I got the Pentothal and the next thing I heard were the words of the surgeon - "Osborne, here's your prize!" it was a rivet from the GIRAFFE. Ah, well if Billy Bishop could keep a souvenir from his Newport, why couldn't I keep one from my Sherman tank?

MONTREAL MILITARY HOSPITAL

One winter evening as I lay on the bed at M.M.H., a German lady that I had known before the war came to visit me. Mrs. Himmelmann (not her real name) had come to Montreal during the twenties. Her husband had a very good position with a European importing firm. She used to spend her summers at the Glenbrook [resort] on Sergeant's Bay, Lake Memphremagog. The adjoining property was owned by Dr. Wilder Penfield, the well-known Montreal brain surgeon. As a boy, I used to spend my summers at the Glenbrook where my mother took summer work in order to eke out her meagre salary as a school teacher in Magog and to give my sister and me a country holiday. Here, we hobnobbed with the children of the wealthy from Westmount and Hampstead, suburbs of Montreal. Mrs. Himmelmann brought her children to the Glenbrook and they were always accompanied by a German governess. She taught us German folk songs accompanied by her playing on a zither. Somehow Mrs. Himmelmann heard that I had been invalided home and was in the Montreal Military Hospital so on this cold winters night she came to visit me. She hadn't changed much since the early thirties and seeing her brought back memories of happy childhood days playing in the woods, swimming in the lake and climbing the Hogs Back Mountain. She asked me, "You don't really hate the German people do you?" I suppose the question was one for which she had to have an answer. It must have been hard for her living in Montreal with the jingoism of war all around her. I replied that I was certain there were many fine folk in Germany, though I had not met any. She reminded me of the great German culture - of the contributions of the German race to the world of music and art and science. I said that I was aware of that, but felt that the German people had to answer before the world for Hitler and the Nazis. I said that I no longer hated the German people - but I considered the Nazis a blot on the escutcheon of Germany. My time for hating was over. "A time to love, and a time to hate. A time for war and a time for peace."

This winter I have been shuttled back and forth between M.M.H. and St. Annes. Dr. Gerry, the plastic surgeon, seems to operate out of M.M.H., so anything he does takes me in there. One evening a woman

At the time of his death, Doug McNight was serving as Loader/Operator for Capt P.V.B. Grieve. In a conversation with Pat Grieve, he told me that Doug was killed instantly when their tank was hit by an 88, or something equally powerful, in the attack on Udem. His name is listed on the Groesbeek Memorial.

"How many of mine old acquaintances are dead!"
- William Shakespeare (1564-1616)
- Henry IV, Act III, Scene 2 (1597)

KILLED IN ACTION — Cpl. Douglas Delbert McKnight, of North Hatley, son of Chester McKnight, who has been reported killed in action Overseas.

Cpl. McKnight joined the 1st B. N. Canadian Grenadier Guards of Montreal, July 21st, 1940, proceeding Overseas in September, 1942, as a Wireless Operator of the 22nd Canadian Armored Regiment.

Photo taken by Colonel John Gardam, O.M.M. [Officer of the Order of Military Merit], C.D. [Canadian Forces Decoration] at the Groesbeek Memorial. The Groesbeek Canadian War Cemetery and Memorial is located about three kilometres north of the town of Groesbeek, Netherlands. The cemetery contains 2,338 Canadian soldiers of World War II. Thousands of Dutch children tend the graves of the soldiers buried here as they do throughout the Netherlands.

came to visit me whose husband had been killed in Normandy. Somehow she found out that I had been with the Guards. I knew her husband and I had heard that he had been killed, a couple of weeks after the battle at Hill 195. Some of the boys had told me about his death - a single mortar bomb had landed near the tank while they were stopped for a bite to eat and he had been the only casualty. The woman was convinced that her husband was not dead - that he would turn up as a prisoner of war. Nothing I could say would persuade her otherwise. I suppose eventually, when the war was over and he did not return, she would realize that he was gone, or would she go on thinking that he was an amnesia victim lying in a hospital somewhere waiting for someone to recognize him? By strange coincidence, this week I have been reading James Hilton's Random Harvest which is based on just such an incident in the First World War.

STE. ANNE DE BELLEVIEW

It seems strange but when you have been immobilized for some time you have to learn to walk again. Of course you don't remember the first time you learned to walk so in a way it is like going back in time - and recapitulating those first hesitant baby steps. They had parallel bars for you to place your hands on and you walked along a ramp. It reminded me of those ramps that they have in vaudeville shows for show girls to walk on. I got along very well. After a few sessions of this physiotherapy I was doing fine but I still needed my crutches for longer walks. One day, when I was returning to the ward along a corridor, some workmen suddenly started one of those pneumatic drills - Rat-tat-a-tat-tat. I threw my crutches and hit the deck! There I was clutching the cement floor. I couldn't help but laugh as I picked myself up and gathered up my sticks. I suppose it will take time to forget that a sudden outburst of noise like that is not a Schmeizer [M30 submachine-gun]. The reflex action that once saved our lives is now something that we have to unlearn.

THE WINTER OF 1945

The winter was a long one for me. I do not know what the statistics were for snowfall that winter but the snowdrifts were half way up the hospital windows at St. Anne de Bellevue. I was on crutches, so got out very seldom. However, there were compensations. Hospital can be a wonderful place to be. You no longer have to "compete" or in our case "fight." Everything is looked after for you - meals, laundry, everything! I discovered the Library at the hospital and read everything by Daphne du Maurier - "Rebecca", "Jamaica Inn", "Frenchman's Creek". They brought back memories of England and Cornwall. Then I got into Hemingway and James Hilton. It was toward the end of this long winter and just before Easter that I read in the Montreal Star the announcement of Doug McKnight's death. "Killed in Action" it said. So, poor old Doug had got it at last. I had hoped that since he had gone through the shootout at Hill 195, he might have lived to see the end of the war. It was not to be. His picture in the paper brought back so many memories. I felt an acute sense of loss. We had both enlisted from the Eastern Townships and had served together for five years. Although we had ended up in different squadrons, we were, nevertheless, inseparable pals and always tried to get our leave together. He was my only really close friend in the Guards. The "Twins" they called us. I felt a wave of depression sweep over me. It was like losing a brother. We had shared so many experiences together. If Doug had come back I'm sure the Regimental Reunions would have meant so much more. Now there was no one to share these memories with. I later learned that it was on the twenty-sixth day of February in the assault into the Hochwald that Doug was killed. I had last seen Doug in Normandy. He had taken part in the raid on La Hogue on the 5th of August, 1944, and he came out of that raid carrying a Jerry machine gun over his shoulder. We had gone to gather camouflage together and came upon the two dead Germans behind a machine gun. That's the way I will always remember him - just as I last saw him, with his hand raised in a farewell salute, before he disappeared into the darkness.

It was just after this, on the 26th of March, 1945, that W/C Robertson told me that I would never walk without pain unless they tried to do a bone graft on my left ankle. The operation was done under a spinal

Major H. A. Smith,
M.C.
Dauphin, Man.

1956 - Robert E. Osborne

anaesthetic. I can still remember the nurse saying - "Oh, how I hate that noise!" when the surgeon cut into the bone with the surgical saw. It was a long operation and I suffered a lot of pain in my shin when the morphia wore off. I could feel the hammer and chisel taking the bone out. The operation was a great success and I remember Dr. Robertson coming into the ward on Good Friday to show me the X-Ray plates. "Don't lose them!" I cautioned. Very soon after that he was transferred to Shaugnessey Hospital in Vancouver. I shall always be grateful for his surgical skill.

During this long winter in St Anne's Hospital, the ladies from the Grenadier Guards Women's Auxiliary came out from Montreal to visit us regularly. I looked forward to these visits. It was a contact with the world outside. One visitor in particular was especially kind to me, Mrs. Smith, the wife of Major H.M. Smith. On one of her visits she arranged with the Hospital authorities to take me out for a drive on her next visit. What a treat! It was springtime. Life was coming back again after a long hard winter. Her chauffer drove us to a cosy tearoom on the north side of the Island. After tea, we were driven to her home in Westmount where she entertained me, and her mother-in-law, on the piano. What a lovely and gracious person. That outing remains vivid as the highlight of a long and depressing winter.

MONTREAL MILITARY HOSPITAL

I was getting very irritated with Canadians. Too many had become fat-cats making money out of the war boom. I thought of all the splendid young men who had laid down their lives so that these bloodsuckers might live on in comfort. I despised these people far more than any poor zombies. As I lay in the hospital bed brooding over this, I began to wish I had never come home and longed to return to England. One night I wrote these nostalgic lines à la Rupert Brooke [Rupert Brooke (1887-1915) - The Old Vicarage, Grantchester (1912)]:

"God! I will pack, and take a plane,
And get me to England once again!
For Sussex is the one place, I know,
Where Canadian servicemen may go;
Do they still play cricket on the green
Opposite the pub at Rottingdean?
Ah God to watch the raging sea
Leap the wall on Shoreham quay!
And westering sunset's parting spell
Light golden windows in Arundel.
And Sussex, of all England,
And of that district I prefer
The cathedral city, Chichester.
And does the Rother flow as sweet
And at Pulborough the Arun meet?
And sunrise shimmering along the sea
From Eastbourne to Winchelsea.
Stand the Seven Sisters white and clean
From Birling Gap to East of Dean?
St. Leonard's girls are pert and pretty
And so are those of Brighton city.
Is the Clock Tower still the place to meet
To chase the hours with flying feet?
Is Sherry's still the place to quaff

Victory in Europe Day
May 8th, 1945

A shandy with a pretty W.A.A.F.?
And is there a fighter station still
under the hill, under the hill?
Sound the tank engines beyond the lea
From Devils Dyke to Amberley?
God! I will pack, and take a plane
And get me to Sussex once again."
- Robert E Osborne (1945)

V-E DAY - MAY 8th, 1945

V-E [Victory in Europe] Day found me in the Montreal Military Hospital on Queen Mary Road. The ward was half deserted. All those who could walk went out to celebrate. I got on a street car and went down Park Avenue. People seemed to be in a celebrating mood. I recalled pictures I had seen of Armistice Night in London in 1918. I felt I wanted to be in on the rejoicing. There were many young people on the street car - university students I guessed. They were in a boisterous mood and started rocking the street car. I felt panicky. What if they suddenly seized me and hoisted me on their shoulders crutches and all? They were looking at me. They knew that I had been wounded in the war, which today had ended after six long years. I suddenly wanted to get back to the security of the hospital ward. I got off the streetcar at the Pine Avenue stop, swung across the street on my crutches and caught the next car back to Queen Mary Road.

There were only a few of us in the ward that night. Some of the "walking wounded" decided that we should have a little celebration of our own. The occasion demanded it. Tonight we were the forgotten heroes. No visitors came to the ward and only a skeleton staff was on duty. What could we do? We were a motley crew - some on crutches, others hobbling on canes, some with eyes and ears missing, a couple with half their faces burned away and some with the owl-like faces which showed them to be tank men whose goggles had protected their eyes from the burns. We passed through the swinging doors that led out to the reception desk. The duty nurse was not there. She was away in some other part of the wing probably celebrating with some of the officers. Who could blame her? We went into the small kitchen and helped ourselves from the fridge. Well loaded up with tomatoes, oranges, apples and eggs. We returned to the ward and shared our loot with the lads who were bed-ridden. Then we went to the window and opened it quietly. We were on the second storey. Down below we could see the poor sentry standing in front of his sentry box. One man gave the fire order and a barrage of fruit descended on the unsuspecting victim. A tomato caught him between his jaw and neck - an orange knocked his hat off! The poor man threw up his arms, dropped his rifle and fled inside the hospital. We roared with laughter, slammed the window down and scurried back to our beds. We had all just got safely tucked in when we heard feet running down the corridor and the door to the ward burst open and a breathless medical officer and several nurses appeared. "Who did it?" the officer shouted. Not a sound other than loud snoring from many beds. "All right you guys," the officer threatened, "we know those fruit and vegetables came from this ward. The Colonel will deal with you in the morning." The officer went out accompanied by the two nurses but no sooner had the doors swung shut than there was a loud whoop from the whole ward. The officer returned. Again silence in the ward except for loud breathing and a snicker here and there. "You'll all be crimed for this," he said, and went out again. This time the bed patients, who still had their ammunition, sat up and rained a deadly barrage at the door. Eggs and tomatoes bracketed the crack in the door in a murderous hail of fire. We could hear yelling outside but no one dared to enter. We had the range and woe betides the officer or nurse who got caught in that splattering crossfire! The officer shouted something from the other side of the door. "Go to hell!" we yelled in one defiant chorus. "That goes for the Colonel too!" somebody added. And that's the way Victory in Europe was celebrated by the boys in our ward at the M.M.H. I fell asleep wondering what the boys in the

CITY OF TORONTO
PROCLAMATION

A Civic Service of Praise and Thanksgiving to Almighty God
Will be Held When Victory is Achieved in the
Present European Conflict

- - - - - - - - -

*in front of the City Hall
at 12.30 o'clock in the afternoon*

on the Day Following Official Announcement
Of "V-E" DAY

All Citizens are invited to attend

THANKSGIVING SERVICES—DEMONSTRATIONS AND CELEBRATIONS ON

"V-E" DAY
in various Civic parks

Arrangements have been made to hold community services, demonstrations and celebration programmes in each of the undermentioned parks

During The Day That "V-E" DAY Is Officially Announced

EAST:
  Lakefront Park Beach
  Greenwood Park
  Riverdale Park

CENTRAL:
  Trinity Park
  Willowvale Park

WEST:
  High Park
  Sunnyside
  Earlscourt Park

NORTH:
  Eglinton Park

Ample opportunity will be provided in each of the said parks for an organized celebration with bands, community singing and display of fireworks, in which all classes of citizens may participate.

Tune in local radio stations for further details, particularly on "V-E" Day.

On "V-E" Day citizens are urged to observe the following requests:

Participate in the service and celebration in the park nearest your respective locality.

Refrain from driving vehicles into the down-town area and do not create pedestrian congestion in this district.

Remove all non-essential vehicles from the streets.

Remember, Victory in Europe is not final victory.

ROBERT H. SAUNDERS, K.C.
Mayor

GOD SAVE THE KING

THE "52 NATURAL"

Regiment were doing tonight and I thought of Doug and wondered if somewhere from the battlements of heaven he was celebrating too.

ST. ANNE'S MILITARY HOSPITAL

St. Anne de Bellevue is the site of Macdonald College. This is where the Protestant teachers and agriculturists are trained. I had made up my mind that I was not going back to work in the Dominion Textile plant in Magog, Quebec. I had done a lot of instructing during the War and had enjoyed it, so I thought I would go in for teaching. I knew that in order to attend Macdonald College I would need to get discharged from the Army. One Saturday afternoon, when things were very quiet in the ward because all those who could were away on weekend leave, I bearded the Colonel in his office. "May I speak to you sir?" "Yes, corporal, what is it that you want?" I explained to him that I would like to take up teaching and that Macdonald College School for Teachers was located right here in St. Anne, but that I could not enrol as long as I was in the Army. However, if I could get discharged and come under D.V.A. [Department of Veterans' Affairs] it would be possible. He listened attentively to my proposal. When I had finished he said, "Corporal, you're the first man that I've seen around here who wants to do anything. All the others are just hanging around waiting for a pension. I like your proposal. However, you realize that you still have more work to be done on you. Your leg is still in a cast and there are several more operations scheduled for you. If you are willing to go to college, realizing that we may call you back right in the middle of term for an operation, then I'm willing to recommend your discharge." "I would appreciate that very much, sir," I replied.

In a couple of weeks I was sent home on a month's leave and told to report to Longueil for my discharge when the leave was over. I hitchhiked home and had no trouble getting a lift.

That summer my brother-in-law, Dr. Leslie Shaw, was also vacationing at Magog and as he was a keen golfer I decided to accompany him on some of the holes. I found that it was a little awkward to play with a walking cast because it made my left leg higher than my right, but I soon got the hang of it. I rode my bike around and went bathing in the lake, keeping one leg out of the water! By the time the month was up, the cast was a mess - covered with green grass stains and getting quite soft from the beating to which I had been subjecting it.

THE "52 NATURAL"

"Cpl. Osborne was wearing his boots for the first time since he was wounded and is walking without crutches or cane but he will have to take it easy or awhile. He has to wait about a year before he will have his next operation so he is planning on going to Macdonald College in the meantime."
- Mitt Shaw - Montreal, August 15th, 1945 - Voice of the Canadian Grenadier Guards (Vol I. Issue 22 - Sept 28, 1945)

THE PADRE TO THE RESCUE

At last, the day came for me to report to Longueil. I soon found myself in a stream of men all waiting for their ticket out of the Army. However, I was the only one with a cast on my leg. Before we got to the medical end of things we had to see a lot of other people - personnel officers - vocational guidance people - dentists - chaplains - paymasters and so on. Just before lunch I saw the Padre. He was quite interested when I told him that I wanted to be discharged so that I could attend college. He ticked off his approval of my plans and said, "Well Osborne, I guess all you need now is to get your clearance from the medical people." After lunch I headed toward the medical centre. Just as I approached it, I saw a fellow coming toward me

**Leopard Tank
Lahr, W. Germany
March 4th, 1982**

**(Left) Sergeant Mike Hogan, Crew Commander
(Centre) Robert E Osborne
(Right) Corporal W. Kennedy, Driver**

with whom I had once had an altercation. He had been a corporal in the Medical Platoon in the Regiment but he had left us in Debert when we proceeded overseas. I hoped he would not recognize me because he was now wearing three stripes and a crown [Sergeant]. "Osborne, what are you doing here?" I did not like the tone of his voice. I realized that he had it in for me. "I'm here for my discharge," I said, as nonchalantly as possible. "Oh, no you're not!" he retorted. "We can't discharge you with that cast on your leg. Now you just turn right around and report back to the hospital. That's an order!" I knew he had me over a barrel, so I didn't stay to argue but turned around and began walking toward the office of my new-found Padre friend. I just prayed that he would be in his office. My prayers were answered for I saw him sitting at his desk. "Hello." he said, "What brings you back here?" I explained to him that it was like the game of Monopoly - DO NOT PASS GO - and I told him about the staff-sergeant who had queered the pitch for me. "We'll see about that," said the Padre, "if he wants to pull rank on you, I guess I can pull a little rank on him! A Major out ranks a staff-sergeant! Now Osborne, can you remember the name of the Colonel that you spoke to in the hospital at St. Anne's?" I could, and I did, and the Chaplain put through a phone call to the Hospital. My luck was in, as he was able to get through to the Colonel who confirmed my story and said he would call through to the Medical people. I thanked my Padre friend and hastened back to the Medical building. I was lucky and did not run into the staff-sergeant. In no time I was being examined by a medical officer who had received the message from the Colonel at St. Anne's Military Hospital. After an hour of tests I walked out of the Medical wing, completed my documentation and received my discharge papers. It was about 5 o'clock when I was finally released. I slept at the barracks that night as a civilian and, the next day before I left, I made a little visit to the Medical Centre hoping to run into my irritable friend the staff-sergeant. I did and I waved my discharge paper in front of him. "You can't, Osborne ... you're still in a cast ... I'll ..." he spluttered. "You go stuff yourself!" I said as I walked away with the most glorious sense of freedom. After all that's what we'd been fighting for all these long years, wasn't it? The date was the 7th of August, 1945. I had been in the Army for 5 years and 36 days. The next day the United States Air Force dropped an atomic bomb on Nagasaki and brought the War to an end.

FULL CIRCLE

On the 4th of March, 1982, I visited the Officer's Mess of the Royal Canadian Dragoons in Lahr, West Germany. I sat drinking coffee while Major Sproule and eight other young officers asked me questions about what it was like to "fight in a tank." I felt like "Biggles", when in 1944 one of the leading fighter pilots was asked by a reporter from an English Sunday newspaper to what he owed his success, and he replied "Biggles". This sent the reporter scurrying to find out who "Biggles" was. Captain Bigglesworth, to give him his proper name, was a pioneer air fighter of the Royal Flying Corps, whose exploits first appeared in The Modern Boy about 1932, and whose creator, Captain W.E. Johns, had been a fighter pilot himself. It was a strange feeling to sit with these young tank men and tell them about my war so long ago, and to realize that not one of them was born when I was wounded in 1944. It made me feel awfully old in one sense, and in another I suddenly felt the exhilarating stirrings of youth. Here we were, just as in the old days, talking about our tanks. More than 40 years separated us, but some things had not changed much - how you "bail out" of a blazing tank - or what it is like to get "hit". I tried to remain nonchalant about it all and to answer their questions directly and not get off into reminiscing. They told me that in a few weeks they were going to retrace the route we had taken in OPERATION TOTALIZE in August, 1944. Their leader on this scheme was to be a much decorated Canadian tank man, Brigadier-General S. V. Radley-Walters, C.M.M. [Commander of the Order of Military Merit], D.S.O. [Distinguished Service Order], M.C. [Military Cross], C.D. [Canadian Forces Decoration]. How I envied them! I wonder if the church steeple from which the sniper nearly got me, is still standing at Bretteville-le-Rabet and if Hill 195 looks anything like it did forty-two years ago? They had arranged for me to spend some time with their Leopard [Leopard 1 Main Battle Tank] tank and, as I stood up and shook hands with each of them, I felt confident that these

**Canadian Grenadier Guards Regimental Reunion
Montreal, QC 1980**

**Crew of the GIRAFFE (Left to Right)
Don Ross - Bob Osborne - Gordie Hatch - Jack Kane**

"boys" would uphold the traditions of the Royal Canadian Armoured Corps laid down by their fathers. The future of the Corps I felt was in good hands.

Outside the Mess, I was introduced to Sergeant Mike Hogan, the Crew Commander, and Corporal W. Kennedy, the tank driver. They showed me how to climb aboard their 42-ton Leopard. It was as different from my old Sherman as Captain Bigglesworth's Sopwith Camel was from a modern CF-18 Hornet. As I let myself down into the turret, the old familiar smells of petrol and oil came back to me. That hadn't changed, nor had the white cleanliness inside.

"Perhaps the plaintive numbers flow
For old, unhappy, far-off things,
And battles long ago."
- William Wordsworth (1770–1850) - The Solitary Reaper (1803)

The gunner's sophisticated equipment was hardly recognizable - lasers, computers, television sets, searchlights, snorkels, light-intensifiers, and a 105-mm gun that made the 75-mm, and even the 17-Pdr on the old Sherman Firefly, look like a peashooter. If only we'd had a tank like that at Hill 195! This tank had a crew of four where we had had five. The driver had a steering wheel like the one on a Boeing 707 airplane. We had tiller bars like a tractor. And the driver's seat was so comfortable I wondered how he would ever keep awake! It seemed to me that the radio operator's job had been greatly scaled down. With the modern wireless sets the frequencies were pre-set and Morse code was never used, but the gunner's role was greatly increased. He had to master all sorts of hi-tech equipment. They took me for a ride in their tank and I stood on the commander's seat where I had last stood forty years ago. It was a thrill to feel the power of the 830-H.P. engine and the speed of the Leopard was exhilarating. Sergeant Hogan ordered his driver to "Halt" but first he cautioned me to hold on tight. The tank bucked as she almost stood on end. Then he ordered "Back Up!" and with lightning speed we whipped round in a manoeuvre that would confuse the enemy and place us in a new position for a quick return shot. I climbed out of the Leopard glad that our lads had a tank that was second to none. She is a real beauty and she is made by our former enemy. They always did make superior tanks!

June 1982 Protestant Chaplain's retreat RMC - Photo by Colonel D Estey

EPILOGUE

Our War was different from the First World War, which ended in so much cynicism because of the awful futility of it all. Men like Siegfried Sassoon, the poet, came home from the carnage on the Western Front and threw his Military Cross into the river. For us, it was clearly our life of freedom or to live under the jackboot of Hitler's Nazis. I think most of us felt that some things were worse than death in battle and one of them was slavery. It was a frightening thing during the era of appeasement and "Peace In Our Time" to watch the ominous dark shadow of Nazism creeping across Europe until only the little island of Britain was left. When we listened on the radio to the orchestrated "Sieg Heils!", we wondered how we could ever beat such a bunch of swastika waving fanatics. They seemed to be winning everywhere and their arrogance knew no bounds. But we did beat them and today we live as free men and women. It makes you believe in miracles! It was one hell of a party but I wouldn't have missed it for the world.

"The voice of rejoicing and salvation
Is in the tents of the righteous;
The right hand of the Lord does valiantly.
The right hand of the Lord is exalted;
The right hand of the Lord does valiantly.
I shall not die, but live,
And declare the works of the Lord.
The Lord has chastened me severely,
But He has not given me over to death"
- Bible (NKJV) - Psalm 118:15-18

In Memory of

The Reverend Doctor Robert Ernest Osborne, B.A., B.D., S.T.M., Ph.D (1920-1986), Captain Royal Canadian Army Chaplain Corp, C.D.

Many years after my father passed away, I came across a draft of a book he started. The roughly typed pages and blurred photocopied images were loosely bound in a 3 ring binder. The importance to my father was obvious, he had a story to tell. I suspect that he had hoped to complete the work on this project during his retirement, however, cancer claimed his life within a year of that milestone. I can only imagine the time and work involved to write and type the pages by hand. It had obviously meant a lot to him as he continued to work on it up until his death.

Like many, my father rarely spoke of his war experiences, or the early years of his life. At the time of his passing I was in my early 20's and was still too young to really understand the importance of the sacrifices made by all those who serve. It was a phenomenal experience to read and learn about my own father's life story, particularly since it was so different from the part of his life that I was familiar with.

It has been my honour and privilege to play a small part in keeping his story "alive".

David Osborne (2019)

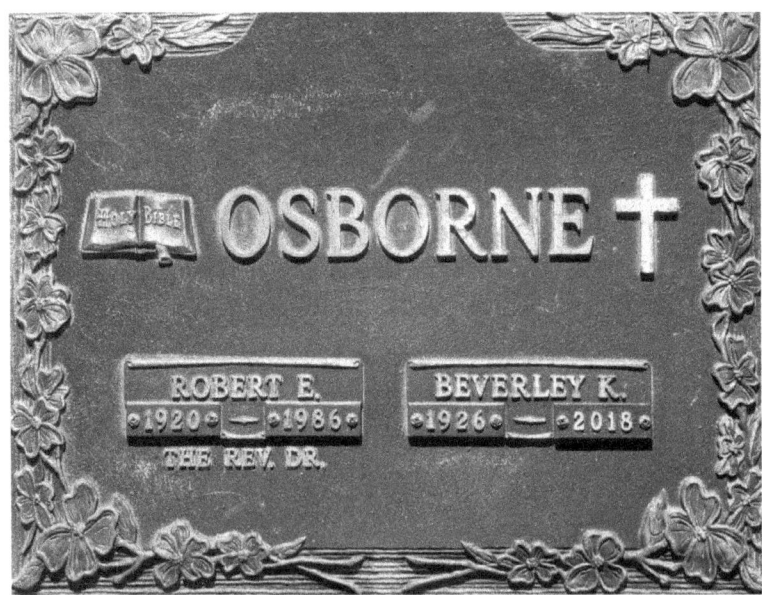

Grave Location: Capital Funeral Home & Cemetery (Arbor Memorial)
3700 Prince of Wales Drive, Ottawa, Ontario, Canada K2C 3H1

OTTAWA CITIZEN

The Citizen, Ottawa, Tuesday, February 4, 1986

DEATHS

OSBORNE, Rev. Dr. Robert Ernest

On Sunday, February 2, 1986, in Victoria, B.C. Rev. Dr. Robert Ernest Osborne. Survived by his wife Beverley; sons John of Victoria, Robert of Chicago, David of Ottawa, daughter Mrs. Margaret Bedok of Ottawa; 2 grandchildren; sister Mrs. Shirley Shaw of Brockville, Ontario. Friends may call at Hulse and Playfair, Central Chapel, 315 McLeod Street on Thursday 2 to 4 and 7 to 9 p.m. Service at Riverside United Church on Friday at 2 p.m. Cremation Capital Memorial Gardens. Donations to the Canadian Cancer Society would be appreciated.

THE OTTAWA CITIZEN G13
SATURDAY, NOVEMBER 19, 1988

**Rev. Prof. Robert E. Osborne
1920-1986**

Robert E. Osborne was widely respected and loved both as a Religion Professor at Carleton, and as a United Church Minister. His enthusiasm for the message of the New Testament inspired all who knew him. In his honour, Carleton has created the **"Robert E. Osborne Memorial Scholarship"** to be given annually to a deserving Religion student. Donations (tax-deductible) can be made by making a cheque out to "Carleton University", Development Office, Ottawa, Ont. K1S 5B6. Please include your name, address and the name of the Scholarship. Thank you.

This Week

CARLETON UNIVERSITY

Bob Osborne dies in Victoria

Bob Osborne, Professor of Religion at Carleton until his retirement last June, died in Victoria, B.C. February 2 of cancer.

Robert Osborne

Professor Osborne was a specialist in New Testament studies. He had an eclectic mind and an enthusiasm for life and learning that was infectious. He won the prestigious OCUFA teaching award in 1978, and shared his talent as a teacher and his knowledge of religion and many other subjects with a wide audience. He was among the first at Carleton to teach courses on ITV, and enjoyed an unprecedented popularity.

He was much loved by his students and respected by his colleagues.

Professor Osborne served with the Grenadier Guards in the Second World War, and was wounded at Normandy in 1944. After the war, he taught school, studied theology at McGill, and was ordained into the United Church, which he served with great distinction for 10 years. He completed Ph.D. studies in Edinburgh then taught at Emmanuel College, University of Toronto for seven years. He joined the faculty of the Department of Religion at Carleton in 1968.

When he retired last June he returned for the first time in 40 years to Normandy; then, with his wife of 38 years, he established residence in Victoria, B.C. where he was putting the finishing touches on his biography of St. Paul.

Chairman of the Department of Religion, Leonard Librande said, "the department has many memories of Bob Osborne. They all revolve around his enthusiasm for life. His office was the place to sit over lunch or tea and enjoy friendly conversation. When you couldn't find him there he would probably be racing his bicycle which was nearly as old as he was. Each winter he skated the length of the Canal, seeking ever to improve his time.

"Bob's passion was teaching. This love spilled over into his preaching in the United Church and into his participation in the Ottawa Lay School of Theology. His concern and love for his students was public knowledge. Less well known is the extent to which his spirit and energy contributed to the quality of teaching in the Department of Religion. Hidden too are the many occasions when his generosity and compassion touched students and members of the Carleton community.

"We will remember him, in our continuing contact with his students and friends and in our role as teachers."

The department will create a memorial award to be presented annually to a deserving student in Religion. Donations gratefully accepted.

He is survived by his wife Beverley and four children: John, of Victoria, David and Margaret of Ottawa, and Robert of Chicago. The funeral service will take place on Friday, February 7 at 2:00 p.m. in Riverside United Church, 3191 Riverside Drive.

Canadian World War II Service Medals
Awarded to Robert Ernest Osborne

1939-1945 Star **Defence Medal** **War Medal (1939-1945)**

France and Germany Star **Canadian Volunteer Service Medal with Maple Leaf Bar** **Canadian Forces Decoration (CD)**

1939-1945 Star: *The Star was awarded for six months service on active operations for Army and Navy, and two months for active air-crew between 02 September 1939 and 08 May 1945 (Europe) or 02 September 1945 (Pacific). The ribbon consists of three equal stripes: dark blue, red, and light blue (representing the navy, army and air force).*

France and Germany Star: *The Star was awarded for one day or more of service in France, Belgium, Holland or Germany between 06 June 1944 (D-Day) and 08 May 1945. The ribbon consists of equal stripes of blue, white, red, white, and blue. The colours represent the Union flag and those of France and the Netherlands but not of Belgium.*

Defence Medal: *Although the medal was usually awarded to Canadians for six months service in Britain between 03 September 1939 and 08 May 1945, the exact terms were: Service in the forces in non-operational areas subjected to air attack or closely threatened, providing such service lasted for three or more years. Service overseas or outside the country of residence, providing that such service lasted for one year, except in territories threatened by the enemy or subject to bomb attacks, in which case it was six months prior to 02 September 1945. The award was established on 16 August 1945. The light green ribbon is 1.25 inches wide with a central stripe of orange (0.5 inches wide) and a narrow black stripe in the middle of each green stripe. The orange (flame colour) represents the enemy attacks on the green land of England and the black represents the black-outs.*

The Canadian Volunteer Service Medal: *The Canadian Volunteer Service Medal is granted to persons of any rank in the Naval, Military or Air Forces of Canada who voluntarily served on Active Service and honourably completed eighteen months (540 days) total voluntary service from September 3, 1939 to March 1, 1947. The medal was established on 22 October 1943. The ribbon is 1.25 inches wide with a royal blue centre (0.5 inches) flanked by two equal stripes of scarlet and dark green, the dark green being on the edges. The ribbon was issued during the war; the medal after the war.*

Bar: *A silver bar (clasp), a maple leaf at its centre, was awarded for 60 days service outside Canada. A silver maple leaf is worn on the ribbon in undress.*

War Medal 1939-1945: *The War Medal was awarded to all full-time personnel of the armed forces and merchant marines for serving for 28 days between 03 September 1939 and 02 September 1945. The award was established on 16 August 1945. The ribbon is 1.25 inches wide and consists of 7 coloured stripes: red, dark blue, white narrow red (centre), white, dark blue, and red.*

Canadian Forces Decoration: *Awarded to officers, and to the men and women of the Canadian Forces who have completed twelve years of service. The medal is awarded to all ranks, who must have a good record of conduct during the final eight years of claimed service. The medal may be awarded to persons in possession of any long service, good conduct or efficiency decoration or medal clasps, provided that the individual has completed the full qualifying periods of service for each award and that no service qualifying towards one award is permitted to count towards any other. The service need not be continuous.*

Additional information is available from the Honours and Awards Section, Veterans Affairs Canada, Ottawa, Ontario K1A 0P4.

*Record of Service of **OSBORNE** (Surname) **Robert Ernest** (Christian No's) Regimental Number **D.26348**

4551 P

QUALIFICATIONS

Military	NO
Business or Professional	NO
Trade or Civil	NO
Technical	NO
Languages	English

EDUCATIONAL QUALIFICATIONS

High School or Collegiate	4 years (years completed)
*College	
*University	
Graduation or Matriculation	Matriculation (specify)

* (Name of institution, courses or years completed, and degrees obtained to be shown)

All personnel whether G.S. (General Service) or N.R.M.A. will be taken on strength as private soldiers. Postings, appointments and promotions should be shown in the spaces below.

This column for checking purposes only	Record of Postings, Promotions, Reductions, Transfers, Casualties, Rejoints, etc., from and including date taken on strength.	Rank Shown	Effective Date	Unit	Place	AUTHORITY Part II D.O. No. Com. List, etc.	Dated
2-7-40	T.O.S. Canadian Grenadier Guards C.A.S.F.	Gdsm.	2-7-40	C.G.G.	Mtl.	Pt. 2 No. 17	2-7-40
	Proceeded on Command to Internment Camp "S" for all purposes.	"	27-7-40	"	St. Helens Que.	D.O. 47	9-8-40
	Returned from on command at Internment Camp "S" 0900 hrs. 14-8-40 Is proceeding on command to Central Tech Toronto (Quarters Dist. Depot) to attend a Vocational Course Instrument Mech(Sim'l)"a	"	14-8-40	"	"	D.O. 60	24-8-40
	Att. to DD 2 C.A.(A) for rations, quarters and discipline	"	23-1-41	"	C.Border,Ont.	D.O. 18	23-1-41
	Cease to be attached to No. 2 D.D. For all purposes except pay on return to C.G.G. Valcartier, Que. eff. 7-5-41	"	23-1-41	DD 2	Toronto	D.O. 24	29-1-41
	Is granted furlough w.e.f. 0600 hrs 12-5-41 to 0800 hrs. 26-5-41	"	7-5-41	"	Valcartier Camp,Que.	D.O. 108	7-5-41
	Has returned from on Command at Central Tech. Toronto	"	12-5-41	C.G.G.	"	D.O. 94	9-5-41
	w.e.f. 895-41	"	8-5-41	"	"	D.O. 95	10-5-41
	Ret'd from furlough w.e.f. 2359 hours 26-5-41	"	26-5-41	"	"	D.O. 106	26-5-41
	Promoted to rank of A/Cpl.	A/Cpl.	14 Feb 42	22 Armd. Regt.(C.G.G)	Debert	5	13 Feb 42
	Grtd. furlough to 27 Feb 42	"	14 Feb 42	"	"	5	13 Feb 42

4351 P

Regimental No. D-26348 Rank A/Cpl. Sheet No. 2

M.F.M. 1 & 2 (a)
50M—3—1 (4002)
H.Q. 17-439-1846

Name OSBORNE Robert Ernest

Record of Promotions, Reductions, Transfers, Casualties, Reports, etc.—	Rank Shown	Effective Date	Unit	Place	Authority D.O. Number	Authority Dated
Att. for rations to Camp Borden, Ont. while on Course	A/Cpl.	28 Feb 42	22 Armd. Regt. (CGG)	Debert	17	28 Feb 42
Qual. W.T. Operator Class III at Course of Instruction, Camp Borden, Ont.	"	11 Apr 42	"	"	55	30 Apr 42
Grtd. special leave to 9 Sep 42	Cpl	5 Sep 42	"	"	134	7 Sep 42
Qual. as Loader Operator Group "C"	A/Cpl.	15 Sep 42	"	"	144	22 Sep 42
To draw T.P. as loader operator group "C"	"	15 Sep 42	"	"	144	22 Sep 42
EMBARKED CANADA-SAILING LIST NO 2016		25 Sep 42				
DISEMBARKED ENGLAND 7 Oct 42						
S.O.S. Cdn. Army (Canada) 25 Sep 42. T.O.S. Cdn. Army O/S 26 Sep 42. Disembarked U.K. 7 Oct 42	"	26 Sep 42	"	At Sea	1	30 Sep 42
Grtd. 7 days priv. leave and F.T.W. with money allce. in lieu of rations to 29 Oct 42	"	16 Oct 42	"	U.K.	5	20 Oct 42
Confirmed in rank of Cpl.	Cpl.	2 Dec 42	"	"	7	16 Dec 42
Grtd. 7 days priv.leave with money allce. in lieu of rations to 11 Feb 43	"	5 Feb 43	"	"	8	20 Feb 43

4351 P

Regimental No. D-26348 Rank Cpl. Sheet No. 3

M.F.M. 1 & 2 (a)
50M—8-44 (4009)
H.Q. 1772-30-1645

Name OSBORNE Robert Ernest

Record of Promotions, Reductions, Transfers, Casualties, Reports, etc.—	Rank Shown	Effective Date	Unit	Place	Authority D.O. Number	Authority Dated
Grtd. 7 days priv. leave with money allce. in lieu of rations to 3 Jun 43	Cpl.	28 May 43	22 Armd. Regt. (CGG)	U.K.	26	12 Jun 43
Relinquishes qual. of Dvr. Oper. "C" on being remustered and is qual. Operator CAC "C"	"	20 Jul 43	"	"	35	3 Aug 43
Grtd. T.P. Operator CAC "C"	"	20 Jul 43	"	"	35	3 Aug 43
Grtd. 7 days priv. leave with money allce. in lieu of rations to 4 Aug 43	"	29 Jul 43	"	"	37	16 Aug 43
Proceeded on CMHQ Course 859A AFV Compass and Navigation and att. to AFV School f.a.p. from 25 Aug 43 to 8 Sep 43	"	25 Aug 43	"	"	41	13 Sep 43
Ret. from CMHQ Course 859A and ceases att. f.a.p. to AFV School	"	8 Sep 43	"	"	42	20 Sep 43
N-of-K now: Mrs. Bessie Osborne, Magog, Que.	"	--	"	"	51	21 Nov 43
Grtd. 7 days priv. leave plus 48 hrs. pass with money allce. in lieu of rations to 20 Nov 43	"	12 Nov 43	"	"	53	29 Nov 43
Awd. C.V.S.M. & Clasp	"	15 Jan 44	"	"	5	28 Jan 44
Grtd. 7 days priv. leave plus 48 hrs. pass with money allce. in lieu of rations to 19 Mar 44	"	11 Mar 44	"	"	14	27 Mar 44

4351 P

Regimental No. D-26348 Rank Cpl. Sheet No. 4

M.F.M. 1 & 2 (a)
5034—3-44 (4002)
H.Q. 1772-39-1945

Name OSBORNE Robert Ernest

Record of Promotions, Reductions, Transfers, Casualties, Reports, etc.—	Rank Shown	Effective Date	Unit	Place	Authority D.O. Number	Authority Dated
Embarked U.K. 20 Jul 44. Disembarked France 22 Jul 44	Cpl.	22 Jul 44	22 Armd. Regt. (CGG)	21 Army Group	37	9 Aug 44
S.O.S. to X-3 List CAC "C"	"	10 Aug 44	"	"	40	26 Aug 44
T.O.S. from 22 Armd. Regt. C.G.G.	"	11 Aug 44	X List CAC "C"	"	37	28 Aug 44
S.O.S. to Y-3 List #3 C.A.C.R.U.	"	13 Aug 44	"	"	43	15 Sep 44
T.O.S. from X-3 List CAC "C"	"	14 Aug 44	Y List #3 CAC RU	U.K.	199	21 Sep 44
S.O.S. to #1 N.E.T.D.	"	11 Oct 44	"	"	222	21 Oct 44
T.O.S. from Y-3 List #3 C.A.C.R.U.	"	12 Oct 44	#1 N.E.T.D.	"	214A	13 Oct 44
S.O.S. Cdn. Army O/S and #1 N.E.T.D.	"	25 Nov 44	"	"	245B	27 Nov 44
RET. CANADA DEC 8, 1944 S/L 601						
T.O.S. from Cdn. Army O/S 26 Nov 44. Reported 9 Dec 44	"	26 Nov 44	#4 D.D.	Montreal	302	11 Dec 44
Grtd. leave and ration alloc. to 8 Jan 45	"	10 Dec 44	"	"	302	11 Dec 44
Continues T.P. Group "C" Dvr. Oper.	"	26 Nov 44	"	"	309	19 Dec 44

4351 P

Regimental No. D-26348 Rank Cpl. Sheet No. 5

M.F.M. 1 & 2 (a)
50M—3-44 (...)
H.Q. 1772-...-1646

Name OSBORNE Robert Ernest

Record of Promotions, Reductions, Transfers, Casualties, Reports, etc.—	Rank Shown	Effective Date	Unit	Place	Authority D.O. Number	Authority Dated
Adm. to Montreal Mil. Hosp.	Cpl.	9 Jan 45	#4 D.D.	Montreal	13	13 Jan 45
Removed from Montreal Mil. Hosp. to Ste Anne's Hosp	"	13 Jan 45	"	"	18	18 Jan 45
Ceases T.P. Group "C" Dvr. Oper.	"	7 Feb 45	"	"	39	12 Feb 45
Ceases T.P. Group "C" Dvr. Oper.	"	7 Feb 45	"	"	43	16 Feb 45
Removed from Ste Anne's Hosp. to Montreal Mil. Hosp.	"	24 Apr 45	"	"	103	27 Apr 45
Disch. from Mtl. Mil. Hosp.	"	7 Jul 45	"	"	168	12 Jul 45
S.O.S. on discharge under R.O.1029(10). Grtd. $100.00 clothing allce.						
and 30 days' pay of rank	"	7 Aug 45	"	"	191	7 Aug 45

Regimental No. D.96346 Rank
Name OSBORNE R. C.

Sheet No. 1

Record of Promotions, Reductions, Transfers, Casualties, Reports, etc.—	Rank Shown	Effective Date	Unit	Place	D.O. Number	Dated
RET. CANADA 1944						
S/L						
TOS from C.A. 4/5.	Cpl.	26 Nov 44	F.D.O.	M.T.C.	302	11 Dec 44
Attd. Gen. 2 P.JAN.45	"	10 Dec 44	"	"	202	11 Dec 44
Cnd. Fatigue pay C (Ron. fee)	"	2 Nov 44	"	"	203	11 Dec 44
admitted to Mont Milt Hosp	"	9 JAN 45	"	"	13	
trans from Mont Milt Hosp to S e Annes Hosp.	"	13 JAN 45	"	"	18	
Trans from St Annes Hosp to Mtl Mil Hosp.	"	24 Apr 45.	"	"	103	27 Apr 45
Disch from Mtl Mil Hosp.	"	7 Jul 45	"	"	168	12 Jul 45
	Cpl.	7/8/45	"	"	191	7/8/45

SOS DISCHARGED:- (R.O. 1029 para 10.)
ADD. ON DISCHARGE:- 1 Mary St Magog, Que
Granted $100.00 Clothing Allowance (Art 106 (2) Fr & E)
and 30 days pay of rank (R.O. 4415).

CANADIAN NATIONAL TELEGRAPHS

DAY LETTER [x]
NIGHT LETTER [ ]

CASUALTY (REPORT DELIVERY)

OTTAWA

16 AUGUST 1944

TO:-

MRS BESSIE OSBORNE
MAGOG P Q

10320 MINISTER OF NATIONAL DEFENCE SINCERELY REGRETS TO INFORM YOU D26348 CORPORAL ROBERT ERNEST OSBORNE HAS BEEN OFFICIALLY REPORTED WOUNDED IN ACTION TENTH AUGUST 1944 NATURE OF WOUNDS DESCRIBED AS PETROL BURNS FACE SHELL FRAGMENT WOUND BUTTOCK LEFT KNEE STOP WHEN ADDRESSING MAIL ADD WORDS IN HOSPITAL IN BOLD LETTERS AFTER NAME OF UNIT FOR QUICK DELIVERY STOP WHEN FURTHER INFORMATION BECOMES AVAILABLE IT WILL BE FORWARDED AS SOON AS RECEIVED

DIRECTOR OF RECORDS
OFFICER I/C RECORDS

PREPAID

CANADIAN ARMY (ACTIVE)
DISCHARGE CERTIFICATE

M.F.M. 7 (LINEN)
500M—2-45 (8061)
H.Q. 1772-30-1653

This is to Certify that No. D-26348 (Rank) CORPORAL.

Name (in full) Robert Ernest OSBORNE. enlisted or was enrolled in the "CANADIAN ARMOURED CORPS"

the **CANADIAN ARMY (ACTIVE)** at Montreal Que. on the 2nd. day of July. 1940.

~~She~~
He served in Canada - - -UNITED KINGDOM-CONTINENTAL EUROPE- - - - -

and is now discharged from the service under Routine Order 1029 Para...10 by reason of UNABLE TO MEET THE REQUIRED MILITARY PHYSICAL STANDARDS.

Medals, Decorations, Mentions, awarded in respect of service during this war: Canadian Volunteer Service Medal. Ribbon & Clasp.

THE DESCRIPTION OF THIS SOLDIER on the DATE below is as follows:—

Age 25 Years. 1 Month.
Height 5' 9½"
Complexion Fair
Eyes Blue
Hair Fair

Marks or Scars
Vaccination left arm.

Other Active Army Service (This War)
- - - - - - NIL - - - - - -

Signature of Soldier: Robert E Osborne

Date of Discharge

Issuing Officer
S. ECHENBERG, Lt Colonel,
COMMANDING...
Rank
Date 7th August 19 45.

N.B.— As no duplicate of this Certificate will be issued, any person finding same is requested to forward it in an unstamped envelope to the Director of Records (Army), Department of National Defence, Ottawa, Canada.

In Memory of

Lieutenant Donald Armitage Ross (1916-1992)

Canadian Grenadier Guards

"Souvenirs of War"

Shrapnel and Dog Tags belonging to Lt. D. A. Ross

Content provided by and used with permission from Donna Ross

Lieutenant Donald Armitage Ross

Canadian Grenadier Guards

Introduction – Donna L. Ross

November 2019

My father never spoke about his war years. It seems this is the case for most who fought in World War II.

It was their time, their memories and their world, as awful as it was.

Why would they want to share stories about the cruel world of fighting, maiming and killing?

Mostly they kept silent.

And so, my father's life from September 1942 to December 1944 was mostly a blank for his five children.

However, there were a few reminders of his war years as well as a memory of him and Mum going to the Regiment's annual parties. I sensed he had a good time and that the time spent with his fellow soldiers was special. Not sure where his war things were kept, but they materialized after his passing in July 1992 when things from our family home were being organized and distributed to family members. I was given the honour to be the keeper of all things war, including photographs, letters and post cards, strategic war maps, a piece of shrapnel and dog tags. His younger sister, by 15 months, Georgina wrote a story about his arrival home in Montreal, December 1944. As well, she and her younger sister and then later, their brother, travelled to Normandy and stood on the battle ground, Hill 195, where Dad was gravely injured.

All of this intrigued me, so much so, I wanted to learn more about Dad's time as a soldier in the armoured division of the Canadian Grenadier Guards. Who would know more about these times than the four other men that served with him overseas and fought together in their Sherman tank, Giraffe? But how to find them or their families? And so, from looking through what material I had of my father's, asking questions to his sisters, and visiting the Guards' Armoury on Esplanade Avenue in Montreal, I eventually connected with John Osborne, one of two sons of Bob Osborne, a crew member with Dad in Giraffe. Meeting John in Ottawa in October 2014 was unbelievable; I felt connected to him without even ever knowing him.

And then the story I heard from one of the fellows at the Armoury on my visit there in 2012 became a reality: that Bob Osborne had written a book. I learned from John Osborne that his brother, David had edited his father's letters home to his Mother and memoirs into a book, *Pax in Bello - Peace in War*. Like John, David lived in Ottawa and I began communicating with David through e-mails, sending him many things I had of Dad's.

It was my extreme pleasure to finally meet David and have both him and his brother, John to our home for lunch in August 2019. Our fathers' time spent together, first in the UK training and then later in Normandy fighting, brought the three of us together. I think they would be happy to know that we are connected because of their time in World War II, an outcome from those wartime years, that has a peaceful ending.

Content provided by and used with permission from Donna Ross

Lieut. D. Armitage Ross

Lieutenant Ross, of the 22nd Armored Regiment (Canadian Grenadier Guards), whose wife, the former Mary Louise Allyn, lives at 43 Brock avenue north, Montreal West, is a son of Rev. A. S. Ross, D.D., and Mrs. Ross, of Montreal West. He received his education at Stanstead College and Queen's University, and has been overseas since September, 1942. He was a pre-war member of the Canadian Grenadier Guards.

The Montreal Gazette - 5 May 1942

Wedding Attendants

At the marriage of Miss Mary Louise Allyn, youngest daughter of Mr. and Mrs. Alfred W. Allyn, of Montreal West, to Lieutenant Donald Armitage Ross, Canadian Grenadier Guards, elder son of Reverend Dr. Andrew S. Ross and Mrs. Ross, also of Montreal West, which is taking place on Saturday afternoon, May 9, at half-past three o'clock in Montreal West United Church, the bride will be attended by Mrs. David Olive, as matron of honor. Miss Helen Moxley, Miss Betty Ross, sister of the bridegroom, and Miss Barbara Mauroyenis, of Claremont, N.H., will be bridesmaids, and the Misses Mary Ann and Jane Allyn, of West Orange, N.J., nieces of the bride, will be flower girls.

Lieutenant Gordon Trower will act as best man and the ushers will be Pilot Officer George Sprague, of Ottawa, Mr. Horace W. Allyn, of West Orange, N.J., brother of the bride, Mr. John F. Edwards, of Kingston, Ont., Mr. John Dobie, of Ottawa, and Mr. O. A. (Sandy) Seeber, of Sudbury, Ont. The reception will be held in the Town Hall, Montreal West.

The Faces of War

Photo by Lt. Charles H. Richer,
Canadian Army Film and Photo Unit

Lt. D. A. Ross in a motivational photo post amputation. Taken at Leavesden Hospital in England, 1944

Content provided by and used with permission from Donna Ross

"Close to the Heart"

(Top 3) Ross family members and (bottom 3) pictures carried in the uniform pocket by Lt. D. A. Ross

Content provided by and used with permission from Donna Ross

The Postcard
By Donna Ross

The postcard always sat on my Dad's dresser. As children, we got used to seeing the sketched card, leaning up against a pewter cup. Who would think to ask about it?

Dad died in 1992 and when clearing out the family home, we found other postcards stuck into a red leather-bound 1943 Dominion Diary. In the inside cover, he had written: "Return to: Donald A. Ross, 22nd Can. Arm'd Reg't (C.G.G.)". The 13 postcards all depicted the same theme: changing of the guard on Parliament Hill, Ottawa.

But the 14th one, the one we got used to seeing as kids, was different, yet all 14 were dated August 10 of different years and from the same sender: Bob Osborne.

My Dad, Lieutenant Donald Armitage Ross, a World War II veteran, was with the Canadian Grenadier Guards of Montreal. Through my research, I know that his Regiment left the port of Halifax and sailed on the SS Athlone Castle September 29, 1942, arriving in Liverpool October 7, 1942.

It was not until the summer of 1944 that he was engaged in battle. In the evening of July 24 a convoy of ships left for France, and anchored at Juno Beach on July 25. Dad was part of the TOTALIZE operation beginning on August 8. And herein lies the story of the 14th postcard.

One of the objectives of TOTALIZE was to secure Point 195, on the Caen-Falaise highway. On the morning of August 10, the Regiment started out and by mid-morning was established on Point 195, yet under heavy German anti-tank gunfire for the rest of the day and throughout the night.

Who knows when Dad's tank, Giraffe, was hit, except the 14th postcard tells the story in vivid colour: Dad's Sherman tank, clearly marked, Giraffe, appears to be on fire; in the distance a German Panzer tank is firing; in the forefront is a stick figure man carrying another man over his shoulders; the inscription on the card reads: Falaise, Hill 195, 10 Aug. '44. On the reverse side of the postcard, is a note with a Toronto return address: "Dear Don, Here's a little reminder of what you were doing 19 years ago today. As ever, Bob Osborne."

Dad never really spoke about this. I never asked him about the postcard that had a prominent place on his dresser. Like my Dad, Bob Osborne has passed away. Only the postcard can tell the story now.

Epilogue to the story: Dad was the stick man with the man over his shoulders. His tank, Giraffe, had been hit and on fire. Dad was catapulted out of the tank but went back to get the unconscious Bob Osborne from the inferno. In doing so, he was hit by shrapnel. As Dad writes in a letter to his parents, dated 13 Aug. '44: "I was wounded in the left leg and am in a Cdn hospital in France waiting evacuation to England when I can travel. This closes the war off for me as it will be 4-6 mos. before I get out of hospital."

Reprinted with permission from: OMMCINC ©2013 Organization of Military Museums of Canada
Web Site: https://www.ommcinc.ca/publications

Postcards from Robert (Bob) Osborne to Don Ross

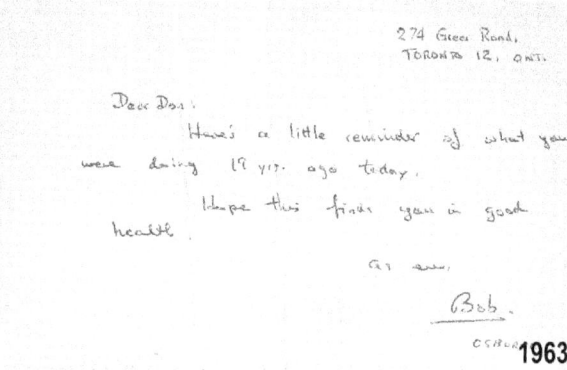

1963

1969

Content provided by and used with permission from Donna Ross

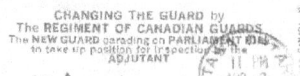

1970

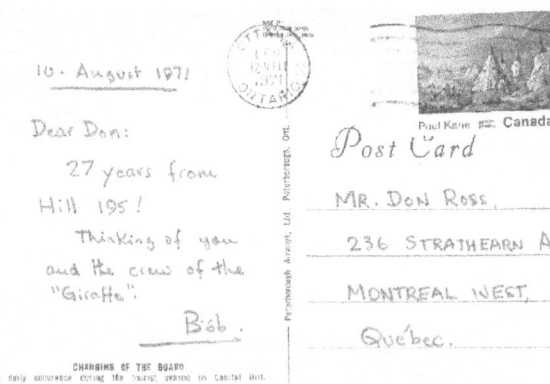

1971

1972

Content provided by and used with permission from Donna Ross

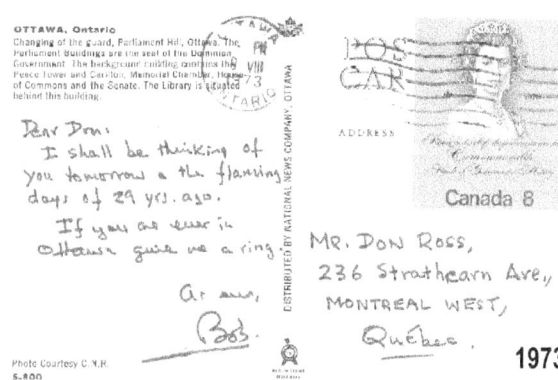

Dear Don:
I shall be thinking of you tomorrow & the flaming days of 29 yrs. ago.
If you are ever in Ottawa give us a ring.
As ever,
Bob.

Mr. Don Ross,
236 Strathearn Ave,
MONTREAL WEST,
Québec.

1973

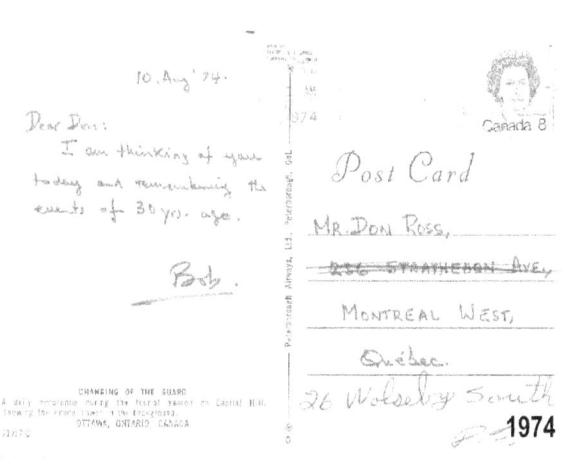

10. Aug. '74.

Dear Don:
I am thinking of you today and remembering the events of 30 yrs. ago.
Bob.

Mr. Don Ross,
~~236 Strathearn Ave,~~
MONTREAL WEST,
Québec.
26 Wolseley South

1974

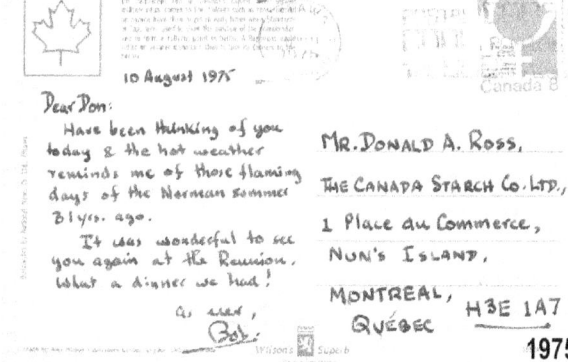

10 August 1975

Dear Don:
Have been thinking of you today & the hot weather reminds me of those flaming days of the Norman summer 31 yrs. ago.
It was wonderful to see you again at the Reunion. What a dinner we had!
As ever,
Bob

Mr. Donald A. Ross,
The Canada Starch Co. Ltd.,
1 Place du Commerce,
Nun's Island,
MONTREAL,
QUÉBEC H3E 1A7

1975

Content provided by and used with permission from Donna Ross

1980

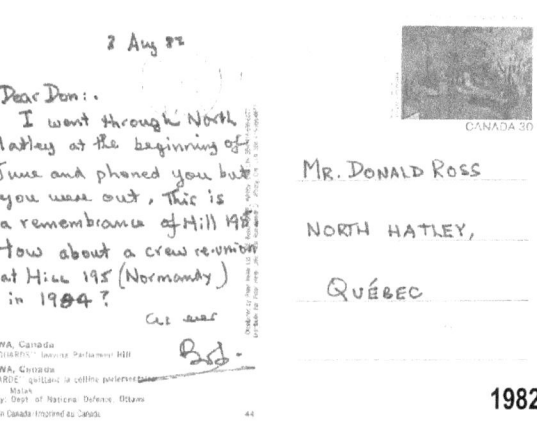

1982

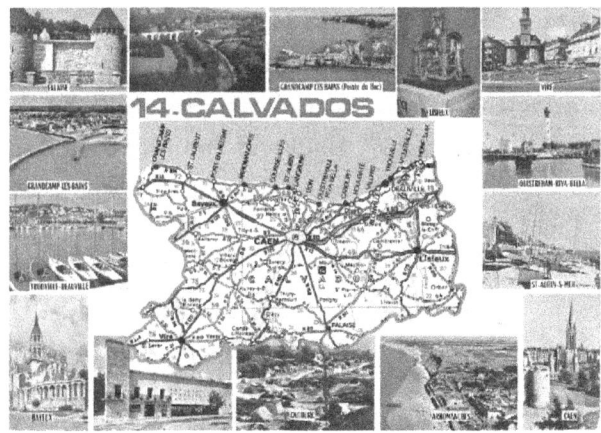

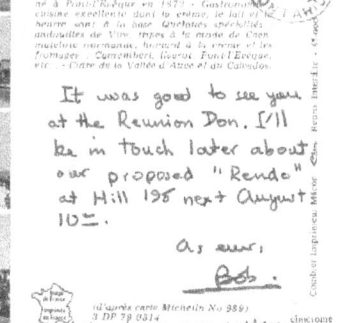

1983

Content provided by and used with permission from Donna Ross

Image of the painting by Adam Sherriff Scott (1887-1980), hanging in the Canadian Grenadier Guards Museum in Montreal, Quebec, Canada commemorating the capture of Hill 195 presented by the Molson Family. Also featured in The Standard, Montreal, August 25th, 1945 and The Montreal Daily Star, January 28th, 1946.

Robert (Bob) Osborne used one of these sources as inspiration for his postcard to Don Ross in 1963.

Content provided by and used with permission from Donna Ross

Salute to Victory
1945-08-25
The Standard, Montreal

Caption: During the bitter fighting along the Caen-Falaise Road, the Canadian Grenadier Guards were ordered to seize Hill 195 dominating a large area vital to the success of further Canadian Army Operations.

The Guards attacked and after two hours [of] severe fighting during which several tanks were lost, captured their objective.

And, through twelve hours of murderous concentrations of shell and mortar fire and of desperate counter attacks during which numerous enemy robot tanks, S.P. Guns and tanks were destroyed, the Guards held the position until relieved by a stronger force.

The Standard, Montreal © 1945

The Homecoming
Lieutenant Donald Armitage Ross, Canadian Grenadier Guards

Georgina H. Matthews

My brother, Lieutenant Donald Ross, joined the Canadian Grenadier Guards in Montreal in the early years of the Second World War, and after training at Farnham, Quebec, and Camp Borden, Ontario, left for England on 12 September 1942. Almost two years later, on 24 July the Guards, as one unit of the 4th Armoured Brigade, 4th Canadian Armoured Division, embarked for Normandy and by 5 August were deployed in battle.

Meantime, Lieutenant Ross's wife went to live in Montreal West at her parents' home. I too had returned to my family's home, also in Montreal West, after my husband Flight Lieutenant D.J. Matthews, had joined an RAF Squadron in England. Along with many other war wives, Mary Lou and I anxiously followed news of the battles in Normandy, ever dreading delivery of a telegram from the Defence Department.

One morning the ringing of the doorbell summoned my Father, my Mother and me to the front hall where we huddled together as Dad slowly opened the official-looking envelope. We waited almost breathless. Would it be, "We regret to inform you..."?

No, the dreaded news was that Don had been wounded on 11 August. With a deep sigh I whispered, "Thank goodness, now he will be out of the fighting." Mother's eyes brimmed with tears; Dad looked heavenwards in prayerful thanks.

Then began the days and weeks of waiting for news, for some details of Don's wounds, for exchanging with his wife any scraps of information she had gleaned. In mid-September a letter addressed to Dad in Don's own handwriting was mulled over endlessly. When he said he was "fine" how should that be interpreted? How could he be "fine" if he was being treated with sulpha, penicillin and morphine and acknowledging his left leg was "a bit painful"? What about his shaky handwriting What about his estimate of four to six months in hospital?

One sorrowful day news came his left leg had been amputated because gangrene had developed. I realized Mother's anguish as she had to accept the brutality of that wound to her adored firstborn.

Weeks went by, letters were sent or were received, friends tried with jocularity to assuage our worries about Don's serious disability. By October's end we began to hope he might be home for Christmas. More waiting, more days of expecting word of his return. At last a notice in the newspaper: a Red Cross ship had docked in Halifax with soldiers invalided home, and the train carrying Montreal-bound men would arrive on December 22. What excitement ensued!

A Christmas tree! We must have a Christmas tree, but where could one be found? This was wartime; the vacant lots usually stacked with freshly cut fir trees were empty. One day on a return trip from downtown Montreal I spied a corner lot with a sign advertising "CHRISTMAS TREES." Still miles from home, without a car to transport a tree, what could I do?

The next day I retraced my journey and purchased one of the few remaining trees. It was no beauty, meagre and scrawny and somewhat

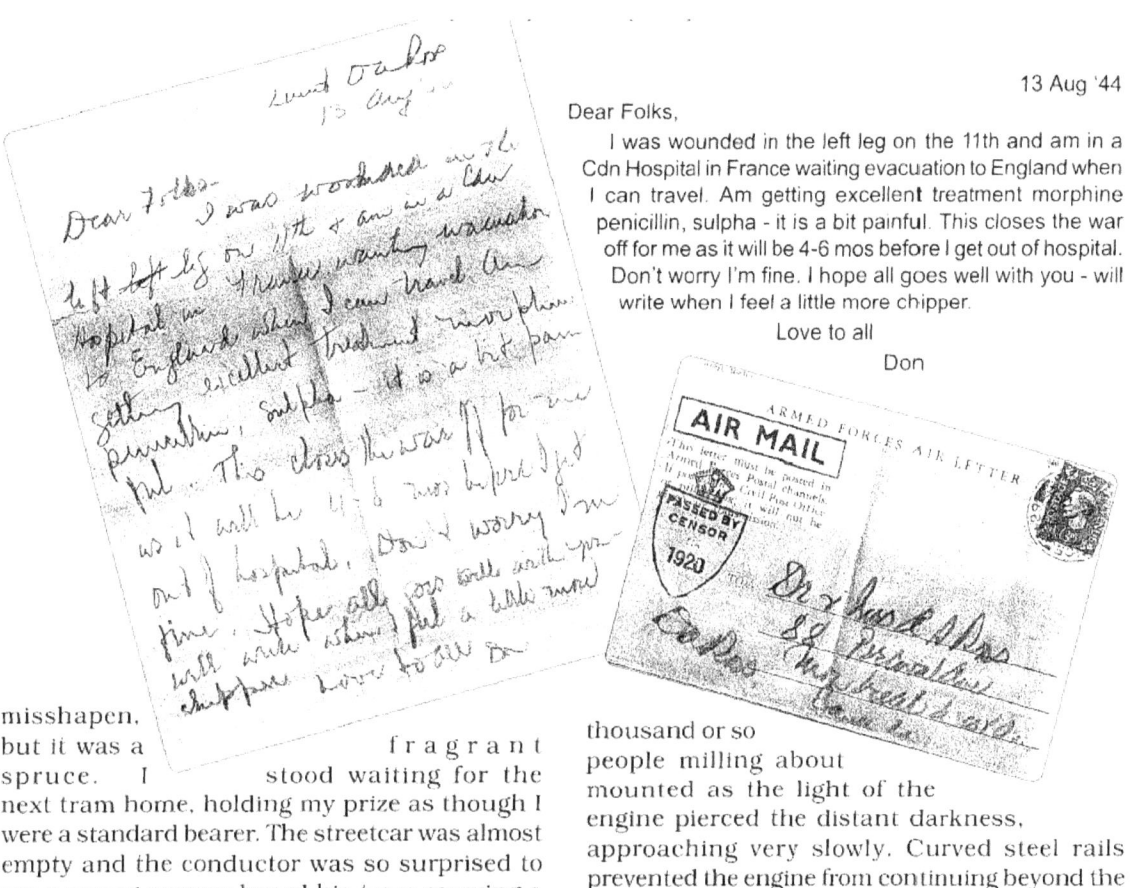

13 Aug '44

Dear Folks,

I was wounded in the left leg on the 11th and am in a Cdn Hospital in France waiting evacuation to England when I can travel. Am getting excellent treatment morphine penicillin, sulpha - it is a bit painful. This closes the war off for me as it will be 4-6 mos before I get out of hospital. Don't worry I'm fine. I hope all goes well with you - will write when I feel a little more chipper.

Love to all

Don

misshapen, but it was a fragrant spruce. I stood waiting for the next tram home, holding my prize as though I were a standard bearer. The streetcar was almost empty and the conductor was so surprised to see a young woman board his tram carrying a tree he raised no objection as I took a place at the rear of the car.

The next hurdle was the long walk from the last tram stop. In the snow and darkness of that December night I hoisted the tree to my shoulder, chuckling at the sight I must have presented to passersby, and trudged home with my treasure.

The Armed Forces' train was to arrive at Montreal's Bonaventure Station on 22 December between 11 pm and midnight. Each wife of a returning soldier was sent three passes to allow her and two others entry to the platform. It was a surprise when my sister-in-law phoned to invite me to go with her and my Father to meet Don's train, and my heart overflowed with gratitude at her recognition of what this would mean to me.

The Bonaventure CNR Station was an ancient building with no amenities. Wide double doors along the side opened onto a wooden platform that stretched the full width of the station, looking out on several sets of tracks which ran at right angles to the building, each having cement walkways adjacent. We stood out on the platform as close as permitted to where the train would stop. Excitement among the thousand or so people milling about mounted as the light of the engine pierced the distant darkness, approaching very slowly. Curved steel rails prevented the engine from continuing beyond the safety point as it shuddered to a stop and coughed up a last blast of steam.

No one who was there that desperately cold midnight of 1944 will ever forget the sight of hundreds of soldiers streaming down the walkways, on stretchers, on crutches, with empty sleeves, with empty trouser legs fastened high, all purposefully making their way towards us. Don was one of those on crutches, one leg missing. We signalled to him excitedly and at last caught his eye, and, in a crush of people and as he grasped his crutches tightly he was embraced first by Mary Lou, then by Dad, then by me. I felt useless trying to clear a way to the exit. Don gently tapped a bystander on the shoulder. "Can we please get through?" Immediately the crowd melted back.

A taxi was found and we were on our way to Mary Lou's place where her parents and Mother awaited us with hot beverages. Don and Mary Lou disappeared but startled us all as an alarming thump was heard and a clatter followed that could be nothing but his crutches hitting the floor. We stilled, fearing an injury for him, but soon voices and laughter bubbled from the next room.

An "O" Group for the personnel of No.1 Protective Troop, Headquarters Squadron, 4th Canadian Armoured Brigade, Vaucelles, France, 7 August 1944. Lieutenant Ross is third from the right with the cigarette.

The following day Mary Lou, along with Don and their 20-month-old daughter came to Mother and Dad's to see all the family. I shall never forget Mary Lou's remark to me as they left. Her two-year vigil for an absent husband had just ended; mine was to continue for almost a year more. She turned to me, "I hope Joe will be home with you next Christmas." Touched by her kindness, I looked aside and bowed my head lest she see the shimmering of my tears.

* * * * *

Years later, in September 1991, Lieutenant Ross, accompanied by one of his sons, returned to the Normandy battlefields. Standing on Hill 195 which had been the Regiment's objective of 10/11 August 1944, he spoke into a mike and was filmed as he pointed out the railway line, the orchard, and Quesnay Woods where German tanks and guns had been concealed on that fateful day long ago. He talked of his tank being hit and of being catapulted out of it. As it burned he returned to check for a missing crew member. Bob Osbourne, badly injured and helpless, was still inside. Hauling him out, Don hoisted him to his back, and as the tank exploded, he himself was struck by shrapnel. One of his crew crawled forward and dragged him to the cover of a shallow ditch where he lay for nearly four hours before he and Osbourne were picked up.

For the rest of his life, every year on the anniversary of that battle, Bob Osbourne sent a note of gratitude to Don, and, once a pen and ink sketch of their tank Giraffe in flames and a wounded man being carried on another's back away from the inferno.

* * * * *

In June of 1999 I had the rare good fortune to join a study tour of the Normandy battlefields led by Terry Copp. We visited Hill 195, and as we stood on that open hillside hallowed by the blood of those young soldiers of long ago we marvelled at how that ancient land was now liberated and peaceful. The fields of ripening wheat gently undulated and a phantom breeze softly whispered "Lest We Forget".

* * * * *

Lieutenant Donald Ross died on 10 July 1992.

Right: Lieutenant Donald A. Ross

Below: The wreck of a Canadian Grenadier Guards Sherman tank with Quesnay Woods in the background. Photographed in 1946.

World War II Memorial

In editing and publishing this record of events, I was saddened as I searched for information on the people my father named in its pages as friends, schoolmates and fellow military. Name after name came up on the many wonderful memorial sites honouring those who made the ultimate sacrifice, their lives. Almost all stricken down in their 20's. It also made me realize just how lucky I, and the rest of my siblings, are to be here today.

Thankfully, many survived the war and returned home to families, friends and hopefully a country that welcomed them back to start a new chapter in their lives. It is my hope that this memorial section will not only honour those who died, but also honour those that served in World War II and all past and present military personnel whom we take for granted.

I was surprised at the effort many have gone to in gathering information, designing and maintaining websites and making valuable historical data available, particularly at no cost (or at least for the sites I found) or by donations of money, time and/or resources. Although I did not have much to offer, I did find some pictures and documents that I was happy to share along with a few corrections and clarifications along the way that I hope will make their way to relatives researching their family roots in the future.

In particular, I would like to acknowledge the following sites for their hard work and the primary sources of the content in this section:

CWGC - Commonwealth War Graves Commission
Website - http://www.cwgc.org
Funding: Government (United Kingdom, Canada, Australia, New Zealand, South Africa, India) and PayPal Donations Gratefully Accepted

Canada At War
Website - http://www.canadaatwar.ca/memorial/world-war-ii/
Funding: Privately run - PayPal Donations Gratefully Accepted

Find A Grave
Website - http://www.findagrave.com/index.html
Funding - Privately run - Volunteers / Advertising Revenue

Canadian Virtual War Memorial
Website - http://www.veterans.gc.ca/eng/remembrance/memorials/canadian-virtual-war-memorial
Funding - Government of Canada - Veterans Affairs Canada

Fallen Heroes of Normandy
Website - http://fallenheroesofnormandy.org/
Funding - Privately run - PayPal Donations Gratefully Accepted

David Osborne, 2016

CWGC

The Commonwealth War Graves Commission owes its existence to the vision and determination of one man - Sir Fabian Ware.

Neither a soldier nor a politician, Ware was nevertheless well placed to respond to the public's reaction to the enormous losses in the war. At 45 he was too old to fight but he became the commander of a mobile unit of the British Red Cross. Saddened by the sheer number of casualties, he felt driven to find a way to ensure the final resting places of the dead would not be lost forever. His vision chimed with the times. Under his dynamic leadership, his unit began recording and caring for all the graves they could find. By 1915, their work was given official recognition by the War Office and incorporated into the British Army as the Graves Registration Commission.

Royal Recognition

Ware was keen that the spirit of Imperial cooperation evident in the war was reflected in the work of his organisation. Encouraged by the Prince of Wales, he submitted a memorandum to the Imperial War Conference. In May 1917, the Imperial War Graves Commission was established by Royal Charter, with the Prince serving as President and Ware as Vice-Chairman.

The Commission's work began in earnest after the Armistice. Once land for cemeteries and memorials had been guaranteed, the enormous task of recording the details of the dead began. By 1918, some 587,000 graves had been identified and a further 559,000 casualties were registered as having no known grave.

Establishing principles

The Commission set the highest standards for all its work. Three of the most eminent architects of the day - Sir Edwin Lutyens, Sir Herbert Baker and Sir Reginald Blomfield - were chosen to begin the work of designing and constructing the cemeteries and memorials. Rudyard Kipling was tasked, as literary advisor, with advising on inscriptions.

Ware asked Sir Frederic Kenyon, the Director of the British Museum, to interpret the differing approaches of the principal architects. The report he presented to the Commission in November 1918 emphasised equality as the core ideology, outlining the principles we abide by today.

The Commonwealth War Graves Commission ensures that 1.7 million people who died in the two world wars will never be forgotten. We care for cemeteries and memorials at 23,000 locations, in 154 countries. Our values and aims, laid out in 1917, are as relevant now as they were almost 100 years ago.

What We Do

Explore this section to gain an insight into the variety of work we do.

History of CWGC

Find out more about the history and origins of our remarkable organisation.

Our Organisation

Find out more about how the CWGC is structured, who we are, how we are funded and how to contribute to our work.

Our Partners

The CWGC works in close association with many other organisations to achieve its task of commemorating those who died in the two world wars. Meet some of our partners here.

Common Questions

We don't always have the answer to your query or hold the information you need but we will try to direct you to someone who can help.

Careers

All you need to know about working for the CWGC and applying for any of our current vacancies.

In Memory of

Sergeant W.Op./Air Gnr.

Norman Sargeant Ball

R/55463, 150 (R.A.F.) Sqdn, Royal Canadian Air Force who died on 28 August 1942 Age 24

Son of Ezra and Anna Westover Ball, of Magog, Province of Quebec, Canada.

Remembered with Honour
Bergen General Cemetery

Commemorated in perpetuity by
the Commonwealth War Graves Commission

CWGC

BALL, NORMAN SARGEANT

Rank:	Sergeant
Trade:	W.Op./Air Gnr.
Service No:	R/55463
Date of Death:	28/08/1942
Age:	24
Regiment/Service:	Royal Canadian Air Force
	150 (R.A.F.) Sqdn
Grave Reference:	Plot 1. Row A. Grave 6.
Cemetery:	BERGEN GENERAL CEMETERY
Additional Information:	Son of Ezra and Anna Westover Ball, of Magog, Province of Quebec, Canada.

In Memory of

Flying Officer Pilot

William Henry Laurie Bellingham

J/25376, 412 Sqdn., Royal Canadian Air Force who died on 19 November 1944 Age 21

Son of William and Bertha Bellingham, of Magog, Province of Quebec, Canada.

Remembered with Honour
Reichswald Forest War Cemetery

Commemorated in perpetuity by
the Commonwealth War Graves Commission

CWGC
Commonwealth War Graves Commission

BELLINGHAM, WILLIAM HENRY LAURIE

Rank:	Flying Officer
Trade:	Pilot
Service No:	J/25376
Date of Death:	19/11/1944
Age:	21
Regiment/Service:	Royal Canadian Air Force
	412 Sqdn.
Grave Reference:	14. F. 6.
Cemetery:	REICHSWALD FOREST WAR CEMETERY
Additional Information:	Son of William and Bertha Bellingham, of Magog, Province of Quebec, Canada.

In Memory of

Lieutenant

David Harold Bindman

Royal Canadian Regiment who died on 10 December 1943 Age 24

Son of Carl and Margaret Marcuse Bindman, of Thetford Mines, Province of Quebec.

Remembered with Honour
Moro River Canadian War Cemetery

Commemorated in perpetuity by
the Commonwealth War Graves Commission

CWGC

BINDMAN, DAVID HAROLD

Rank:	Lieutenant
Date of Death:	10/12/1943
Age:	24
Regiment/Service:	Royal Canadian Regiment
Grave Reference:	X. C. 9.
Cemetery:	MORO RIVER CANADIAN WAR CEMETERY
Additional Information:	Son of Carl and Margaret Marcuse Bindman, of Thetford Mines, Province of Quebec.

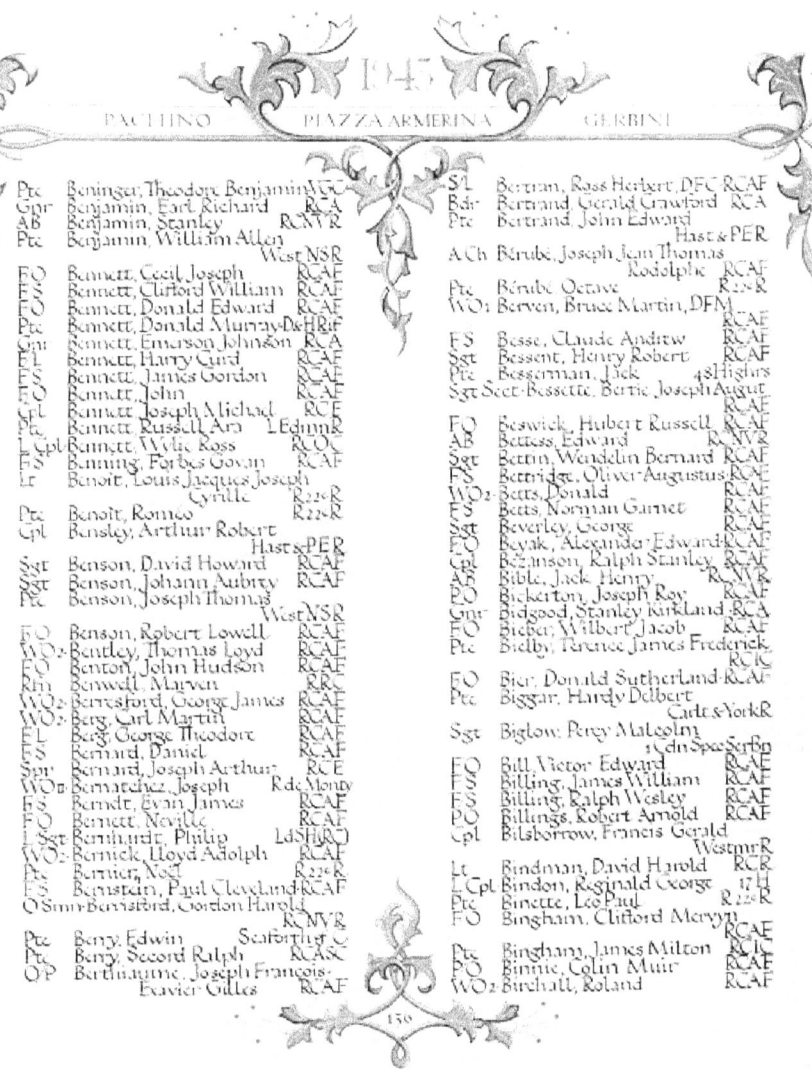

In Memory of

Private

Richard Everard Milne Connor

D/175677, Royal Hamilton Light Infantry, R.C.I.C. who died on 28 October 1944 Age 21

Son of Henry and Jane Elizabeth Barbour Connor, of Magog, Province of Quebec. King's Scout.

Remembered with Honour
Bergen-Op-Zoom Canadian War Cemetery

Commemorated in perpetuity by
the Commonwealth War Graves Commission

CWGC
Commonwealth War Graves Commission

CONNOR, RICHARD EVERARD MILNE

Rank:	Private
Service No:	D/175677
Date of Death:	28/10/1944
Age:	21
Regiment/Service:	Royal Hamilton Light Infantry, R.C.I.C.
Grave Reference:	7. C. 2.
Cemetery:	BERGEN-OP-ZOOM CANADIAN WAR CEMETERY
Additional Information:	Son of Henry and Jane Elizabeth Barbour Connor, of Magog, Province of Quebec. King's Scout.

PTE. RICHARD EVERARD CONNOR, 21, was killed in action October 28, according to word received by his parents, Mr. and Mrs. Henry Connor, of Magog. Pte. Connor was born near Belfast, Ireland, May 24, 1923, and came to Canada with his parents in June, 1926. He attended Magog High School and was a former King Scout. Prior to enlistment he was employed by the British Overseas Airways Corp. at Dorval as an airplane engine mechanic. Pte. Connor joined up in May, 1943, and went overseas a year later. He served in France and Belgium as a regimental signaller with the Royal Hamilton Light Infantry for two months. Besides his parents he is survived by five brothers Robert and John of Magog, Lt James Connor, R.C.A., Petawawa Edward, of Waterloo, and Norman of Vancouver, and one sister, Claire of Magog.

In Memory of

Private

Arthur Frederick Cordy

177291, 1st Bn., Canadian Infantry who died on 27 February 1917 Age 23

Son of Eliza Ann and the late John G. Cordy. Born at Sherbrooke Co., P.Q., Canada.

Remembered with Honour
Bruay Communal Cemetery Extension

Commemorated in perpetuity by

the Commonwealth War Graves Commission

CWGC

CORDY, ARTHUR FREDERICK

Rank:	Private
Service No:	177291
Date of Death:	27/02/1917
Age:	23
Regiment/Service:	Canadian Infantry
	1st Bn.
Grave Reference:	C. 20.
Cemetery:	BRUAY COMMUNAL CEMETERY EXTENSION
Additional Information:	Son of Eliza Ann and the late John G. Cordy. Born at Sherbrooke Co., P.Q., Canada.

In Memory of

Captain

Bernard Ernest Ghewy

22nd Armd. Regt., Canadian Grenadier Guards, R.C.A.C. who died on 24 August 1944 Age 28

Son of Gilbert W. and Alice Bender Ghewy; husband of Jane Adams Ghewy, of Montreal, Province of Quebec.

Remembered with Honour

Bretteville-Sur-Laize Canadian War Cemetery

Commemorated in perpetuity by

the Commonwealth War Graves Commission

CWGC

GHEWY, BERNARD ERNEST

Rank:	Captain
Date of Death:	24/08/1944
Age:	28
Regiment/Service:	Canadian Grenadier Guards, R.C.A.C.
	22nd Armd. Regt.
Grave Reference:	XXI. D. 6.
Cemetery:	BRETTEVILLE-SUR-LAIZE CANADIAN WAR CEMETERY
Additional Information:	Son of Gilbert W. and Alice Bender Ghewy; husband of Jane Adams Ghewy, of Montreal, Province of Quebec.

In Memory of

Guardsman

George Holidenke

D/129411, 22nd Armd. Regt., Canadian Grenadier Guards, R.C.A.C. who died on 10 August 1944 Age 29

(served as HOLDEN). Son of Morris and Yetta Holidenke.

Remembered with Honour
Beny-Sur-Mer Canadian War Cemetery, Reviers

Commemorated in perpetuity by
the Commonwealth War Graves Commission

CWGC
Commonwealth War Graves Commission

HOLIDENKE, GEORGE

Rank:	Guardsman
Service No:	D/129411
Date of Death:	10/08/1944
Age:	29
Regiment/Service:	Canadian Grenadier Guards, R.C.A.C.
	22nd Armd. Regt.
Grave Reference:	VIII. C. 12.
Cemetery:	BENY-SUR-MER CANADIAN WAR CEMETERY, REVIERS
Additional Information:	(served as HOLDEN). Son of Morris and Yetta Holidenke.

GUARDSMAN GEORGE HOLDEN

GUARDSMAN GEORGE HOLDEN, D-129411, Canadian Grenadier Guards, of Montreal, died of wounds on August 10, 1944, according to an official announcement. He was buried at Beny-sur-Mer Canadian Military Cemetery, France.

Guardsman Holden enlisted in 1941 and went overseas in 1942. He was attached to the 22nd Armoured Regiment, Canadian Grenadier Guards when he was wounded in France.

Guardsman Holden's sister, Mrs. Betty Holidenke, lives at 1247 Grant Avenue, Bronx, N.Y.

George Holden

1985-05-24 Bob Osborne at George Holden's Grave Berniere-sur-Mer

In Memory of
Lance Corporal

William A. G. Knapp

E/30545, Royal Rifles of Canada, R.C.I.C. who died on 22 November 1943 Age 22

Son of William H. and Shirley Gowen Knapp.

Remembered with Honour
Yokohama War Cemetery

Commemorated in perpetuity by
the Commonwealth War Graves Commission

CWGC
Commonwealth War Graves Commission

KNAPP, WILLIAM A. G.

Rank:	Lance Corporal
Service No:	E/30545
Date of Death:	22/11/1943
Age:	22
Regiment/Service:	Royal Rifles of Canada, R.C.I.C.
Grave Reference:	Cdn. Sec. A. C. 16.
Cemetery:	YOKOHAMA WAR CEMETERY
Additional Information:	Son of William H. and Shirley Gowen Knapp.

In Memory of
Sergeant W.Op./Air Gnr.

Angus MacIntosh

1342558, Royal Air Force Volunteer Reserve who died on 05 May 1943 Age 22

Son of Margaret Mary MacIntosh, of Corpach.

Remembered with Honour
Oban (Pennyfuir) Cemetery

**Commemorated in perpetuity by
the Commonwealth War Graves Commission**

CWGC

MacINTOSH, ANGUS

Rank:	Sergeant
Trade:	W.Op./Air Gnr.
Service No:	1342558
Date of Death:	05/05/1943
Age:	22
Regiment/Service:	Royal Air Force Volunteer Reserve
Grave Reference:	Sec. O. Grave 26.
Cemetery:	OBAN (PENNYFUIR) CEMETERY
Additional Information:	Son of Margaret Mary MacIntosh, of Corpach.

In Memory of

Trooper

Douglas Delbert McKnight

D/26661, 22nd Armd. Regt., Canadian Grenadier Guards, R.C.A.C. who died on 26 February 1945

Son of Mr. and Mrs. Chester G. McKnight, of North Hatley, Province of Quebec, Canada.

Remembered with Honour
Groesbeek Memorial

**Commemorated in perpetuity by
the Commonwealth War Graves Commission**

CWGC
Commonwealth War Graves Commission

McKNIGHT, DOUGLAS DELBERT

Rank:	Trooper
Service No:	D/26661
Date of Death:	26/02/1945
Regiment/Service:	Canadian Grenadier Guards, R.C.A.C. 22nd Armd. Regt.
Panel Reference:	Panel 10.
Memorial:	GROESBEEK MEMORIAL
Additional Information:	Son of Mr. and Mrs. Chester G. McKnight, of North Hatley, Province of Quebec, Canada.

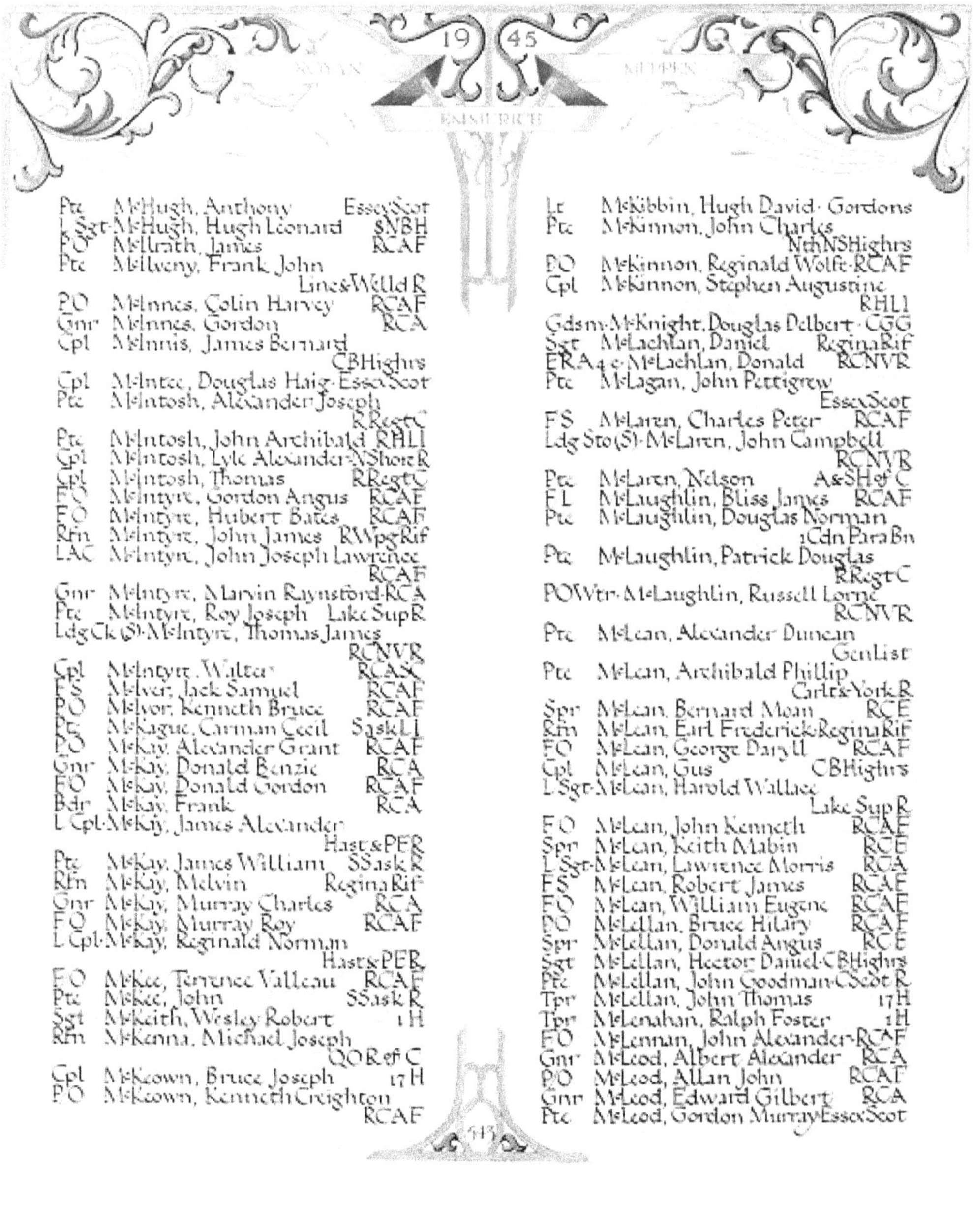

In Memory of

Flight Lieutenant Pilot

Wilbur Lewis Turner

J/8378, 218 (R.A.F.) Sqdn, Royal Canadian Air Force who died on 04 May 1943 Age 28

Son of Grayson L. and Betsy Ann Turner; husband of Miriam Annabel Turner, of Waterville, Province of Quebec, Canada.

Remembered with Honour

Dantumadeel (Damwoude) General Cemetery

Commemorated in perpetuity by

the Commonwealth War Graves Commission

CWGC
Commonwealth War Graves Commission

TURNER, WILBUR LEWIS

Rank:	Flight Lieutenant
Trade:	Pilot
Service No:	J/8378
Date of Death:	04/05/1943
Age:	28
Regiment/Service:	Royal Canadian Air Force
	218 (R.A.F.) Sqdn
Grave Reference:	Plot E. Row 7. Grave 4.
Cemetery:	DANTUMADEEL (DAMWOUDE) GENERAL CEMETERY
Additional Information:	Son of Grayson L. and Betsy Ann Turner; husband of Miriam Annabel Turner, of Waterville, Province of Quebec, Canada.

Document Title: War Diary of 22x Cdn Armd Regt (CGG).

Author(s): Lieutenant-Colonel W.W. Halpenny.

Date(s): July-August, 1944.

Document Type/Physical Description: Textual Records.

Fonds/Collection Name: RG 24, The Department of National Defence Fonds.

Original Archival Reference: RG 24-C-3 Volume 14260 ; Microfilm Reel T-12727.

Item Description: Every unit in the Canadian and British armies kept a daily record of events, titled 'War Diary or Intelligence Summary'. The length of these documents varies by unit, but they all give a detailed and revealing overview of the activities of the unit during its period(s) of operation.

Keywords: Normandy ; Battle of Normandy ; D-Day ; Second World War ; Canadian Army ; Canadian Army ; 22nd Canadian Armoured Regiment ; Canadian Grenadier Guards ; 4th Canadian Armoured Division

*When citing material digitized from other archives, the LMH Archive encourages users to cite the original reference information provided in the above field.

The purpose of the Laurier Military History Archive is to acquire, preserve and make available documents relating to the Canadian and international experience of military conflict in the twentieth and twenty-first centuries.

Website: http://www.lmharchive.ca/   **E-mail:** admin@canadianmilitaryhistory.ca

War Diary – Summary of Events and Information

22 Canadian Armoured Regiment - Canadian Grenadier Guards

Tuesday August 8th, 1944

Lt Phalan's tp was at this time in the woods at 075547 and was ordered to advance having observed flashes from the corner of the orchard, at 079543, Lt Phalan fired HE and advanced, finding he had shot up an 88mm gun. Moving around the north of the orchard, he winged a 2cm gun at the corner, and moving across to the bldgs at 078540 he got two more 2 cms. With his tp covering his advance, he dashed across to 075535 which appeared to be a prepared posn of some kind. Across the open stretch he was fired on by 88s from the hedge running SW from CINTHEAUX. This hedge was plastered with HE and co-ax by his tp sgt and it was found to contain three 88mm and one 2cm all of which were knocked out. On going over the mound at 075536 he saw 3 SP guns, two immediately to his front (same m/r) and one withdrawing at 075531. All three were fired on and halted one of these at 075536 going up on impact with a tremendous flash. Joined by the rest of his tp he proceeded to round up prisoners, and whilst dismounted so doing another SP gun exploded killing one man and wounding five others. Not daunted, they nevertheless rounded up 28 PWs. About 15 dead men were counted around the gun posns. Two of his tks had become X-ray cas. A coy of the A & SH (Maj Farmer) arrived on the scene, and they took over the job of mopping up the town. No. 3 sqn excluding no. 4 tp who remained down in the hollow near the rly, harboured at the orchard 078543 and no. 1 sqn went back to a regtl harbour at Gaumesnil where they were joined by no. 2 sqn. It was then 2000 hrs and it was considered that in view of the fact that darkness was rapidly approaching, the fact that some regrouping and the proper tying up the next advance was necessary, that a dawn attack on Bretteville-le-Rabet would be most likely successful. The adv was tied up to continue at 0315 hrs.

Wednesday August 9th, 1944

Weather - fair. At 0330 hrs no. 2 sqn pushed on to go to phase 1 which was Bretteville-le-Rabet. The order of march was no. 2, no. 1, RHQ no. 3 sqn being left in the orchard at Cintheaux at 079543 to spend the day resting. The move was completed very quickly and by 0600 hrs, when it was just becoming light, no. 2 sqn had reached the low ground at 093507, no. 1 sqn and RHQ being at 095513. Considerable speculative shooting was engaged in and the tracer bullets were about as thick as snow in a snow-storm. Gradually everyone stopped firing, and it was then possible to observe flashes coming from an anti-tk gun at 010501 which was silenced with HE by Lt Grieve. No. 1 sqn then regrouped for the attack on Bretteville, no. 2 sqn and RHQ returning to their previous harbour at Gaumesnil. The clearing of Bretteville was to be carried out by no. 1 sqn and a coy of the LSB, another coy of the LSR being in reserve.

The initial clearing was done by no. 1 tp under Lt McKinnon who entered covered by the fire of the rest of the sqn from the north of the town. Surprised by 88 fire Lt McKinnon's tk was brewed up and he was wounded. Later on Lt Verner's tk ran out of petrol having been running almost steadily since 0100 hrs the previous morning but he was towed back. Apart from these incidents, the operation was most successful and by 1500 hrs the town was cleared. Scores of enemy had been killed by co-ax and HE, the gunners having a fd day. HE rds against single inf was quite in order and speculative shooting on hedges and houses flushed the enemy inf who were then co-axed by the score. The LSR took over 60 prisoners in this operation. No. 1 sqn returned rather weary but still going strong at Gaumesnil shortly after 1700hrs. During the evening Capt C Cassila replaced Capt CHP Smith as Adjutant. No. 2 sqn moved to 091515 with two tps fwd to assume a mobile counter attack role. While the attack on Bretteville was in progress, the BCRs and the GGFGs had pushed on and it appeared during the evening that they would attain their objectives in phase 2, and we were ordered to push on to phase 2-B (see appx _) without delay. The BCRs were supposed to be at 20 but had not been heard from since 1000 hrs. The 21st were headed for phase 2-A but were having trouble south of Grainville La Gannerie. The A & SH were putting in an attack south of the Caen-Falaise rd at 1800 hrs. Our proposed adv was called off when it was heard that the SARs were doing the same thing, but it was soon on again, and the orders having been already issued it was not long until the regt was moving. The order of march was no. 2 sqn with a section of Recce and one FOO from 23rd SP, no. 3 sqn in support, RHQ, and then no. 1 sqn in reserve. The adv was to be in two phases, phase 1 (code word Christmas) being the orchard near the embankment at 087483 and phase 2 (code word New Years) was the objective (phase 2B in sq 120747). No. 2 sqn was to complete Christmas before the rest of the regt moved (for route see map).

Thursday August 10th, 1944

Weather - fair. No. 2 sqn reported "Christmas clear" at 0030 hrs and no. 3 sqn then began to move followed by RHQ and no. 1 sqn. A cross country move from the wood at 090515 was quite difficult since the moon had not yet risen and the night was very dark, but thanks to some guidance from Maj Smith and Amy the two sqns arrived safely at Christmas. Lt Shaugnessy, who was leading no. 2 sqn, later gave Sgt McIsaac of the Recce Tp credit for leading them across this rather difficult stretch. On the way down, the CO's tk, Grenadier, threw a track, and was left behind i/c of Lt RHW Brown.

The Regt was assembled at "Christmas" by 0300 hrs. It was decided to await first light before carrying on to "New Years". During the interim orders were rec'd to go on directly to phase 3, the pt 206, in sq 0943 and to stand by on 10 mins notice to move. Orders to move were not rec'd until shortly after 0800 hrs and by this time the I.O. Lt CL Tomlinson, had liaised with the Lincoln & Welland at 092493 and found out that the A&SH had occupied the high ground at pt 195 (Phase 2C) and that two coys of the L&Ws were at phase 2B with some of the Alq in the area of St Hilaire Fe at 0847. Information was also rec'd from an unknown Lieut in the L&W that there had been a Tiger tk in the orchard that evening. It seemed inconceivable that this tk could still be there for we had been there all night but later on it opened up on a repaired GRENADIER and holed her through the front plate. However, no. 2 sqn moved off at 0815 their first bound being the pt 195. On arriving there they were to form up on the feature allowing no. 3 sqn to pass on to final objective. Two enemy tks were seen in the area south of St Hilaire Fe and fire was experienced from Quesnay Wood 103482 to the east by the main road. Two tks, one 5C and one 75 from no. 2 sqn were lost in at Hilaire Fe area, but the adv continued and by 1130 hrs nos. 2 and 3 Sqns and RHQ had reached the cornfd to the north of pt 195. A 5 barreled mortar on the sky line was knocked out by no. 2 sqn. An Orders Gp was held in the centre of the fd, three tks being parked to form an armoured box at about 087462. One of no. 2 sqn's tks which had ventured to the right of 195 was ominously brewing. It was felt that the adv to pt 206 must be properly laid on with arty and air sp, and targets were picked and given to the arty rep, Maj Talford. At 1150 hrs Lt-Col W W Halpenny attempted to contact Bde to give them his plans and it was discovered that comms bad broken down. At 1155 hrs the regt come under severe 88 fire from the left flank and though no definite clue as to the origin of the fire was given it appeared to come from the left of the crest, the mine at 1045 and the hedge to left of the cornfd. All the comds were at this time out of their tks and comms to Bde were out, so the attack came at a most inopportune moment. Control was soon exercised by Lt-Col Halpenny who issued a regtl fire order to spray the crest and the left front with co-ax and HE. Three ROBOT TKS were launched at us from the right of the row of trees at the crest to increase our difficulties. These were about the size of carriers, carried a white flag on top of their aerial and travelled at about 12 to 15 miles per hour.

They seemed to stop momentarily, and change their course just before their final adv which terminated in their explosion. Hits on the robots were claimed by Lt-Col Halpenny and Major Amy but whether their explosion was caused by our fire or the enemy's desire could not be stated. Their value is problematic, for the blast being practical vertical caused no material injury to us. By 1300 hrs the enemy's attack had diminished in furor. Nos. 2 and 3 Sqns with the exception of seven or eight tks which were brewing in the fd nearest the crest, had pulled down behind the hedge to regroup. Comm with Bde were re-established and Lt-Col Halpenny reported on the situation and explained that further adv, in view of the opposition encountered, would be impractical without inf to clear out the A/Tk guns. We were therefore ordered to remain on the pt 195 and to hold it in conjunction with the A&SH. Lt Stanbury's tk was one of those which had burned and he was wounded. Sgt Forsythe and Sgt Andrews were knocked out. Throughout the remainder of the day the area was periodically shelled. We brought down Typhoons and shell fire on all likely targets on our front. During the afternoon the 21st C.A.R, moved up to the area 080475.

Capt H Hawes had a rather interesting experience at about 1500 hrs when be passed "Christmas" when bringing up tks which had been put back on the rd after previously having been cas. Since the regt had long been in possession of pt 195, he felt that the area near the rly would be relatively safe, but as he was breezing along with his six tks an 88 opened up (the Tiger reported in the morning?) and stopped GRENADIER leaving her with a gaping hole in the front. During the afternoon we were told that we would be relieved by the GGFG but because of difficulties in contacting their Comd Offr, the change was not effected.

Friday August 11th, 1944

Weather - Fair. At 0430 hrs firing was heard from the Foot Guards' area. They were attacked from the west by inf who came in with the German equivalent of the Bazooka. A tremendous display of Browning fire went up and the attack was stopped with heavy losses to the enemy, about 60 prisoners being taken. At 0830 hrs Lt-Col Halpenny left to consult with Brig Booth. During the morning the area was very heavily shot up with 88 HE and mortars and four tks including two from RHQ, were knocked out, there being twelve cas. Arrangements were finally made with the 21st CAR to take over our responsibilities and the regt began to leave the pt 195, a tp at a time, beginning at 1400 hrs. The run down proved a difficult one, 88mm in the wood at 100483 opening up at each tp as it came into the St Hilaire farm area. Six tks were knocked out on the way down, these included Lt D A Ross (who was wounded) Capt Douglas (FOO from 11 Med Regt) Cpl Buck, Sgt A B MacDonald, Lt W D MacDonald (who was wounded). Having run the gauntlet, the tks pulled into a temporary harbour in the orchard, 092495. Capt G D Sherwood had moved up the A1 Ech and the crews refuelled and then had a ration of rum and a bottle of beer a piece. A meal followed and almost everyone had time to wash and generally clean up. The Regt then moved via Lagannerie to the old harbour at Gaumesnil. After dark it moved to the wood at 107557. Reveille for the following morning was set at 1200 o'clock and everyone went to bed with a feeling of complete relaxation to enjoy a well earned full night's sleep. Some mention should be made for the excellent work done by the echelons. Crew going back to T.D.R. after having bailed out of their brewing tks are treated more or less like schoolboys back home on leave. They are immediately given small packs, mess tins, shaving eqpt, blankets, etc., and battle dress and complete change of clothes if so reqd. Cigarettes and candies, square meals and plenty of opportunity for sleep. All assist in getting them over the initial shock and back on their feet for another fight. At leaving pt 195 we rec'd an air photo (Appx 16) showing what we had been up against.

Saturday August 12th, 1944

Weather - Fair. After a good night's sleep the Regt went to work to get in shape for the next show. Truck loads of Tigers and Sherman tracks, salvaged from burned out tks were welded or wired onto tks to thicken their skin. Most of the regts attended a much needed and heartily appreciated bath parade. Cas for the operation were at last compiled and the result was amazingly low. There were; killed 11, wounded 43, tks knocked out and not recovered 21. During the operation it is reasonably estimated we killed well over 500 Germans. At least 100 Germans were taken prisoners by us though they were turned over to the inf. Though we have not knocked out any tks, the score on SP guns, A/Tk guns, MGs and men has certainly been sufficiently high to outweigh our losses. The personnel and veh requirements are shown in Appx _. Lt Hobday and Chevrier rejoined the unit.

Glossary:

tank tp (or just tp) - tank troop
A & SH - The Argyle & Sutherland Highlanders of Canada (Princess Louise')
Alq - The Algonquin Regiment
L&W - The Lincoln & Welland Regiment
GGFG (or 21st) - 21st Armoured Regiment - Governor General's Foot Guards
i/c - In Care of
CAS - Casualty
Tk - Tanks
coy - convoy
LSR - The Lake Superior Regiment
LSB - (?)Landing Support Battalion(?)Logistics Support Battalion(?)
BCR - 28th Armoured Regiment - The British Columbia Regiment, Duke of Connaught's Own Rifles
SAR - 29th Armoured Reconnaissance Regiment - The South Albert Regiment
SP or SP Gun - Self Propelled Artillery gun

Regimental Number **D26348** Rank **Gdsm.**

Name **Robert Ernest Osborne**

Next of Kin **Mrs. B.S. Osborne**

Address **9 Merry Street MACOG Que.**

Relationship **Mother.**

Regiment — Canadian Grenadier Guards, C.A.S.F.

Commanding Officer — Lt.-Col. M. F. Peiler, E.D.

Company **HQ** Co.'. C'm'd'r. **Major Sadler**

Platoon **#1** Pl. C'm'd'r. **Lieut. Shewy**

Section .... Sec. C'm'd'r. ....

Rifle No. **K6653**

Other Information ....

CANADIAN GRENADIER GUARDS

CANADIAN ACTIVE SERVICE FORCE

REGIMENTAL NOTES

for

Warrant Officers, N.C.O's and Guardsmen

Compiled by
MAJOR R. H. DEAN
LIEUT. G. R. WHISTON
and approved by
LT.-COL. M. F. PEILER, E.D.
Lt.-Colonel Commanding
Canadian Grenadier Guards, C.A.S.F.
MONTREAL, QUE.

June, 1940

CHAPTERS	Page
I. A brief history of the Regiment	3
II. The Spirit of the Regiment	11
III. Regimental Orders	12
IV. Order of Dress for Warrant Officers, N.C.O.'s and Guardsmen	12
V. Books and Pamphlets	14
VI. Discipline	14
VII. Drunkenness and Detention	16
VIII. Salutes	16
IX. Applications and Leave	18
X. Absence without Leave	19
XI. Health and Cleanliness	19
XII. General Advice	21

CANADIAN GRENADIER GUARDS

A Brief History of the Regiment

THE BRITISH ARMY took possession of Montreal September 8th, 1760. Within a fortnight from that date, the first steps were taken towards establishing a Canadian Militia under the British Flag. On September 19th, General Amherst, the first British Governor of Canada, instructed Colonel Haldimand to assemble the militia of Montreal who had served under the French regime.

Under certain conditions, and upon taking the Oath of Allegiance to the British Crown, the officers were re-commissioned and the men recruited to form the first Militia under British rule.

Tracing its origin from this body, in 1807, the first Battalion, Montreal Militia was organized.

From this Battalion the present Regiment is directly descended. In 1811, an order was issued raising the Battalion again, together with other units of the Montreal Garrison. The Commanding Officer was the Hon. James McGill, founder of McGill University, and many well-known citizens' names were on the Roll of Officers, among them Forsyth, Ogilvy, Logan, Gillespie, Badgley, Porteous, McTavish, Selby, Busby, Griffin. Several of these are commemorated in our street names of today.

In 1812, the United States declared war against Great Britain, and the First Battalion was immediately called upon. A detachment was present with the British forces in a successful raid on Plattsburg in 1813, and a Company fought with great distinction under DeSalaberry at the Battle of Chateauguay, in October 1813. The Battalion was presented with Colours by the Prince Regent for its services on this occasion. It continued under arms until the Declaration of Peace.

Among the officers of those days was Lieut. William Hallowell, whose uniform worn by him as a bugler before he obtained his commission, was recently presented to the Regiment by his descendants.

The Regiment's next active service was in 1837, when a Company under Major DeBleury fought at St. Eustache. One of the Lieutenants of the Company was William Meredith, afterwards Chief Justice Sir William Meredith. DeBleury was a grandson of the first Seigneur of Bleury, after whom Bleury Street was named.

In 1854, a special Company, called the Montreal Rifle Rangers, was formed under the command of Captain Theodore Lyman. The first private enrolled was George Washington Stephens. Among other citizens who joined were R. L. Gault, Thomas D. Hood, E. E. Beaudry, George Fraser, G. E. Starnes, L. A. Dufresne, Charles Nelson, R. G. Starke, Richard Thomas, W. L. Haldimand, William Farrell. A privates' uniform cost £17, a large sum in those days, and was of the same material as the officers' uniforms. In 1855 a Defence Act was passed, by which the Montreal Rifle Rangers was officially recognized, and became not only the senior militia body in Montreal, but the senior VOLUNTEER unit in the whole British Empire. The Rangers were then absorbed into the First Battalion, Montreal Militia, and eight other companies were quickly added. There is some interesting information available regarding these nine companies.

No. 1 (The Montreal Rifle Rangers) was composed of prominent citizens. Nos. 2 and 3 consisted largely of members of the City's Volunteer Fire Brigade. Nos. 4 and 5 were composed entirely of Irish Roman Catholics, No. 6 of Orangemen, No. 7 of Scottish Highlanders, and Nos. 8 and 9 were entirely French-Canadian. Surely a conclusive demonstration of the truth of the City motto, "Concordia Salus".

In 1859 these nine Companies were formally gazetted as the First Battalion, Volunteer Militia Rifles of Canada, the Commanding Officer being Lieut.-Colonel Thomas Wiley, and the Majors, Bernard Devlin, afterwards Mayor of Montreal, and Thomas Alfred Evans.

In 1860, H.R.H. the Prince of Wales, who was then in Canada, consented to give his name to the Battalion, and it was forthwith called the "First or Prince of Wales' Regiment, Volunteer Rifles of Canada". The status was then changed from a Battalion to a Regiment.

During H.R.H.'s stay in Montreal it furnished nine Royal Guards.

A Company of the Regiment served at Sandwich, Ont., from December, 1864, to May, 1865, during the alarm caused by the so-called St. Albans Raids. The Company was commanded by Capt. Frank Bond.

In 1866 and again in 1870, the whole Regiment was on active service in the Fenian Raids, but saw no actual fighting. It was commanded by Lieut.-Col. Bernard Devlin in 1866, and by Lieut.-Col. Frank Bond in 1870.

The Regiment was called out for active service in the Northwest Rebellion of 1885, but as there were indications of renewed Fenian activity on the borders of the Province, it was kept under arms in camp on the old Exhibition Grounds, where Mount Royal Avenue is today. It reached a very high state of efficiency at that time.

An amalgamation took place in 1898 of the First "Prince of Wales" Rifles and the Sixth Fusiliers under the name First "Prince of Wales" Regiment. Fusiliers, and H.R.H. honoured the Regiment by becoming the Honorary Colonel, retaining the appointment until his death.

The First "Prince of Wales" Regiment, Fusiliers, sent a detachment to the South African Campaign, thus gaining for the Regiment the battle honours "South Africa, 1899-1900".

A further change took place in 1912, when the Regiment was thoroughly reorganized under command of Lieut.-Col. J. W. Carson, afterwards Major-Gen. Sir John W. Carson, C.B. An unprecedented distinction was conferred upon it. By direct command of H.M. King George V., it was named the Canadian Grenadier Guards, and was thus not only raised to the status of Household Troops (Maison du Roi), but was granted the actual name of the unit which is not only the Senior Regiment of the Brigade of Guards, but of all British Infantry.

In 1914 came the supreme test of the Great War. The Regiment first sent overseas sufficient officers and men to constitute one-third of the 14th. Battalion C.E.F. It followed this up by sending one complete Company with the 23rd. Bn. C.E.F., and another with the 60th. Bn. C.E.F. In 1915 it raised a complete unit, the 87th. Bn. C.E.F., which, by permission of H.R.H. the Duke of Connaught, fought under its own name "Canadian Grenadier Guards". Two Companies of the 87th. Battalion were sent to the 1st. Battalion C.E.F., and were replaced from our reserves. Finally, it raised the 245th. Battalion C.E.F., "Canadian Grenadier Guards" under Lt.-Col. the Hon. C. C. Ballantyne. Unfortunately, this last was not given the opportunity to serve as a unit in France, as the Canadian Corps was already complete, but was used as reinforcements for the 87th. The Regiment thus practically furnished three Battalions for Canada's Overseas Forces.

The 87th. Bn. Canadian Grenadier Guards made a splendid record with the Fourth Canadian Division, and was one of the outstanding units of the Canadian Corps. It took part in all the great battles and it is a significant fact that in the four supreme and victorious engagements, the Somme, Vimy, Drocourt-Queant Line and Canal du Nord (Cambrai) it was selected to attack the most important and difficult point of the German defences, Regina Trench at the Somme, Hill 145 at Vimy, Dury Mill at Drocourt-Queant, and Bourlon Wood at Canal du Nord. In the last named battle it made four separate attacks in the five days of the battle and came out of action with only 125 left of all ranks. At Regina Trench it was the only Battalion of the Fourth Division that was called upon to make two attacks in the struggle which resulted in the capture of that defiant enemy stronghold.

These facts speak for themselves, and prove the confidence that the Higher Command had in its fighting ability.

Members of the Battalion won a long list of honours, among them the Victoria Cross awarded to Guardsman John Francis Young of Montreal.

The Regiment's Battle Honours, emblazoned on its Colours, are:

South Africa, 1899-1900
Ypres, 1915-1917
Festubert, 1915
Somme, 1916
Arras, 1917-1918
Vimy, 1917
Passchendaele
Amiens
Drocourt-Queant
Canal du Nord
France and Flanders, 1915-1918

In addition to the foregoing, the Regiment has the following Battle Honours:

Mount Sorel
Ancre Heights
Ancre, 1916
Souchez River
Hill 70
Scarpe, 1918
Sambre
Hindenburg Line
Pursuit to Mons
Valenciennes

The Grenadier Guards (British) have shown a keen interest in their Canadian namesakes. The Lieut.-Col. Commanding wrote: "We rejoice that the Canadian Grenadier Guards have so well maintained the glorious traditions of the name they bear, and our regret is that it has not been our good fortune to fight side by side during the War. The Regiment has watched with pride the spendid and distinguished services rendered by their Canadian brothers."

Praise from such a source is praise indeed.

In 1923, with the gracious approval of H.M. The King, H.R.H. the Prince of Wales was appointed Honorary-Colonel of the Regiment. In 1924, H.R.H. was given the rank of Colonel-in-Chief to bring the appointment into conformity with the custom in the Brigade of Guards.

The first meeting between His Royal Highness and the Regiment, took place in October 1919,

when it furnished the Royal Guard at Windsor Station on his arrival in Montreal. It was commanded by Captain A. H. Cowie, M.C., with Lieuts. Norman Nicholson, M.C., and A. W. W. Kyle, M.C., Lieut. Kyle carried the Colour. It numbered 100 men.

The first time, however, that His Royal Highness saw the Regiment, after he had become Colonel-in-Chief, was on August 1st, 1927, when it furnished the Royal Guard at the City Hall. The Guard of 100 men in full dress was under the command of Major H. D. Rolland, with Lieut. W. W. Gear and Lieut. J. C. F. Reid carrying the Colour. This was the first occasion that a parade bearing arms had worn the Guards full dress uniform in Montreal since 1865, when the British Grenadiers had a Battalion stationed here, on Le Royer Street.

On his return to Montreal from the West at the beginning of September, 1927, His Royal Highness visited the Armoury, where the Warrant Officers and N.C.O's were presented to him. He then went to the Sergeant's Mess and inspected their trophies and Honour Roll, being much interested in the latter. He then visited the Officers' Mess, where he presented an oil painting of The Changing of The Guard at St. James' Palace. An hour was then spent in social intercourse, the Prince chatting freely with the officers, and joining in the singing of old army songs.

In May, 1939, the Canadian Grenadier Guards, in association with the Governor-General's Foot Guards of Ottawa, with whom our unit is now brigaded in the Fourth Division, Canadian Active Service Force, had the honour of Trooping the Colour before His Majesty, King George VI, on the spacious grounds in front of the Federal Parliament Buildings, Ottawa. This was the first

occasion on which a reigning British monarch had visited Canada, and the first time in the history of the Empire that the King's Colour had been trooped in His Majesty's presence outside of England.

Prior to receiving orders to mobilize (June 3, 1940) the Regiment had furnished approximately 20 officers and 125 other ranks to other units and staffs of the Canadian Active Service Force.

On June 28th 1940, Regimental History again was made. On this date the Regiment was authorized to raise a second battalion. This battalion commanded by Lt.-Col. H. D. Rolland, with Mjr. A. C. Barwick as second in command became the 2nd (N.P.A.M.) Battalion Canadian Grenadier Guards.

From the above brief outline of history, it will be seen that the Regiment has a long and honourable tradition, and that it is a unit of the Forces of the Empire to which it is an honour to belong.

REGIMENTAL NOTES
The Spirit of the Regiment

The Canadian Grenadier Guards has the honour and privilege of bearing the name of the senior and most famous regiment of infantry in the British Army, the Grenadier Guards. Besides living up to this famous name, the Regiment has also to maintain a reputation in keeping with that made by the representatives of the Canadian Grenadier Guards who served with the 1st., 14th., 23rd., 60th., 87th., and 245th., Battalions of The Canadian Expeditionary Force, 1914-1918.

A Regiment of Guards, because of its splendid traditions, must always consider itself bound to the exact discharge of all its duties more than any other Regiment.

For this reason, the greatest activity, alertness and precision must be shown at all times. Guardsmen must never relax in the smallest degree from the strict discipline of the Regiment. It is not sufficient that a Guardsman merely do his duty; he must do more, on all occasions, on the side of law and order.

In a Regiment of Guards intelligence is expected to be distinguishable in every individual. All ranks should be able and ready to act, independently and separately, from one another.

When on duty every Guardsman must appreciate that a confidence is reposed in him which it is unworthy to him to betray, and he must, therefore, exert himself to perform every duty in a military manner, and with scrupulous exactness.

When off duty, his actions are sure to be noticed, and by them the Regiment will be judged. By behaving, therefore, at all times in an orderly manner he will reflect the greatest credit upon the Regiment.

REGIMENTAL ORDERS
Warning for Duty

Orders are made known to soldiers by being posted in a suitable place in the Company quarters. Soldiers are generally warned for duty by orders or details similarly posted. They may be warned verbally. Soldiers are responsible for making themselves familiar with orders and with the details of duties posted in this way.

ORDER OF DRESS FOR WARRANT OFFICERS, N.C.O'S AND GUARDSMEN

WALKING OUT:

1. Cap — Field Service.
2. Blouse.
3. Trousers.
4. Boots.

Waist belts and anklets will not be worn when walking out, except when greatcoats are worn, the waist belt then being worn over the greatcoat.

The greatcoat will be worn when necessary.

Only issue clothing may be worn.

Sticks will not be carried by other ranks.

N.C.O's of the rank of Corporal and above will wear sidearms when walking out in greatcoat.

SUMMER DRILL:

Khaki Drill clothing with helmet, if ordered. Puttees will be worn when shorts are worn. Warrant Officers will wear hose tops of officers' pattern when wearing shorts and puttees.

MARCHING ORDER:

Battle dress with anklets or Summer Drill, as ordered.
Water bottle filled.
Ammunition S.A. (on active service only).
Respirator (on occasion).
Cap (F.S.).
Field Dressing (on active service only).
Gloves — worsted (Winter only).
Haversack (containing, cap comforter, hold-all, spare socks, spare underwear, knife, fork, spoon).
Helmet — steel (to be worn sufficiently often to accustom troops to its use).
Iron Ration — (on active service only).
Pay Book (on active service only).
Ground Sheet — (on occasion).
Mess Tin and cover.
Webb equipment complete.

Duty Guards, Picquets, etc., wear Marching Order. In Marching Order the haversack is worn on the back; water bottle in the haversack.

FULL MARCHING ORDER:

As above except:
1. Haversack on left side.
2. Water bottle on right side.
3. Pack on back.

DRILL ORDER:

Battle Dress with anklets or Summer Drill as ordered.
Respirator — on occasion.
Webb equipment complete.
The following will not be worn, unless ordered:
Helmet — steel.
Ground sheet.
Mess tin.
Water bottle.
Haversack.

BOOKS AND PAMPHLETS

A number of books and pamphlets on Infantry Training are available. These books should be studied, and in them, soldiers will find the answers to most questions on training, saluting, etc., which occur to them. They should apply to their N.C.O's for any other advice or assistance they require. Soldiers are recommended to study other books, particularly the official manuals of training.

DISCIPLINE

Obedience is the first duty of a soldier.

An order given by an Officer, Warrant Officer, or N.C.O. is to be obeyed instantly without hesitation or remarks.

Guardsmen should be distinguished by their smartness and cleanliness, by their sobriety and honesty, by their patience under difficulties, and by their resolution to overcome obstacles; in short, by their exertion to do their duty as well as possible, and in a manner which will bring greatest credit to the Regiment to which they have the honour to belong.

In the absence of officers or non-commissioned officers, the responsibility of maintaining and enforcing discipline always devolves on the senior Guardsman present.

A soldier will not leave his quarters unless properly dressed. He will not smoke in the streets when on duty.

When ordered to escort a prisoner to the Guard Room, it should be done with the greatest possible alacrity as promptness in this will often prevent a man confined from aggravating his offence.

Guardsmen must not saunter leisurely across the main floor of the Armoury or any outdoor parade ground. Parties of two or more will walk together smartly or be paraded.

No unauthorized ornament or emblem will be worn with uniform. However, all ranks when not on duty are permitted to wear national flowers or emblems on their uniform headdress on days specified. Ref. K.R. (Can.) 1270.

All ranks of the C.A.S.F. are warned against communicating, either verbally or in writing, any item of information respecting Naval, Army or Air Force matters which may be of value to the enemy.

In particular, private correspondence should make no mention of the following: (a) The disposition, movement, or projected movement of warships, merchant ships, troops or aircraft; (b) Details as to numbers, armament, equipment or condition of ships of all kinds, troops or aircraft. (District Order No. 189, December 22nd, 1939).

Reference K.R. (Can.) 420: "Under the existing law, any person who shall maliciously and advisedly endeavour to seduce any person or persons serving in His Majesty's Forces by sea, land or air from his or their duty and allegiance to His Majesty, or to incite or stir up any person or persons to commit any act of mutiny, or to make or endeavour to make any mutinous assembly, or to commit any traitorous or mutinous practice whatsoever, may, on being convicted of such offence, be sentenced to imprisonment for life."

DRUNKENNESS AND DETENTION

A private soldier who is drunk will be placed under close arrest in a Guard Detention Room. About 24 hours will be allowed to elapse before he is brought before an Officer for investigation. A private soldier will be dealt with for drunkenness under the provisions of Section 46 of the Army Act. Having regard to the attendant circumstances in each case, fines for drunkenness may be imposed as laid down in K.R. (Can.) 492.

SALUTES

Guardsmen will always salute officers of the Navy, Army and Air Force, whether they belong to their own Regiment or to another Corps, whether in uniform or not, when they know them to be officers.

If a number of men are standing together, the senior N.C.O. or man will call the whole to attention and will alone salute; if men are walking out, all will salute, any N.C.O. who may be present saluting with the men; time will be taken from the N.C.O. or man nearest the officer saluted. If sitting at meals, Other Ranks will salute by sitting to attention.

On meeting a Battalion or other party, soldiers not on duty will halt, face the party, salute the officer in command only, and remain at attention until the party has passed. Soldiers on duty as orderlies, etc., will salute the officer in command in the usual way, without halting, and will proceed on their duty. Colours, if present, will also be saluted.

If in sight when a parade is being formed or when a battalion or duties march off, soldiers will stand to attention.

On approaching an officer to address him, soldiers will halt two paces from him, salute, state application, salute again, turn about correctly and march away.

If in a room with caps on, soldiers salute with the hand in the usual way. If not wearing caps, or if the hands are engaged, they will, if halted, stand to attention and face the officer; if on the move, they will salute by turning the head and eyes in the direction of the officer. If riding a bicycle or driving a motor vehicle, they will salute in a similar manner without removing the hands from the steering gear.

Salutes should always be smartly given.

If a soldier not carrying a rifle is halted and an officer passes, the soldier will come to attention and salute with the hand.

If a soldier carrying a rifle is at the order, he will salute by turning towards the officer and standing at attention; if he is at the slope, by striking the rifle at the small of the butt with the right hand.

If improperly dressed, jackets undone, etc., or if in canvas order, (fatigues), soldiers will salute by taking their caps off.

If in a civil court, the cap will be taken off when the magistrate is present, except when on duty under arms.

N.C.O's and men will be careful to salute all officers, whether they are walking, riding or driving.

A Warrant Officer, (Reg't. Sergeant Major, Reg't. Quarter Master Sergeant, Company Sergeant Major, Platoon Sergeant Major, etc.) is addressed as "Sir" but is not saluted.

N.C.O's and men when given an order by an Officer or Warrant Officer will answer by saying "Sir". Such replies as "Yes Sir" and "Very Good Sir" are not according to Regimental custom. To N.C.O's their juniors will reply by saying "Yes Sergeant" or as the case may be.

APPLICATIONS AND LEAVE

Soldiers having applications to make will give their names to the Company Sergeant-in-Waiting half an hour before breakfast. A soldier desiring to see an officer, either to make a complaint or for any other reason, must always apply through a non-commissioned officer. Under special circumstances, and when recommended by the Officer commanding his Company, a soldier will be allowed to see the Commanding Officer.

Passes are granted as an indulgence, not a right, and on the understanding that a man, if summoned, will return at once. Passes which interfere with training will only be granted for exceptional reasons.

ABSENCE WITHOUT LEAVE

Absence without leave is a very serious offence and men absenting themselves without leave forfeit pay and will be dealt with under military law or, under certain circumstances, by civil prosecution. On civil prosecution punishment may include imprisonment with hard labour.

HEALTH AND CLEANLINESS

Soldiers will be careful of their health and will promote and preserve it by scrupulous personal cleanliness in their habits in barracks and in camps.

When soldiers feel ill, or have any disease or sores, they will give their names to the Company Corporal-in-Waiting at Reveille in order that they may see the Medical Officer. If they are taken ill at any other time of the day, they will report to the Company Sergeant-in-Waiting.

They will not treat themselves or consult private practitioners.

On going to hospital they will take their devotional books, hair brush, tooth brush, shaving brush, cleaning material, comb, razor, canvas shoes and greatcoats, in addition to what they are wearing. Arms and accoutrements must be packed and placed in Company stores before going.

Soldiers are responsible for their arms and accoutrements which must always be kept perfectly clean and ready for use. They will clean their rifles and bayonets with great care so as to avoid damage. The dull parts of rifles, bayonets, etc., will be wiped clean, but not made bright. They will not take any part of their rifles to pieces, repair or re-mark their accoutrements or scour or cut their belts and straps. Whenever anything is required in the way of repair or alteration, they will at once report to their Company Quartermaster Sergeant.

They are responsible for the care and repair of their clothing and necessaries. They must supply themselves with cleaning materials.

A soldier on joining the Canadian Active Service Force is given a full kit. This must be kept in order and repair, but articles of clothing worn out by fair wear and tear will be replaced after being found unserviceable by a Board of Officers.

No distinguishing marks are to be placed on clothing and equipment other than that which is authorized at the time of issue.

Barrack Rooms will be arranged as laid down in an Appendix to Battalion Standing Orders, copies of which will be posted in the Barrack Rooms.

Kits will be laid out for inspection as shown in the diagram or photograph which will be posted in the Barrack Rooms.

Every soldier must show a full kit on inspection. Any deficiencies will have to be made up and their cost will be charged against the soldier's pay.

Soldiers must not lend to or borrow from one another articles of clothing or necessaries.

Soldiers finding any lost articles, will take them to their Company Sergeant-in-Waiting at once.

Soldiers will be careful not to waste or mis-use their food. They should acquire the habit of being very careful in everything affecting its cleanliness and economical use as these are points of great importance at all times and especially on active service. They are also enjoined to husband their allowance of fuel, never throwing half-burnt stuff away; not to waste or foul clean water, nor to allow waste or unnecessary use of gas or electricity.

GENERAL ADVICE

You are again reminded that you must always take a pride in your Regiment, and be a smart Guardsman. Clothing and equipment must be clean and properly put on. Quarters must be tidy and men orderly. That is necessary for the comfort and health of all. Be considerate of the rights of your comrades and no matter what happens, or what inconvenience or discomforts you meet with in the course of your service, always be cheerful. Grumbling, or as it is called in the Army, "Grousing", is a bad habit. No grouser will ever get on, and no unit which suffers from grousers will be a happy one. In the ups and downs of service do what you can to make things go smoothly for yourself and comrades. Remember, that all ranks in the Battalion are working to the same end. All have made sacrifices to go on service, and all have the interests of the service, which are your interests, thoroughly at heart.

NOTES

The first Guards in the British Standing Army now the GRENADIER were raised by the Cavalier Colonel Russel.

It became customary to add an extra grenadier company to the twelve companies then in each regiment, consisting of the tallest strongest men.

The white plume, now worn by the Grenadier Guards, was supposed to represent the smoke of a grenade fuse. They wore caps instead of hats, for convenience in slinging off their fire arms before throwing bombs.

NOTES

Arrived Aldershot Oct 7-43
Arrived Hadley Jan 11-4?
Bruce - Pet.

Joined July 2 1940
July 17 left Aldershot
for Petawawa
Oct 16 left St Helens Island
" 17 arrived Camp Borden
Jan 7/ changed camp site at
/41 Camp Borden
Jan 27 arrived at Petawawa
transferred to Regina Rifles
30th of [?]
May 7th arrived Valcartier Camp
May 31 left Valcartier
June 1. Arrived Halifax
Aug 3rd arrived Sussex NB
Oct 8th landed at Hurst-
pool England.